About the Author

Monika Rossa Wheatley was born in Warsaw, Poland, in 1960. From a very young age, she knew she wanted to be an artist. She studied art, but the politically challenging times didn't let her pursue her career. She had an opportunity to leave Poland one month before martial law was imposed, in 1981. She went to art schools in Spain and France, before moving to the United States in 1984. She has exhibited her work in the United States, Europe and Mexico. She has also published a few short stories. Her paintings are in many private collections. She lives in Tucson, Arizona.

Bipolar: A Difficult Life

Monika Rossa Wheatley

Bipolar: A Difficult Life

Olympia Publishers
London

www.olympiapublishers.com
OLYMPIA PAPERBACK EDITION

A CIP catalogue record for this title is
available from the British Library.

ISBN: 978-1-80074-771-5

This is a true story.
Names have been changed to protect privacy

First Published in 2023

Olympia Publishers
Tallis House
2 Tallis Street
London
EC4Y 0AB

Printed in Great Britain

Dedication

To all mothers

Acknowledgements

Thank you to all who helped me through the difficult times.

PART ONE

Chapter 1
A promise

I was standing in front of the hospital door looking at the large metal sculpture representing a tree. The parking lot was busy with cars moving in and out. The emergency vehicles ramp was flooded with yellow and red lights when an ambulance pulled in. The paramedics ran out and opened the back door. I turned back to the tree sculpture.

My eyes followed the tiny leaves and ended up at the bottom, where a big metal plaque was welded to the iron bark. *'Behavioral Services'*, it read across its whole width.

It was a late evening in November 2008. While I was looking at the iron leaves and guessing why I was in this place, the events from the previous night played in my head.

My husband, Earle, and I were planning to go out to dinner, since it was his birthday. We didn't make any reservation; it wasn't our style. We liked to do things spontaneously. Just as we were leaving the house, my son, Alex, showed up. He was oblivious to the fact it was his stepfather's birthday. He also ignored the fact that both of us were dressed as if we were going out, too. Alex was eighteen years old. I am Polish, so I often called him 'Oles', his Polish name. He was the fourth of my five children. This fall was his first semester at the University of Arizona. He came to our place and told us he wanted to talk about his new business.

"Look at this," he said. He stood by the table and pulled out two notebooks from his backpack. Alex was tall and very handsome. His hair was blond with a slight trace of a mustache. Under his tall forehead were his deep blue eyes. His jaw was square and his full lips seemed always ready to smile. Alex had a low, deep voice with a particular timbre that made it impossible not to recognize him. Above all, he was a very healthy young man. Now though, his hands were shaking and he was talking unusually fast. Also, it didn't look as if he combed his hair in a while. I looked at my husband, thinking that our outing wasn't going to happen. He also knew that going out wasn't in the picture. I took off my "better" shoes and I stepped into my house flip flops. Earle got up from the table and went to the bathroom to change. He came out in his house clothes, his curly black hair combed to the back. Earle was muscular and shorter than Alex. He was fifty-five years old, but looked much younger.

"Do you want to eat something?" I asked. We were hungry. After all, we were planning to go out to eat at our favorite Thai restaurant. I still had some old spaghetti in the fridge and I was going to warm it up.

"I can't think about food now," Alex said. "Too many important things are going on. I wonder how you two can think about food. Well, it will change after I show you what we need to do."

I heard the 'we' and I didn't like it. I didn't like how Alex looked, either. He was way too skinny, his cheeks were sunken, his nose seemed overgrown. His forehead was covered in sweat and his blond hair was a little bit too long.

"Sit down," I said. I pulled out the pot with the spaghetti in it and divided it into three plates. Alex didn't want to sit down, or rather, he just wasn't capable. It seemed as if his legs had two motors of their own and they were carrying him around the room without stopping. We started to eat our spaghetti. Alex finally sat down, but only to move his plate away. He spread out one of his notebooks and started flipping the pages. They were all covered in his neat, almost printlike writing. The drawings between the lines were executed with a precision particular to Alex. The drawings were mostly circles and other geometric figures, accompanied by tiny descriptions. In a few places, I spotted a mathematical equation of some sort.

"Here, look. This one," Alex said.

He stopped flipping pages and pointed to a circular shape.

"This one can take us out of the Solar System," he said. My husband looked at me. I looked back but then I saw Alex's phone flashing Tessa's name. It was his girlfriend, or rather fiancée, since he had proposed to her recently. He was eighteen, and he still would have to wait for her, since she was only seventeen, although looked a little older. She was a small, skinny girl with a round face and blue eyes. Her hair was straight and dark, almost black. She kept it in a ponytail.

"Tessa is calling," I said. "You silenced the phone?"

Alex gave me an angry look. He covered the phone with a palm of his hand, then he put it on the table, face down.

"Was it her?" I made sure.

"Yes," he said. "It's my wife. She can wait."

Tessa wasn't his wife, but a fiancée. I tried to continue eating but found I had lost my appetite, too. I didn't have to ask Alex 'what's the story', he was more than eager to tell.

"We need to build it. It's a spaceship. I know, talking about spaceships sounds crazy, but I'm not crazy. Mom?"

"Of course, you're not." I forced a few noodles into my mouth. Earle was finishing his share of the spaghetti.

Alex pointed out the details of his drawing to Earle. Then he started explaining how to build that spaceship which would be able to go across the solar system and beyond, without requiring an external source of energy.

"After the initial kick-off, it powers itself. It's essentially a yo-yo," he said.

My husband reached for an ice tea. He poured honey into it, and was now mixing it with a spoon. He tried not to make noise.

"You know how to build stuff," Alex said. "And I calculated the costs. It would be something like fifty grand."

Alex was right about one thing; his stepfather knew how to build things. I met Earle through the art gallery which he owned. The gallery was in a big building Earle had bought and renovated. Earle was an artist himself. He painted on clear acrylic with spray paint. His paintings were mostly large and very colorful. They were abstract. Being an artist and entrepreneur, he wanted to add to the art community, and he was having openings for other artists every month. He was also renting the studios very cheaply to artists who had no space to work. Earle loved art and he was supporting it in any way he could. I was selling the house after my divorce, therefore looking for a temporary studio until I could move into a new place. I asked around and that's how I met Earle. He offered me an affordable space. The gallery was Earle's 'baby', as he called it himself. It didn't matter to Earle that the mortgage on the gallery building was high, its primary business was a small plastics company where he did fabrication and thermoforming. There was no prototype which he couldn't or wouldn't make.

His plastics company was doing very well, and he could afford to pay the mortgage for his gallery.

"Okay," I said, cautiously. "Fifty thousand dollars is a lot of money."

"For a spaceship? Mom, go talk to NASA," Alex said. I didn't say I wasn't interested in talking to NASA.

While Alex was showing the details of the drawing to my husband, my mind was racing. I knew he had to be evaluated by a doctor. Tessa kept calling Alex, and he kept silencing his phone. One time he even talked to her and simply told her to leave him alone. I thought I heard a '*fuck off*', but I wasn't sure.

The round spaceship in Alex's booklet got my husband's attention, or at least that's how it looked; maybe he was just being polite. He didn't raise Alex. We got married when the boy was seventeen. While we were dating, Alex worked in Earle's shop. Now, he was looking at Alex's sketches and sipping his iced tea.

"And this? What is this?" he pointed at something on the page.

Alex didn't answer. Instead, he pulled out a yo-yo and started playing. I moved away. Then, I got up and moved a flower pot away as well. I also picked up a few cups from the table.

"This is exactly the motion that's needed to make it work," Alex said. Now he was throwing the yo-yo in a horizontal direction.

"So, Earle, are you up for this?" Alex asked.

Earle was still studying the drawing but I wasn't sure if he was only trying to buy time.

"We don't have fifty grand," he finally said.

Alex caught his yo-yo. He stopped moving, too.

"Maybe thirty? Thirty would do if we were cautious with the money," he said.

Earle shook his head '*no*'.

"I'm afraid…" he started to say.

"Then, fuck you, guys. You don't know what you are missing out on. This one thing I'm asking you, and you say '*no*'. Fuck you. I need to go, now."

He picked up his notebooks and left. He slammed the door, but it jumped back open. Earle got up and closed it gently. When he turned around and looked at me, I saw that he was crying.

#

The next day, all day long, I was begging Alex to go to the hospital and just check himself out, health wise. I knew things weren't going well, obviously. Tessa talked to me, too. I met her in a coffee shop, and she said she was afraid.

"Of what?" I said. "Of him?"

She didn't want to give me a direct answer. With a long spoon she kept mixing her latte without looking me in the eye. The espresso machine was making noise, but when it stopped, Tessa lifted her head and I could look into her blue eyes. She said Alex would sit on his bed for hours at night, watching the bubbles in his lava lamp.

Alex and Tessa lived in a small, old house. We called it 'Flanwill House', since it was on Flanwill Boulevard. It was our house and we had decided to rent it to them, since they were insisting on getting married at this young age.

Alex ignored most of my phone calls all day long, but to

my surprise, he showed up at our house in the late afternoon. While still holding onto his bike, he started to take his helmet off. He looked the same as yesterday; skinny and tired.

"I don't have much time," he said. "What do you want from me? You don't want to pay for my spaceship, do you? Why would I need to do anything for you?"

I was very careful while choosing my words. It seemed to me Alex was a ticking bomb.

"Let's just go to the hospital. It's close by, right on Grant Road," I said. "I will drop you off at your house when it's over."

I wanted to do it quickly, before he changed his mind and stormed out again.

"Put your bike in the gazebo," I said.

He went outside and I texted my husband that I was taking Alex to the hospital.

It was a short but intense drive. At every stop sign and red light, I was afraid Alex would open the door and jump out. He was constantly talking, moving, and slapping his thigh. I was focusing on traffic. I didn't want to make a mistake. I wanted to be in the hospital, now. I wanted Alex to be in the doctor's office. There was one scary moment in the parking lot, when he said that it was all ridiculous, that he was fine, that hospital is for sick people and that he would way prefer me to take him to IHOP, a restaurant where he usually enjoyed a tall stack of pancakes.

"I will bring you food," I said, while opening the car door. He hesitated, but eventually, he opened his door, too.

After we walked into the lobby, I could immediately see a difference between a regular ER and this Behavioral Unit. Here, almost all the chairs were empty. I saw one person in the darker corner of the waiting room, curled up on two chairs. I couldn't tell if it was a man or a woman. It was very quiet. We approached the counter and the woman behind a thick acrylic window asked us how she could help. I guess that thick acrylic screen startled me. The counter looked more like a bank than a hospital. After a short introduction she asked for an insurance card. Looking back, this is when things became either obvious, or simply strange. I felt that this was the first turning point of revealing the truth about Alex's state of mind. Out of his pocket, he pulled a yellow yo-yo, and he placed it on the counter.

"What insurance card? This is my insurance card," Alex said, pointing at the yo-yo.

I started to fumble in my purse in search of an insurance card. Alex wasn't on my plan. His father, a University Math professor who had taken early retirement, was still paying for his children's coverage. Being Polish, he had moved back to Poland after our divorce, but he could still afford the plan that was way better than mine, and our children were on it. I used to carry my kids' cards, so I thought that maybe I still had this one. It turned out I didn't.

In the meantime, Alex was trying to convince the receptionist of how good his yo-yo insurance was.

"Never heard of it? Then, it's time to hear now," he said.

"Please provide the insurance card," the receptionist repeated for the tenth time.

"Listen, lady," Alex said. He leaned against the counter. His face was red and his forehead sweaty, again. "This is the best insurance, and you guys should be introduced to it. In fact, I want to talk to the manager, director, president, CEO or whoever is the highest rank, here, in the hospital. Fuck that thing. If you don't…"

I was trying to whisper to the lady, by just moving my lips and pointing behind Alex's back. She pretended she didn't see me. I wondered who hired that lady for the welcome desk in the Behavioral Unit. She obviously had an attitude and no imagination. The yo-yo was sliding back and forth between Alex and the receptionist. As I was losing hope for any improvement of the situation, a nurse came in.

"What's going on?" he asked. He was dressed in a blue jumpsuit, with a name '*Jerry*' stenciled in red on his chest pocket. He was tall and fairly young. His head was shaved bald and his black skin reflected the hospital light. He looked as if he was smiling. His face was warm and pleasant.

"Man, maybe you will know better," Alex said.

"I'm sure I can help you, young man. What's your name?" Jerry asked.

"Alex. Nice to meet you. Listen, man, this lady," Alex started to say and he pointed several times to the receptionist. He also picked up his yo-yo.

The nurse looked at me.

"You will tell me all about it, Alex, just come with me. My name is Jerry." The nurse reached out to Alex and they shook hands. Without letting Alex's hand go, Jerry led him through the double doors into the unit.

#

The door closed itself right in front of me, so I had to follow them through a regular door, the one controlled by the receptionist with a help of a green, plastic button. She pressed it, and I entered the hospital corridor. I passed several open doors, then I saw Alex in the last room along the hallway.

Jerry and another nurse, a woman, were trying to take his blood pressure. I could tell that even though the female nurse was short, she was very strong. She had Alex pinned down on the chair while Jerry was trying to put the blood pressure cuff on Alex's arm, while holding his legs. The female nurse's face became very red. Her face and hair looked sweaty now. Alex kept protesting. I was holding my breath and praying for him to loosen up and not fight, so they wouldn't have to immobilize him in any way. At a certain point, Alex ran out of the room and started peeing into the trash can in the hallway. Nobody stopped him. Both nurses were still waiting for him, knowing he wouldn't get far.

"I said I'm hungry. I'm out of here. Mom!" Alex looked at me as I was sitting across from the trash can. "You said you would bring me food,"

"Of course, what do you want?" I asked.

"Chipotle." He didn't care about zipping his pants.

I made sure that I would be able to come back, even if it would take me half an hour or so to get food. Chipotle, a popular fast-food takeaway, wasn't far from the hospital. I also told the nurses Alex's stepfather was on his way.

I don't know how long I was gone, but when I came back, Alex was walking around the small room, constantly opening the door which was being closed repeatedly by the hospital staff.

"Your Chipotle," I said, and gave him a steak burrito, his favorite.

Alex sat down on the floor and started to eat it using his fingers. He left the plastic fork on the floor. He must have been starving because picking up food with his hands wasn't enough. He finally put his face into the bowl, like a dog, and kept eating.

"No food on the hospital floor. Did you read the sign?" a voice said.

I looked up. I didn't even realize that I, too, was sitting on the floor now, across from Alex.

A security guard dressed in black uniform was standing by the door. He was probably in his fifties. He had a big belly and a spider tattoo on his neck. His face was red with visible blue veins on his fat nose.

"Oh, I didn't know. I'm sorry," I said.

"Take it away from him. If you don't do it, I will. He's making a mess. Somebody could fall down," he said.

I knew I wouldn't win that battle, but I also knew that I could buy time and maybe Alex would be able to finish his burrito. He was licking the bowl and burping.

"Madam, did you hear what I said?"

"Can we just wait for the doctor, before we take the bowl away from my son?" I asked.

I was terrified. I knew that my husband was somewhere close by, too, and I thought that I should ask to look for him. I wanted to distract the security guard, but it didn't work. The security guard made taking the bowl away from Alex his priority. But as he came closer to my son, the doctor came in with my husband. It turned out that when I was away, they had already drawn Alex's blood. They had a hard time collecting his urine, since he had peed into the trash can earlier and didn't want to cooperate.

The doctor, a tall man in his forties, didn't spend too much time in the room. I figured that he had done all his assessments while I was gone, and later on my husband confirmed that. He did introduce himself though, and he gave me several paper forms.

"Please fill these out, unless you want to take him home,"

he said. "I think that he should stay, though."

I didn't want to take Alex home. Which home, anyway? Ours? His? His, meaning another one of ours, where he currently lived with Tessa? Right, Tessa! I knew he wouldn't go to his classes tomorrow. And I knew he needed help.

"Did you hear what he said?" I heard a question. It was Alex, standing tall next to me, now. "Did you hear it? Let's go home, now. We are losing time here. I did what you told me. I was checked by the doctor." It seemed as if Alex hadn't heard the second half of what the doctor said.

I didn't know I was crying before, but now, when I felt the tears streaming down my neck, I went to the bathroom. I looked in the mirror and behind my swollen, red face, I saw myself, a terrified mother, who was about to abandon her child.

I washed my face, dried it with a paper towel and came back to the room. I told my husband that we needed to sit down in the lobby to fill out the paperwork.

"You, wait," I told Alex.

"Wait?" he asked.

"I will be back," I said.

He started to play with his yo-yo and I snuck out of the room taking advantage of his distraction. I went to the lobby where my husband was sitting, holding the papers. We started to fill them out in order to commit Alex. We couldn't do it any other way. Alex was legally of age, and it didn't matter that he had turned eighteen just three months ago. I wasn't capable of filling in the lines. My tears were dropping on the page, dissolving the ink. Earle was helping. He filled in the pages and I only signed, at the bottom. Still, I saw the last sentence of what he had written in a large description box: '*Doesn't eat, doesn't sleep. Alex thinks he can travel to other planets.*'

.

24

Chapter 2
First hospitalization

"You can leave, now," the female nurse said. She just came into the waiting room. She wasn't sweating any more. The cool air of the waiting room immediately chilled her skin. "Somebody will contact you. He needs to be taken to a different hospital. He will have to stay there for some time."

"Can I drive him there?" I asked. I knew they wouldn't let me, and I knew I didn't want to. But I needed to ask. I thought that, if they agreed, I would take a chance. With Earle, it would be easier.

"No, madam. He needs to be taken by ambulance," the nurse said. She took off her blue head cover.

I didn't insist. But I didn't have a good feeling about the ambulance, either. It was just a feeling which I dismissed. A month later, though, a bill came to the house. It was for Alex, and since he was eighteen, he was responsible for it. The bill was for nine hundred dollars. It was for an eleven-mile-long ambulance ride between the hospitals. Who was supposed to pay that bill? Alex? Me? And why nine hundred dollars? Alex wasn't on life support. He wasn't a danger to himself or anybody else.

The lobby was as quiet as when we first walked in. The sleeping person across the waiting room had disappeared. Suddenly, I heard screams behind the heavy doors, leading to the unit floor. The screams were faint and muted, but I still had no problem in recognizing Alex's voice, which was deep and very distinct. The female nurse looked at me.

"He will be fine," she said. "We just asked him to go to the patients' waiting room, not this one. It is inside the unit. You can see him, if you want."

"Can I?"

"Yes, follow me."

Earle and I both got up and followed the nurse through a new set of double doors. There, the nurse led us to a big, glass window. Behind it was a large, carpeted, empty room. There was Alex. He was only in his underwear. His clothes were crumpled in a corner. He was building a tower from the white, plastic chairs that were in the room.

Alex turned and our eyes met. He came closer and spat on the window that separated us. I stepped back. He turned away.

When two security guards with yellow jackets came in, Alex wanted to run. He didn't give up even when they got him and held him. They dragged him out of the room. He still turned his head to me and I thought I could read his lips; "*Are you leaving me? You said you would come back.*"

#

Alex was taken to Northwest hospital, and the next day, in the morning, I went there. I was told that he would have to stay there for two weeks, unless the doctors decided otherwise. It looked like he would stay those two weeks, though; at least for now. A tall, skinny woman in blue scrubs was discussing this information with me. She was looking at me from above her thick glasses.

26

"But," I said, "what if he behaves himself? What about if there's nothing wrong with him?"

"This isn't about behavior," she said. "It isn't a jail."

My eyes moved to the panel with the names of the units and obviously the 'Behavioral Unit' was the one where we were.

"This is about a correct diagnosis and treatment. We have to do what's the best for him," the woman in blue said.

I also wanted to do what was best for my son, so I took a note from the hospital and I rushed to the University to talk to the Dean's office. But here, again, it turned out that it wouldn't be easy to help Alex. Since he was eighteen, nobody wanted to talk to me without his consent.

"I would like to present a note. Alex was hospitalized and he will miss classes." I was talking to a young woman sitting behind a large desk at the administrative building. She was my first obstacle. The black arrow pointing to the Dean's office was past her desk.

"I'm sorry to hear that," she said. "Was he in an accident? How is he? Can he call us?"

"I'm afraid he can't," I said and left it at that, hoping that she would just let me in. I didn't want her to see the note with the Behavioral Unit stamp. The woman fussed a little but then she let me in.

I didn't talk to the Dean but only to his staff. They arranged for Alex's medical leave. Exams were coming and I knew Alex would want to show up for the finals. I didn't know what to do in general,, but for now at least, I wanted Alex's absence to be justified.

Right after I was done at the University, I rushed to the hospital. On the way there I called Tessa. She told me that she would be waiting for me at Alex and her place after all my errands.

I didn't see Alex that day. I thought maybe I would be able to talk to his doctor, but the doctor had either left or wasn't available. A young woman in a long skirt and white blouse told me that Alex was doing well, but he didn't want to see me. I felt my eyes filling with tears, and I turned my head away. I saw the box of Kleenex on the small table in the middle of the waiting room, and I walked toward it. I wiped my eyes and blew my nose.

"Okay," I said and I came back to the woman. She reached for my arm and squeezed it. I saw the tag on her blouse. She was a social worker.

"Does he need anything from home?" I asked.

She said, "no".

I left and I drove to Alex and Tessa's house to meet Tessa.

#

Alex and Tessa lived in our small rental house in a central part of town. It took me fifteen minutes to get to their house.

Earle and I had bought a new house and moved away from that house. Our new home was in the Foothills, on a street called Piedra Seca; therefore, our nickname for it was Piedra Seca house. It was far from the University area, so it seemed that it would be best if Alex lived closer, in our rental house, so that was what was decided; Alex would move there. We all started to look for a roommate for Alex. The potential roommate showed up promptly, along with his parents. We all met at Flanwill house. The roommate was a pharmacy student form Minnesota; freshman, just like Alex. We all came to an agreement. The boys would move in together right after the summer.

Alex's roommate only lasted one semester. During finals, he let me know he was going to move out. He was polite, but I knew that he he'd had a hard time staying with Alex. Once during the semester, he actually called me and asked for help.

"He's up all night. I can't sleep. And then I'm exhausted during the day and I fall asleep in class," he complained.

"Well," I said. "I'm sorry to hear that. But did you try to talk to Alex yourself?"

"Several times. Nothing happened. That's why I'm calling you," he said.

I couldn't help Alex's roommate much. I tried. But when I only mentioned the roommate's name to Alex, he got angry.

"Yeah, I know. Maybe he's a good guy, but guess what, everybody has to adjust. Me, too."

They both made an effort and agreed to live with each other til the end of the semester. By then, Alex had already proposed to Tessa, and he wanted her to move in with him. She never "officially" moved in since she was under age, but she practically lived with him.

Tessa carried all sort of problems of her own, and Alex really tried to help her. She was young and depressed and seemed lost in the world. I remember one evening when Alex called me on my cellphone. He was crying.

"Can Earle come here?" Alex said. "I need help, now. I can't put the phone down. I'm holding Tessa with my other hand."

Holding Tessa? I had no idea what was going on, but Earle went to Flanwill house immediately. He found them both behind the refrigerator which had moved away from the wall.

Alex was holding Tessa to the ground. In one hand, she was holding a kitchen knife.

"She wanted to kill herself," Alex cried.

Earle called 911, and the police came promptly. After a short assessment of the situation, the policeman and Earle explained to Tessa that she didn't do anything wrong, that nobody was accusing her of anything, but it would be best if she went back to her grandma's. She did, but she only lasted two nights. So again, I started to arrange therapy sessions for Tessa and trying to help Alex at the same time. They were glued to each other. Unfortunately, there weren't many options for Tessa's therapy. She had government insurance, and the only therapy place I found was actually close to my house. I was gladly taking Tessa there, but then Alex wanted to do it and even attend the sessions. It turned out that Tessa wanted him to attend, too. They were very disappointed in therapy, and really, it was hard to blame them. The therapist, who was an older lady, told Tessa that she needed to poke her forehead with her fingers several times a day and do yoga. That was supposed to help Tessa's depression. But when I mentioned medication, Tessa was opposed and so was Alex.

#

Alex finished high school and the summer came. Around June or July almost every year I went to California, camping. In the past, I would take the kids with me, but now they were big. With the three older children out of town, I only had Alex and his younger brother, Andrew. I don't quite remember where my youngest son was spending the summer that year, but he wasn't in town. It turned out, too, that Tessa had never seen the ocean. I felt compelled to show it to her, especially because Alex also badly wanted to come with me. We packed the car with the tent and other outdoor gear. I already had the reservations made for my favorite campsite. We left, all in a very good mood. When we crossed the Arizona/California border and approached the gate with the Border Patrol, the dog sniffed our car, and the agent told me to pull over. To me, it seemed it was a mistake. But not to the dog! We all got out of the car and the dog jumped in. It took him a few seconds to get Alex's red back pack, and pull it out. The agent searched it, and found a small plastic container filled with marijuana, a glass pipe and some other paraphernalia I didn't recognize. There were two agents; a young and an older one. The young agent was really young. He must have been older than Alex, but not by much. He was tall, with black hair sticking from under his hat. He seemed very confident. The older one must have been about my age, in his mid-forties. He was short and muscular. He was obviously the boss. But he walked away with his dog for a moment, and we were dealing with the young one only. He showed me the pouch.

"Is this yours?" he asked.

"It's mine," Alex jumped in. "My mom and my girlfriend have nothing to do with it."

The agent came back to Alex and told him to raise his hands. He was searching him, now, while muttering under his breath.

"Drugs, right? You like your little drugs? Well, that will be the end of it." This agent must have been no more than five years older than Alex. After searching Alex, he turned to me.

"You are the mother? And you don't even react when your son is doing drugs? What kind of mother are you?"

I didn't know what to say. I only felt anger. Luckily, the older agent came back. He came without the dog. He picked up Alex's pouch, and showed it to me again.

"You know what that is, right?" he asked.

I confirmed by nodding my head.

"Will you deal with it?" he said. The younger agent was watching.

Again, I confirmed. The boss-agent told us to get back to the car. With one gesture he silenced the young agent who had started to talk, and we drove away.

I was very angry. Alex apologized in the car. But I was angry. I didn't know what to do. *'Should I go back home?'* I thought to myself. But why, and what for? What to do? I didn't talk to Alex all the way to the campsite. Tessa looked scared, but I didn't want her to be scared of me. It wasn't her fault. We continued to our vacation.

As I was driving, I was thinking about Alex and Tessa. They had met at the Sacred Heart Catholic Church Youth Group meeting. The group met on Wednesday evenings. While focusing on the freeway and the cars passing us, I was thinking that after their church meetings, they mostly smoked pot. The group leader and teacher, was a very devoted man that genuinely wanted to help teenagers. The main theme of the meetings was God and Jesus, but being a musician himself, the teacher also formed a band. Tessa was singing in this very band.

In short, Tessa and Alex fell in love and decided that they wanted to be together, forever. I didn't know about Tessa, but when it came to Alex, I knew that his decisions were irreversible. Alex was always pushing his ideas to the end, until the crash or success would come.

We ended up having a really good vacation. At least Tessa and Alex had, or so I thought. Every evening we were sitting by the campfire eating and watching the flames. We talked little, and never about marijuana. But it was on my mind all the time.

#

With Alex in the hospital my schedule evolved between his visiting hours, my work and spending time with Tessa. After his third night of hospitalization, late one evening I was with Tessa in Flanwill house kitchen. Tessa prepared us hot herbal tea. We went then to the small living room and made ourselves comfortable on the couch.

"Can I visit him?" Tessa asked.

"I don't see why not," I said. "But maybe I will try at least to find out the hours, and visit him once before we schedule anything."

Tessa was trying to leave her family of divorced, drinking, out of town parents, and be on her own. In Tucson, she was living with her grandmother. Legal guardianship still belonged to her mother, but it was in the process of changing. Tessa was sensitive and hard working.

She showed me the bedroom, where Alex spent hours sitting on the bed watching his lava lamp. Here and there I saw several yo-yos. The bedroom smelled like marijuana. There were school books on the wooden desk.

We agreed I would take Tessa to see Alex the next day; that is, if that was okay with him.

Chapter 3
Halfway house

Today, I think that I was in too much of a hurry signing Alex out of the hospital. Not that it was my decision, not at all. It was the doctor's decision, but she was very agreeable and she could see that I really wanted Alex home. She told me that, according to her knowledge, Alex would have to go to a half-way house. I decided that I would investigate that issue and the concept of a half-way house was explained to me. I was given a list of some of them. I was supposed to go and visit them, and then make a choice.

I will never forget the day I went.

I looked for the address of the first one for a long time. I had the number, and even a map, but for some reason the house was hiding from me. I finally found it.

I knocked on the door and waited for a longer than usual before it opened. Immediately, I was overwhelmed by the strong smell. The only way I could describe it would be dirty laundry mixed with toilet cleaner solution.

"How can I help you?" A small woman with black colored hair opened the door.

I didn't like her and I don't think she liked me, either. I'm talking about first impressions. I did put mine aside though, and I smiled as warmly as I could.

"Is this a half-way house?" I asked.

"Yes, it is. How can I help you?" she repeated. She wasn't impatient per se, but I could see that she wasn't thrilled by my presence.

I explained what I had come for. She told me she had one bed available, and that she could show it to me. She led me through the house. We passed the kitchen.

"They eat here," she said. "They are also supposed to clean the kitchen by themselves. But you know, what can I say? It doesn't always work. I have to do it. Otherwise, it wouldn't look so good."

I didn't like the way she said *'they'*. The kitchen wasn't dirty. It was mopped and the dishes were done. It only had paper towels and bags with Styrofoam plates. It wasn't friendly. I didn't like it. I was trying to make a nice comment, but the lady was already leading me through a narrow hallway with a low ceiling. On both sides of the hallway were small bedrooms. She was opening and closing the doors, as we moved forward. Every bedroom looked almost the same; two beds with a night stand between them, a window with a gray curtain which hadn't been washed for years, or at least it gave that impression. Most of the beds weren't made. When we got to the fourth bedroom and the lady opened the door, we saw a man asleep in the bed by the window. He looked like a homeless man.

He was on his side, facing us, but he didn't open his eyes, even though the lady kept talking, pretty loudly, too. I couldn't tell how old he was. His skin was tanned, but it still looked gray against the sheets. His salt and pepper hair, was long and tangled in many places. He was very skinny. I could see his ribs and the sunken skin between them, rising and falling according to the rhythm of his breathing. He wasn't wearing a shirt, but he had his very old and very dirty jeans on, while lying in his bedsheets. On the floor by his bed, there was a half-opened small backpack, which probably used to be black but now simply had no color. *'Nothing in this room has color'*, I thought. Even the small stuffed animal that was sticking out of the backpack didn't have a color. After looking carefully at the toy, I decided that it must have been green, a long time ago.

"This one is available," I heard the lady say. She was talking all the time, in the background of my thoughts, but that last sentence got my attention.

"Available?" I asked.

"Yes. This bed," she said. She was pointing to the other bed in the room. "Your son would be sharing this room, if he chooses to come here."

I thanked the lady and left. I went to my car and started the engine. I slowly drove out of that area of the neighborhood, without even knowing where I was going. I was terrified. *'If your son chooses to come here'*, these words were echoing in my head. *'Son?' 'Chooses?'* I thought. Who is here choosing what? Is Alex choosing anything today? Am I choosing something? Is *'today'* the result of my choices, Alex's choices, any choices? If it really is a result of my choices, then I don't see any possible redemption to it. When do we really start to choose? I think that this word is just overused. In fact, I would throw it away from any dictionary, from the language altogether, if only I could.

#

The image of that empty available bed didn't leave me. Like in a dream, I was envisioning my boy asleep there, curled up, knees against his chin. In my imagination, I saw Alex hanging out with his roommate and the others who lived in that house

When I almost missed a stop sign and a big truck zoomed in front of me, I pulled over. I couldn't give up. I had to find a half-way house. I checked the addresses given to me, and I proceeded to the next one.

The lady that opened the door was a little friendlier than the previous one, but the house looked almost the same. We walked into the kitchen. I looked around, and through a large window, I saw one resident, sitting on the patio and smoking a cigarette. I was shown the pantry and also, to my astonishment, the whole closet full of various medications.

"They have to take their meds," the lady said. She also had a black hair, but not as black as the previous lady.

"Ah," I said. I looked at the bottles, containers and boxes. They were all labelled and had pills in them.

"It looks like lots of pills," she said, while locking the closet with a little chain and the padlock. She kept the key on her own key ring, with the other keys. She had a whole bunch of keys. "But it really is just the right amount," she added.

Desperate, I moved on to the next half-way house from my list. This one was easy to find and was closer to the University. It didn't mean anything, but for some reason I made that note to myself.

Before I knocked, I heard a lively conversation coming through an open window. I didn't want to listen, but I heard some words anyway. It had something to do with State funding, a check which wasn't coming and money altogether. Two women's voices were agitated, but they agreed with each other. Their conversation made me think: somebody has to pay for these half-way houses. Is having a house like that a job? I didn't have time to think about it for too long, because the door was opened and I was let into the house. Again, I was shown the kitchen, the rooms and the backyard. All the residents were out.

"So, where are they? Do you know?" I asked.

This lady of the house had abundant, light-yellow hair. She was wearing a red sweater and big, round, golden earrings. She was shaking her head often, and that was setting the earrings into a gentle spin. I thought that she was doing it on purpose.

"Who knows? They just need to be here before ten in the evening, or earlier, if they want dinner. They need to take their meds. And believe me, no drugs here, not in my house. They can smoke on the other side of the backyard, in the second gazebo. And they have to pick up their cigarette butts," she said.

When I was leaving, a man passed by me in the driveway. It must have been one of the residents. I didn't look at him, and he didn't look at me. Nevertheless, I knew how he looked. He looked like a regular homeless man.

I went to my car. I climbed into it, shut the door and started crying. I felt sorry for myself and for Alex. I couldn't believe that my precious son would have to live with a bunch of homeless people—my baby, who I breastfed until he was two years old. I didn't know what to do, how to stop that humongous avalanche, of what I thought was evil, pouring over me. I certainly couldn't stop it. The best way for me would be just going with it, but how? I would have to be constantly drunk not to see the misery of my son. But his misery didn't want to be contained just to himself; it spilled and contaminated the people around him.

From when Alex was about eight, I started a yearly tradition of preparing a dinner for homeless people in our church. One time, I shared my birthday with them. The guests were all men, brought up from the local Salvation Army. The church administrator showed me the paperwork certifying the vaccination status of all these men. I was told that they would be clean and healthy. I didn't pay attention to it then, but I remembered that dinner now, while sitting in my car, in front of a half-way house. I remembered how eagerly Alex was serving soup and how much he enjoyed playing games with some men. One of them somehow got stuck in my memory. This man must have been in his sixties, but who knows? They all look kind of ageless and alike.

He told me a little about himself.

He was traveling, and never wanted to stop, he said. He was lonely, but not too much, since he had two sons. One of them was a veterinarian, and the other one was a dentist. The vet lived in Houston, Texas, and the dentist, I forgot where. The man asked me for change because he wanted to go across the street and call his '"Houston son' from the payphone. He had a one-dollar bill. We exchanged the money.

I wondered, then: How come this man was homeless, sleeping in churches and Salvation Army facilities, while having two successful sons? What little we know about other people's lives... And how quickly we jump to conclusions.

It was getting cloudy, and I started to search for a Kleenex. When I didn't find one, I blew my nose in the old towel that was on the back seat of my car. I wiped my eyes and the screen of my phone, and I dialed Earle's cell phone. I knew he was at work, of course. I knew he was stressed out. I knew he couldn't deal with Alex, but I also knew I couldn't drop off Alex to any of these half-way houses.

I told him that over the phone, calmly and quickly. I don't even know if he registered what I said. I imagined him nodding his head, a phone glued to his ear, while working on some quotes or parts. I heard several '*okays*', and the conversation was over.

As I said before, Alex's first hospitalization was short, about one week, and maybe this is why the half-way house issue wasn't pressed. The judge at the hospital only talked about taking medication for bipolar disorder and explained where to go for the blood tests. The blood tests were supposed to confirm the level of the medication. To put it short, the State needed to make sure that Alex was taking his meds. And as far as Alex was concerned, he said that he was only going back to Tessa, period.

Chapter 4
A room of his own

Since he was little, Alex always got angry very fast. Or maybe I shouldn't say it like that, because it's not entirely true. I would rather say that he simply didn't control his anger once he found himself in the place where things didn't go the way he planned. A good example of this would be the issue of having his own room. That was a problem in our house when Alex was a child. There were five children, my children's father, Matthias, and me, in our four-bedroom Mitchell Street house. The name of the house came from the street name. The master bedroom was taken by my ex-husband, Matthias, and me, and the three remaining bedrooms by the three older children. Alex and his little brother had the living room which was very spacious and the bunk bed easily fitted in there. Even though Matthias had installed a pocket door in a large opening to this room, it still didn't have the 'feel' of a room, only that of an open space anybody could invade. I didn't know how to sort out the bedroom situation.

Personally, I grew up in a small apartment in Warsaw, Poland, in the sixties. My family's apartment was about six-hundred square feet. There was a tiny kitchen with a little annex, where a live-in nanny had her bed. My parents, my two sisters and I, shared two remaining bedrooms and one bigger open room. Sometimes, we had visiting grandparents who stayed for a month or so. We all had to fit in; go to school, play with our toys, do homework, practice piano (which stood in the open room), cook, eat, wash, do our projects, etc. I think I mentioned it once or twice to my children, when they complained about space. I was told "it isn't communism here, Mom. This is America." I was also told I was 'old-fashioned' or something like that. I still was trying to tell them, but they lived in their own reality, the Western one, the one they were born into. After they grew up, they realized that, even though I grew up under communism, in a country which was only lifting itself up after a five-year occupation, I had been privileged.

My family lived in an apartment in Warsaw, Poland. The apartment was cool and warm, according to our needs in the seasons. My family had a telephone in the apartment and very few people had that privilege. My father owned a car. We had a car and phone without belonging to the Communist Party, only because my father was a lawyer and my mother was a journalist working for a Spanish Radio Station. I went to school. I had all the necessary shots. I went on summer and winter vacations, and I was never hungry. So, yes, we lived in a small apartment... My father smoked in it, of course, preferably while reading a paper and most certainly every time when he went to the bathroom. It was difficult to use the bathroom, right after he'd left. So what, that we only had our first washing machine when I was fourteen, and so what, that I remember life without a refrigerator. So what?

Finally, and most importantly, I didn't have my own room. Not even a table which could be called 'mine'.

When my children were growing up, I would tell them the stories from my childhood. I wanted them to know how good they had it. And of course, when the issue of Alex's room surfaced, I was again trying to tell Alex, a child can survive without a room of his own. But he wouldn't listen. He was eleven years old when he 'demanded' his own room and didn't want to have any conversation about it or even discuss the options.

He was getting angry. In fact, over the years, I observed the 'anger pattern' in him. It looked like this: as long as he was busy doing his projects, he was fine and happy, full of hope. His projects were artistic, unusual, elaborate and time consuming. Alex used all recyclable materials; the cardboard boxes, the empty ice cream containers, the old hangers, nails, screws and other odd objects found on the ground in various places where we went. The walk in the park was a goldmine to him and so was looking in our trash. I always let Alex use my studio for his projects. I had total trust he would only use the materials I let him use, not my own paints. Alex watched me working on my paintings very often, and he especially liked it when I painted on big canvases. Sometimes, we would both work at the same time. I would use the easel, and he would paint sitting on the floor.

The time spent on one of his projects was, on average, two months. During those two months, Alex was in his creative mode, so things would go well. All my friends marveled at how much time Alex was patiently spending cutting paper, coloring, painting and gluing. I remember this one time when Alex was a little sick and I was with him at home. He was about four years old. After I made his herbal tea and fed him a freshly baked scone, I saw him disappear into my studio. He told me that he needed to work on his new project and demanded an apron. I put it on him and tied it at his back. That

43

day a friend of mine stopped by with a tub of ice-cream. We opened it in the kitchen. On the table, she left a clear plastic ring which had sealed the ice-cream tub. It was trash. Alex grabbed it from the table and disappeared into my studio. My friend and I chatted over the ice-cream, but then she had to go. We went to my studio to look at my paintings. We found Alex hunched over a world map that he he'd just happened to have drawn. He had a paper hat on his head, which he he'd also just made, since I hadn't seen it before. It looked like the hat of an explorer. In his hand, he held a fake magnifying glass. He'd made it right there, by pinching the plastic ring from the ice-cream tub, and using the clothes pin he he'd gotten from the laundry room. He was playing explorer. He told us he was going on a long trip but he needed to study his map first.

We left him alone. He was obviously in his creative mode then. There was no sign of anger in him.

Things changed though when the creative mood was over. Knowing Alex as well as I did, gave me an opportunity to peek into the future slightly, and to know that the creative wave would be subsiding, soon. At those times, I had to brace myself and look for other creative ventures for him, hoping that one of them would ignite and Alex would jump at it. Often though, I wouldn't succeed with the new venture, and Alex would start being angry. He would only look for trouble. Often one idea would get stuck in his head, and never leave him. Like that one with wanting a room of his own. The first time he asked for it, he must have been about ten years old, and for over a year, I would explain to him the difficulty of finding a separate room for him.

He started to express his anger in various ways, like making scenes, holding onto things, not getting out of the way in the hallway and such like. He was eleven years old, and it was more difficult to discipline him. He didn't listen to anybody. One day, he simply hopped on his bike and rode away.

Before he did that, though, we had a huge fight on the porch. I don't remember exactly how it escalated to a very physical fight. Alex was totally beside himself. He picked up a rubber flip-flop that was on the laundry room floor, ran towards me, and started hitting me with it. I was trying to grab his hand and stop him. Matthias happened to be at home, so he came out to the porch and started yelling. Alex dropped the flip-flop and ran out through the side gate of the porch and grabbed his bicycle.

He didn't have shoes, nor the helmet, and he was very angry. I hopped on my bike and started to chase him. I was yelling for him to come back. I was pleading and trying to bargain. I was running over potholes in the back alley, because this is where we started our chase. At the end of it was a busy street. As Alex was speeding up, I was dreading what might happen if he wouldn't stop.

He didn't stop, of course, and neither did I. We were very lucky, since the light on the closest intersection was red for oncoming cars. We made it across the street right before it turned green, and we zoomed up a different back alley. My bike was bigger and I was fast, but when I caught up with Alex, I couldn't stop him anyway. How was I supposed to do it, riding at full speed?

"Alex, stop!" I said. "Stop or I will knock you over."

I hated threatening him. I didn't know what to do. Pretty soon this back alley ended, too, and we faced an even busier street. I was terrified.

"The cars will run you over, Alex," I yelled. He didn't care. At full speed we found ourselves in the middle of the street. One car stopped right in front of us. Alex didn't stop. "Will you give me my own room?" he asked, while continuing to zoom across.

"No, but you can use my studio," I said, terrified of the oncoming cars. I pedaled faster. "We will put your desk in there; you will only sleep on the bunk bed with Andrew."

I couldn't give Alex my studio as a bedroom. First of all, it was my studio. I worked there every night, most of the time 'til very late. Also, most of the time I slept there, on a small folding foam mattress.

I really hoped that Alex would stop his crazy ride, but he didn't. He was in a great danger on the streets, and I couldn't stop him. I came home, and as I was calling the police, Matthias hopped on his bike and rode away looking for Alex. Using the car was not an option, since Alex could cut through back alleys and other narrow places.

I dialed 911 and a dispatcher picked up the phone. I explained what the emergency was.

"Madam, it's a family matter and this is an eleven-year-old child," she said.

"I know how old Alex is," I said, irritated. "But I can't manage. He's angry. He was beating me with a shoe. He's riding his bike in a dangerous way. What am I supposed to do?"

"I don't know, madam, but we are not going to send an officer for a family matter like that," she said.

"But why?" I asked. I was angry, now. I felt my stomach tighten and the blood rushing to my head. "I can only push him off the bike if I even get close enough, and he would fall down and injure himself. And then," I continued, "then you would send an officer and arrest me for child abuse, right? So, what am I supposed to do?"

I guess I managed to change her mind because, after mumbling a few words she told me an officer would be on his way, shortly.

Matthias came home, but without Alex. He immediately went inside the bedroom and sat in front of the computer. He would always do that when he didn't know what to do. He knew I had called the police and was against it.

"It's all your fault," he managed to say, before he closed the bedroom door. "That's how you raised them. They don't have any respect for their father. Now, deal with the consequences," he said. I wasn't surprised. I fact, I barely noticed his words. He was always accusing me for any of the children's misbehavior, so I stopped taking it to heart.

The officer showed up with Alex. The officer was very tall and muscular. The gun on his belt was approximately at the same level as Alex's neck. He also had dark glasses, which he took off when he stepped inside. With the tall officer inside our house, Alex looked even smaller.

"Hi. Are you the mom?" the officer asked.

"Yes," I said. "And thank you for coming."

"And the father?" the officer raised his brows.

"He's… busy, doing something," I said.

At this moment, Andrew showed up. It seemed as if he came out of nowhere. He was eight years old. He was a very energetic boy. With his blond hair, blue eyes and skinny silhouette, he looked a lot like Alex.

"Dad is home," Andrew said. He started to jump up and down, out of excitement. "He's home, and he beats us and kicks us all the time," he shouted.

The officer looked at me, and then, at the wall behind me.

"I know nothing about that," the officer said.

I looked away.

Alex's brother kept jumping up and down and shouting. There was really no option to excuse myself, so I just grabbed his hand and asked him to try to calm down. It was hard to bribe him. He didn't watch TV, didn't care for video games, didn't want anything and didn't have a favorite food. It must have been something in my eyes though, because he stopped jumping.

"So, what are we going to do here?" the officer asked. "I was told that your son was hitting you, and then, ran away."

"Yes, that's what happened," I said.

"And why was that?" The officer was looking at Alex, now. Alex was red faced, scared and angry. I could tell.

"It's a complicated story," I said, "but putting it in short, we just don't have a bedroom for him. He has to share," I said.

The officer looked around our entry hall. It was really nice. We lived in a very pretty house in a good neighborhood. There was a big skylight that gave the entrance almost a palace-like look, especially as right under it we had a big indoor tree growing. There were whiteish Italian tiles everywhere, which reflected the light. Immediately to the right of the entry door was a living room with a large fire-place. It was Alex's and Andrew's room. Even though it didn't look like a traditional living room because it was furnished with a bunk bed and some miscellaneous pieces of furniture, it still looked classy.

"Well, we have a choice here," the officer said, after he stopped looking around. "How old is your son? And what's his name?"

"Alex," I said. "He's eleven."

"Eleven," the officer repeated. He paused for a moment. I heard Matthias's chair squeaking in the adjacent room. The officer turned to Alex.

"I have to arrest you," he said. Then, he turned to me. "I have to arrest him for domestic violence. I can either take him with me, or he can stay with you, but the arrest will be there and we will have to proceed with the Juvenile Court," the officer said.

"Let him stay," I said, immediately. "But officer, will this arrest have any long-term consequences? Like, will his school know about it or, when he goes to high school, will this be on his record?" I asked.

"No, not at all. He's only eleven. But everything will have to be followed as the procedure requires. The judge will make all the decisions.

"The judge?" I asked.

"Yes. This is a regular arrest and it will go through the Juvenile Court. Let's fill out the paperwork. Date of birth?" The officer was now writing in his notepad.

After doing all the paperwork the arrest required, the officer left. We were told we would be notified by mail about how to proceed.

#

After I closed the door, I came to hug Alex. He hugged me with all his might. He was shaking and crying and ran to the bathroom. I saw that he'd gotten diarrhea. I ran hot water into the tub. Alex got inside and he sat there, crying all the time. I went to the kitchen to get him a glass of lemonade. Matthias was waiting in the hallway.

"See what you did?" he said. He was standing tall, and even though I wasn't touching him, I could feel the tension in his muscles. The skin on his forehead was crumpled, expressing anger and astonishment at the same time. His neck was tense, with one blue vein leading up to his temple.

I closed the bathroom door, but I still was walking fast towards the kitchen. I didn't want Alex to hear us argue.

"What did I do?" I asked. "Did you have a better idea of what had to be done?"

"Of course," he said, "I'm telling you. All this disaster is the outcome of your actions. That's how you are raising the children-without any respect for their father. Who would ever arrest an eleven-year-old? Only you would, because you are simply stupid."

He was saying all this while following me to the kitchen. My mind was racing. Maybe I wasn't teaching the children to respect their father. If so, I wasn't doing it on purpose. They must have seen through my efforts, when I was telling them to respect his decisions, when I didn't agree with them. Like, for example, when he told me to go and close the student checking account. My eldest son, John, and I opened that account together, as a gift to him for his sixteenth birthday. The account lasted only few hours. John proudly showed the paperwork to his father and that was the end of it. I had to run to the bank and close it immediately. My eldest son cried and was humiliated. He stayed in his bed while I went to the bank. When I came back, I thought about having a conversation with my son, but was I was going to say? Justify his father's anger? Apologize? Wipe away his tears?

Matthias was talking all the time when I was pulling out a glass, opening the fridge and pouring the lemonade. Although I was trying to do it as fast as I could, it took enough time for me to hear the details of my stupidity. When I turned to go back to the bathroom, Matthias scratched his head and headed back to his computer. He passed by Andrew who was still standing by the entrance. For a moment, I thought that he might talk to the boy about his shouting at the officer about the children being kicked. He didn't, though. He was always a little afraid of his youngest son; that boy was completely unpredictable. Matthias went straight back to the computer.

The evening after the arrest, when everybody was asleep, I went outside to our backyard, pulled out a cigarette and took a long sip of a cold beer. I was watching the stars and asking myself, what had happened. My treasure, my pride, my beloved, genius eleven-year-old son had been arrested and I was the one who made it happen.

Or was I?

I didn't even think he would be arrested when I called the police. I wanted Alex to be out of danger on his terrible bike ride on a busy street. Nobody could help me and I couldn't stop him. What, then, was I supposed to do? The questions and answers were moving in perfect circles, without a way out.

#

A few days later, the notification from the Juvenile Court showed up in our mailbox. We were supposed to meet a judge the next week, in the morning. I had to take not only Alex, but Andrew as well, since I didn't have anybody to watch him. After a twenty-minute ride I parked in front of the large, red building. It wasn't only a court building. The Juvenile Jail was there as well.

Alex was still under the effect of the arrest, but he already showed signs of anger again. He blamed me for his arrest, telling me that he didn't do anything wrong.

"You were beating me," I finally said.

He got out of the car and slammed the door with all his force.

"Alex," I said. "You better behave yourself. The judge, and all this, it isn't a joke. Look, there's a security guard watching us."

It was true. The security guard was right there, and sure enough, he was watching us.

The meeting with the judge was tense for Alex and for me, but maybe for different reasons. I had a fear that Alex's brother would start talking again,, but at the same time, the same fear told me not to mention anything to him before the meeting. He would only do the opposite, or so I thought.

Alex was tense because he had to answer questions. He was afraid enough not to show his anger. Right after we left though, he was disrespectful to me again.

The judge assigned him lots of hours of community service so, of course, I drove directly to the church we were assigned to, and talked to Sister Jo, the one who was in charge of religious education for the younger children. She was an older woman in her seventies, very skinny, with large glasses which tended to rest on the very middle of her nose. The recent events must have been imprinted on my face in some form, because she pulled me close.

"You don't need to worry, ever," she said. "Just don't worry. Everything will be okay."

Well, how did she know?, and how was I to live, every day?

I dropped Alex off at the church a few times a week, where he was assigned to help cleaning and some other church related activities. Often, when I picked him up, he was very angry with me. I moved his desk to my studio, and I even gave him my favorite chair which I had painted. Alex really liked it. He was very inspired by it and he wanted to paint some other piece of furniture by himself. In the evenings, we would sit in my studio together; me, working on my paintings, and him, doing homework or his projects until he had to go to bed. I have a small painting of him sitting at his desk, then. In this painting, he looks very focused on his project.

Chapter 5
"You should really do something"

After Alex's first hospitalization ended, I picked him up from the Behavioral Unit and we left quickly. Once outside, we found my car and sat in it for a while. The car was new. I had bought it only the previous week. Alex took out of his bag a pile of papers and an even bigger pile of meds, and he put it all on the floor between his feet. He hadn't seen my new car yet and got very excited. All the way to his house he was hitting the armrest with his fist.

"Jeez, Mom, you have such an awesome car. This is awesome. Incredible." He couldn't stop showing his excitement. When we were riding for ten minutes or so, he pulled up the hospital package from the floor and opened it. He started to read out loud the top page of this stack of papers that he'd been given.

"Some bipolar shit," he said. "These people have no idea."

I was watching the road but I didn't like his attitude. I didn't say anything, though. I was questioning my eagerness of discharging Alex that early from the hospital. Seeing his excitement made me think that maybe he should have stayed longer. The doctor was the one who made the ultimate decision, and at the time, I felt happy about it. Now though, I wasn't sure but I remembered Alex wanted to prepare for his finals.

"Are you hungry?" I asked.

"No, just take me to Flanwill house. I bet Tessa has something to eat."

I wasn't so sure, but it turned out that she had ordered pizza. Alex was ecstatic. He devoured two slices while walking around the living room. With his other hand he was playing with a yo-yo.

That evening I left Alex with my heart a little lighter. I was glad I'd managed to bypass the

half-way house. Alex said he would take his meds, 'mostly'.

#

After a few days of peace and calm, Alex started to call me, very often.

"What's up? How are you?" I asked. It was Alex calling me for the third time that day.

"I'm fine," he said. "But Tessa, I think she's holding me back. She's impossible. I don't know how I can possibly study when she's around."

"What does she do?" I asked.

His reply was long. Nothing was right. Tessa wanted this and that. She was demanding. I couldn't picture it. I knew Tessa. She was mature beyond her years, and certainly, she wanted the best for Alex. And all this time, still, she wanted to marry him. A week after this conversation Alex informed me that they'd bought her a wedding dress. They'd also bought bow ties for Tessa's dogs who were supposed to be present at the ceremony.

"Things are going great, Mom," Alex said. "Tessa got her

GED, meaning she worked on her high-school diploma on her own, and she successfully finished it, All As!"

This was very good news, and when Tessa came over to borrow a crockpot, my husband gave her one hundred dollars. Tessa thanked us for the crock pot and invited us to her grandmother's house to talk about the wedding details.

"My family doesn't want us to get married," she said.

"Really?" I said. I didn't say I wasn't surprised.

"Please help us get married," Tessa said.

I said that we would do what we could. We went to her grandma's house the next day.

Tessa's family had decided not to give her their consent to marry, period.

"You have to wait till you're eighteen, that's what we've decided," her grandma said.

We were sitting together on an old couch at Grandma's house where Tessa lived legally. The house was old and old-fashioned, in the central part of Tucson, with embroidered napkins and hand-woven napkins in the kitchen. Above the couch, a white cloth with what I thought was a large duck cross-hatched with blue thread hung over us.

"But I want to get married. Now!" Tessa cried. "And you," she looked at me. "You promised to help me!"

I felt as if I was deceiving her, but how else could I have helped except for what I was doing now? And besides, no matter how much I wanted Alex to be okay, I didn't know what guarantees there were for their having a good life together.

After this very sad visit, we went home. Tessa left, too. She went to the house where she lived with Alex.

Then the situation changed, again.

Things were not going well as Alex told me over the

phone. A few days later, Tessa called me. She wanted to meet. The next day in the morning, we met at a local small coffee shop, close to Flanwill house. There were not many people inside, and Tessa's voice seemed very loud, even though she was almost whispering.

"I don't know what to do," she said.

"Why do you need to do anything?" I asked. "Did you apply to Pima College?"

I really wanted Tessa to go to college. She could start at Pima and transfer to the University. She was smart. She said she would put in an application.

"You know Alex. He hit the wall," she said, suddenly. She put aside a little fork with which she was eating cake and looked at me.

"A wall? What wall?" I was thinking metaphorically, but it turned out it was a real wall which he'd punched, and he'd made a hole in it. It didn't sound good. I told Tessa that maybe she should stay over at her grandma's for a few days. She was disappointed with me. I could see that.

After I left the coffee house, I went to Home Depot to buy a few things. While I was walking between the aisles, my phone rang. I didn't know the flashing number.

"Do you know Alex Wojtkowski?" a woman's voice asked.

"I do. I'm his mother,"

"Okay. This is Danielle from the U of A. Alex isn't doing well. You know, you should do something."

I froze.

"What happened?"

"He was riding his skateboard on the roof of a ten-story building and didn't want to stop when asked. We needed to call security and the campus police."

I didn't know what to ask first, but I tried this one.

"Was he arrested?"

"They let him go. But you should really do something," the woman said.

"Me?" I didn't know that I was actually pointing at myself with my finger. I was in the bathroom department, and suddenly, I saw myself in a large closet mirror, poking at my chest.

"You don't understand," I said, "I've tried. See, Alex is eighteen. There's really not much I can do. I mean, I'm not different from anybody else in this matter. It doesn't make a difference that I'm his mother. He's not going to listen to me. I can't punish him by not giving him candy."

I added the last sentence because of my growing anger. I felt it in my stomach, boiling together with sadness and fear.

"Madam, I'm just saying. Something needs to be done," the woman said.

"Then do it, whatever needs to be done; do it! I feel powerless," I said, before I hung up.

It turned out that it wasn't meant to be for me to remain powerless. In fact, I had to become powerful, and use the power. And who cares if so called 'powerful people' cry at night?

Tessa called me several times the next day, and I told her I would go see her at around four in the afternoon. When I parked the car in front of their house, Alex was leaving for school. They were fighting. Tessa was crying and yelling at Alex, while he was pushing books into his backpack and trying to zip it. A yellow yo-yo fell out of his pocket.

"Out," he yelled. "Get out and leave me alone!" Then, he saw me. "Mom, tell her to leave, now. She's holding me back.

I won't pass my exam. I have an astronomy class in half an hour, and I need to make it there."

He must have been under the influence of something. He behaved as if he was drunk but he wasn't drunk. If anything, he was drunk with anger. I didn't smell any alcohol. The house smelled like pot, but Alex wasn't high, although I wasn't totally sure. To me, all drugs were the same. I knew though that, when he was smoking pot, his eyelids were puffy, eyes squinting, and most of all, he wouldn't be so angry. Now, his face was red and his movements were sharp. Tessa's face was red and swollen from crying.

"Tessa, maybe I could take you over to your grandma?" I said.

"No! I'm not going anywhere. I'm not throwing away a relationship into which I've invested so much. I've given Alex everything. We are together. Period."

"See what she does to me? Mom, deal with her! I'm leaving for school."

Alex grabbed his skateboard and backpack and left. I told Tessa to get her stuff and waited for her in the car, but she came out after a while and told me to leave. She told me her friend would give her a ride over to her grandma's house.

I doubted that for a little while but it must have been true, since Alex texted me the next day that Tessa was gone. I thought things would improve. I was wrong.

If anything, they became worse. I was going over to his house every day, just to chat, maybe help him with the groceries or simply to hang out. But Alex didn't pay much attention to me, and if he did, it was in a negative way. He stopped cleaning altogether, he didn't take his trash out and the house smelled. I asked him several times if he was keeping up with his meds. He only shrugged his shoulders.

"You are not going to lock me up again, are you?" he asked.

I wasn't going to do it. It would simply cost too much. But Alex's Sunday School teacher, the one leading the band which Tessa sang in, said he was willing to help. I called him the next day. We met at the church. I met him in his classroom, after the youth class.

"I'll visit him tomorrow. I'll talk to him," the Sunday School teacher said. His name was Mr Brown. He was tall, very skinny and almost bald. He knew all my children and liked them very much.

That tomorrow was a regular school day, a Tuesday. Alex was supposed to be at the University. Lately though, I sensed that he was only attending his Astronomy class.

Mr Brown went to talk to Alex and later on gave me a detailed recount of the events. He knocked on Flanwill house door several times only to hear nothing. He walked around the house, as far as the fence allowed. Nothing, again. But then, he heard a noise coming from the bedroom. It sounded as if a door was opening and closing.

"Alex?" he called.

It was then when I started to receive a series of desperate text messages from Alex. To say that he was afraid would have been an understatement. He was panicking. I called him. He didn't pick up.

"You know Mr Brown," I texted. "Let him in."

"They are trying to get me," Alex texted back.

Nothing was helping. Alex finally took the problem into his own hands and started to defend himself by throwing yo-yos at Mr Brown through the window, which he opened only for that purpose. It didn't take long for Mr Brown to call the police. In the late afternoon, against his will, Alex was taken to Kino Hospital Behavioral Unit, where Mr Brown filled out the paperwork in order to commit him. I read a copy of it. I remember one line: '*Alex was throwing yo-yos at me*', it said, among other things. It was Alex's second hospitalization.

Chapter 6
Bipolar

During his second hospitalization, Alex became as angry as one could imagine. The day after his hospitalization, Earle and I drove to the hospital to visit him. I remember that day. It was cloudy. The hospital parking lot was almost empty and we parked close to the entrance. We walked in and in the hall-way we met with the social worker. It was a very nice man, short in stature, with thick glasses and brown hair. He took us to his windowless office. There, in the warm yellow light of two table lamps, he explained to us what was going on and what was likely to happen.

"Can we see him? I asked, before he started explaining.

"I don't think it's a good idea," the social worker said. "At least not today."

"Why?" I asked.

"Alex is very angry," he said. Then, after a short pause he repeated *'very angry'*, stressing the word *'very'*, looking me in the eye. I felt a little uneasy. Earle took my hand.

"How angry?" I asked. "What is he doing?"

"Mostly calling his lawyer," the social worker said.

"His lawyer?" I turned to look at Earle. He looked back at me but I didn't see any answer in his eyes.

I didn't know Alex had a lawyer. In fact, he didn't. The social worker had a number which Alex was constantly dialing, and I checked it in my contacts. It turned out he was calling his friend's father, who happened to be a lawyer, and Alex knew him. Now I knew who the lawyer was. The phone that Alex was using hung on the wall in the common area of the Behavioral Unit. It didn't have a dial tone to the city. The patient was first connected to the receptionist. Even that obstacle wasn't preventing a long line from forming along the wall on which the phone was installed. Some patients were desperate to talk to the outside world. According to the social worker, Alex was one of them. Supposedly, he was hogging the phone and other patients held it against him. But when he was on it, he was pounding the wall with his free hand and yelling into the receiver that it was mandatory for him to talk to his lawyer. He was calling on his rights and 'The Constitution'. After a while the nurses and security had it with him. They threatened they would notify the doctor and a new medication would be administered. The medication would put Alex to sleep and the hospital unit would return to normal.

We sat in the social worker's office for over an hour, while he was going in and out and assuring us things were under control. He was constantly fixing the thick frame of his glasses and waving away his brown, unruly hair. Finally, he told us that Alex's paperwork was all done, and that he was put on the government health insurance. At the time, Alex still had health insurance his father was paying for, but the social worker wasn't interested.

"It will be a good thing for him," he said, meaning using his new government plan. Here again, Alex was eighteen, so it wasn't like I could make any decisions. During this hour in the office, we were trying to find out what was wrong with Alex.

"Bipolar disorder," the social worker said.

Until that day, I hadn't heard about bipolar disorder. It seemed as if nowadays everything was a disorder of some sort, and most people needed medication. I raised five children. I gave birth to all of them within seven years. I was familiar with all possible doctors' offices, psychologists and psychiatrists included. One day, when Alex was six years old, he stopped eating. I couldn't convince him to swallow anything at all. I cooked his favorite soups and dishes, made desserts, to no avail. At school he was seen throwing his lunch away. All this time I was finding around the house and in Alex's backpack small pieces of paper with pencil drawings. The images looked like two pipes, or maybe a tree. When I asked Alex what it was, he showed me his throat and trachea. He pointed at his chest, too.

"That's how we swallow food," he said.

He didn't want anything for dinner and went to his room. Later in the evening I went to check on him. I found him in tears. His pillow was wet, too, but after touching it I realized that they weren't tears only. The pillow was slippery and slimy. Alex has been spitting on it. He was afraid to swallow his saliva, thinking that it might go down the wrong way in his throat and eventually kill him.

The psychiatrist prescribed therapy sessions for an unusually strong obsessive-compulsive disorder, also called 'OCD', at the early age of six. We also talked about medication, of course. It was clear to me though, that I didn't want to give Alex any meds.

But now Alex was eighteen and the doctor didn't talk about obsessive-compulsive disorder. The new word, 'bipolar', replaced the old 'OCD'. I'd never heard the word 'bipolar', and because of that, it didn't mean much to me. I wasn't sure that bipolar disorder was a good explanation for Alex's problems.

We left the hospital equipped with a bunch of brochures, papers and other supporting materials. While Earle was driving, I was going through them.

"What are you looking for?" he asked.

"That one paper with a schedule of the meetings. For bipolar people, remember?"

"Look in the yellow envelope," he said.

Earle was not only a gentleman, but a gentle soul, too. Lately, he was a little withdrawn, and I didn't know at the time the depth of his anxiety. He was the owner of a successful small business, a plastic fabrication company. He employed five people and worked very hard. He also had an art gallery. Things were going well for now. The big cloud of the upcoming Great Recession could be visible sometimes on the horizon, but nobody paid attention to it yet. Certainly not Earle. Something was fishy in the business world, though. My paintings stopped selling like they used to, and I saw it as a bad sign. Still, we didn't know what was coming. And I was totally absorbed by Alex's situation. Earle had to work. But he readily agreed to go to the first available meeting. At one of the conference rooms at UMC, University Medical Center, a group of people were meeting one late afternoon. Alex was still in the hospital, but we attended without him.

We entered a large, windowless room. Almost all of it was taken up by many tables put together. Around this group of tables there were twenty chairs. I counted the people in the room. There were five men and seven women, plus Earle and me.

The leader of the group was a middle-aged woman, who

identified herself as Elizabeth. She also said she was bipolar. Then people started introducing themselves and telling their stories. Not all of them were bipolar. Some of them were simply family members of a person with the disorder, who didn't want to or couldn't attend. I particularly remember one older man. He was in his early seventies. He explained how every day, *every day*, for years, he had wanted to kill himself and even now he still struggles in order not to do it. His eyes were red. He must have been tall because, even while sitting, his head was above the others. I remember him particularly, because it was during his speech when Earle stared crying. He grabbed my hand with one hand, and wiping his cheeks with the other, he started talking.

"Forgive, me," he said, looking at the group. "I had no idea."

Nobody asked him what idea and why he was crying, including me. I squeezed his hand back. I had to introduce myself, though, which I did. I told the meeting what brought me to the meeting.

"Alex hates me. My son hates me," I said. I was trying not to be sorry for myself.

"He hates himself, not you. It's very simple. Don't take it to heart," said a woman from across the table.

What she said sounded to me like a quote from a book or a paper. But he *really* hated me. How was I supposed to ignore my son hating me?

#

The next day, I took Tessa to the hospital for a visit. Alex didn't want to see me and I didn't want to insist. I sat in a lobby while

Tessa walked in through the wide doors. I was looking at the abstract prints hanging on the hospital walls when a woman dressed in a blue gown came to me and told me I could actually go inside. I looked at her face. It was large and smiling. Her black hair was curly and neatly tied in a ponytail.

"Is my son waiting for me?" I pointed at my chest.

"They said you can come in," the woman in blue said, without answering my question. I got up and walked in through the same doors Tessa had.

My eyes searched through people in a large open room. There were several tables and plastic chairs, and the patients were in loose pajamas, some of them in hospital gowns. They didn't have shoes. All of them were wearing bright yellow or gray hospital socks, the ones that have a rubber print on the soles. I still have two pairs of those in my closet. My eyes kept searching, and then I saw Tessa and Alex. They were sitting by a small table, not far from where I was standing. I was surprised hadn't seen them before.

When I came close to the table, Tessa got up. It wasn't because she wanted me to take her seat, although it might have seemed so. Instead, it had to do with their conversation. After getting up, she came around the table and pressed Alex's head to her stomach. She was crying. To this day I can hear in my head the voice of this seventeen-year-old girl, choked by tears, whispering, "Baby, I love you." She was passing her fingers through Alex's hair.

Alex was just sitting there. He was obviously medicated. His eyes were squinting and face puffy.

"Mom," he said.

Tessa let him go and sat down. She was wiping away her tears and calming down the sobs.

Alex asked me for cigarettes, which I obviously didn't have. I promised to bring some, although I was surprised the patients were allowed to smoke.

"Hell, yeah," Alex said. "Not only that. Sometimes the guard brings something better than cigs, but one has to be *really* nice to him."

"What does he bring?" I asked, naively.

I didn't get an answer. On the way out, I saw the infamous phone hanging on the wall. Two women in hospital gowns were standing in line while a tall man was talking into the receiver.

#

Alex stayed in the hospital about ten days this time. He repeatedly asked me for cigarettes. He missed snowboarding. The big window in the main room had a view of the mountains, and it only tormented Alex.

"Did you see the mountains? Covered in snow! And what do I do? I can only look at them through the window, because you had a fancy of locking me up. I should be snowboarding now!" Alex cried.

He missed his yo-yos, too. He was allowed to play with a small, rubber ball, which he was constantly squeezing in the palm of his hand. But he wasn't allowed to play with a yo-yo. The string was too dangerous. I even wanted to bring him one yo-yo without a string, but the hospital staff just said no. Alex was only allowed to use a tiny pencil, and not very sharp. With this pencil he was drawing models of a spaceship, very much resembling the yo-yo. Sometimes, a mathematical equation figured on the same piece of paper, right by the very detailed drawing. Alex's nurse posted several of his drawings on the wall, so everybody could look at them and even ask questions. Alex was very eager to explain his theory of a yo-yo spaceship.

With this hospital stay it was obvious that Alex wasn't going to pass the semester. He and I decided on a medical leave option, but he still had some reservations. He really wanted to pass at least his favorite class, Astronomy. He asked me to go and to talk to his professor. I agreed immediately but inside I was opposed to the idea. He was eighteen, and the so-called adult life on campus rejected intervening parents. Although I understood the reasons for such policies, I still wanted Alex's case to be an exception. I took a trip to the campus, and while I was walking through it, my cheeks were wet with tears and my eyes were red and swollen behind the sunglasses. I saw boys, Alex's age, all happy and talking and laughing, holding hands with their girlfriends, riding bikes, walking with headphones on, eating sandwiches, drinking soda. They all looked normal to me, and every tear of mine repeated the question: '*Why isn't Alex like them?*'

Chapter 7
Yo-Yos

I would like to write a story about Alex in a very linear manner, but no matter how many times I try to do that, I fail. This is the reason why I have to write this separate chapter, about yo-yos only. Yes, we are talking about the yo-yos that children play with. We are talking about the toy. We all know how a yo-yo looks like. It is round and could be made from different materials — metal, wood, most often plastic. A yo-yo has a string attached, so it can be thrown and brought back safely to the person playing with it. A yo-yo can be painted with plain colors, or have specific images glued to it on so-called pogs, which are simply round, cardboard pieces glued to the yo-yo's top and bottom. Alex's house was full of this last kind of yo-yo.

The situation with the yo-yos was out of hand. The yo-yos were taking over Alex's life, of course. All the people around Alex had to deal with yo-yos. The yo-yos were virtually everywhere, wherever Alex was, and when he left somewhere, he would leave some yo-yos, too.

When he was still with Tessa in Flanwill house, the yo-yos were taking up most of the space. They were in big cardboard boxes on the floor and in smaller plastic boxes on the shelves in the bedroom closet. The kitchen cupboards were full of yo-yos stored in plastic bags. There were also other things belonging to yo-yo equipment like, for example, strings and empty pogs, waiting for an image. I could see that Alex was organizing the yo-yos. The boxes were marked with a black sharpie, with the yo-yo count and sometimes the color. Before the first hospital stay, Alex was only starting to be fascinated with yo-yos, and he would buy them at random places. It changed after he came out of the hospital. Then Alex seriously hit the internet with the yo-yo campaign and the big and small packages started to arrive to our different addresses: Flanwill house, Desert house and Huachuca Drive, the location of our plastic company. I would wake up in the morning, and even before I opened my eyes, I was already thinking how many yo-yos would arrive today and to which location. I remember when one day when I brought Alex home from his appointment with the psychiatrist and we saw two large packages with UPS labels resting on the porch. Alex couldn't wait for me to stop the car. He jumped out and ran toward the boxes.

"Mom!" he shouted. "More yo-yos! Remember this guy I told you about? He's giving me his whole collection! Not a collection, forget it," he immediately corrected himself. "His whole warehouse!"

"Where's the warehouse?" I asked. Not that I really wanted to know. The number of yo-yos in those two boxes was overwhelming, especially if someone knew the house was already full of yo-yos.

"In his garage, now," Alex said, to answer my question.

"Aha" I said, inspecting the packing slip that didn't really reveal any information about the sender. "And where is the garage, in that case?"

"East Coast, I think. I will have to check my emails," he

71

said.

The two boxes were full of plastic yo-yos that came in two colors, black and yellow. They were all new, with the ropes nicely rolled in separates plastic bags.

"Let's move the boxes to the house; somebody could steal them," Alex said. "I will ask you to store some for me, but not yet. For now, I'm so happy to have them I need just to look at them for a while."

It was easier said than done. The boxes were very heavy, and after we finally managed to push them into the house, I was sweating.

We hugged and I went back to the car. I left Alex in the house and ran back to work. On his seat, I saw the yo-yo that he'd had with him during the visit with the doctor. I picked it up. Green pictures of marijuana leaves were printed on both sides.

During the visit with the psychiatrist, Alex was playing with this yo-yo all the time, impatiently walking around the room. I remember when the doctor had to drop his head to his desk because the yo-yo was flying towards his head. Alex was showing us a new trick.

"Never a dull moment in my life," the doctor said and laughed. He was a muscular man in his thirties. His blue shirt was so crisp I thought I heard a cracking noise when he was bending his elbows. He kept laughing, showing his white teeth, and repeating his "never a dull moment" remark. He was a doctor assigned by the hospital or rather by the agency Alex was assigned to; Community Behavioral Services, 'COPE' for short, was taking care of the psychiatric needs of people who used government insurance or people who needed help from the state. The patients this doctor would see were people without resources, the ones we see on the streets, begging, the ones who occupy the waiting rooms of the agencies assigned to care for the patients registered with the Department of Economic Security, or 'DES'. And the DES required paperwork from these agencies. Only with the proper paperwork could food stamps and other financial assistance be delivered.

This particular psychiatrist had a good time throughout our visit, I could tell. Alex was so entertaining. I presume that this doctor had seen other patients who had all sort of disorders and psychoses but I don't think that he'd seen a yo-yo obsession yet. Who would think of it? Yo-yo spaceship. Yo-yo, the most perfect shape. Yo-yo, the relaxer for tangled nerves. And who knows what else? As Alex was walking and talking around the office, it seemed as if a yo-yo was only a little detail, and the main topic was marijuana, and the ways people should use it. Otherwise, also according to Alex, the world would go to hell quickly.

"He's an addict, I'm telling you, he's an addict," the doctor told me several times, between the laughs about either Alex's jokes or his behavior. The doctor didn't mind Alex's presence, which confused me a little. But Alex, on the other hand, didn't mind the doctor's remarks. He didn't care.

"Never a dull moment," he repeated for the tenth or twentieth time. He was young and I felt comfortable enough to ask him why he chose psychiatry as a specialty. I shared that I had a son in medical school in Poland.

"Exactly. Me, too, I finished abroad. It was hard to get anything else. But this, you know, the salary's great, the entry position at my job in this town is over two hundred and fifty thousand dollars. And the job? Never a dull moment," he said.

After a short while, he added, "It's mostly distributing meds. There's only so much a doctor can do for these people."

I thought it was true. And I also thought how little the doctors knew about those meds they were distributing, how their patients, especially those using government insurance, live on the very border of reality.

We left the doctor's office reinforced with a new prescription of Depakote, which is the most common medication used for patients with a bipolar disorder. It is a mood stabilizer. Alex promised he wouldn't smoke pot; at least, not for a while.

#

Alex's psychiatrist was very understanding about his patient's behavior. Alex played with the yo-yo all visit long and nobody paid attention to it. Not everybody had as much understanding as that psychiatrist did.

I distinctly remember our visit to the DES. It was our first visit there and it was after Alex's second hospital stay. He had government insurance then, and upon his discharge from hospital, he was assigned to COPE agency, who directed us to the DES. Alex was supposed to get food stamps and schedule some other things and follow ups. At first, I was hesitant about the food stamps. In my mind then, food stamps weren't needed by people like us. But with the recession on our shoulders, we had really limited options. Earle was constantly working and there wasn't enough money, even for the bills. Alex wasn't an easy person and he wanted his stuff. Of course, we stopped taking rent from him. We were covering all the bills. Anyway, we went to the DES.

I had never been to the DES before. Alex dressed up for this occasion and it made me cry. He put on a suit that I'd bought him for his wedding. I remember I bought it for five hundred dollars. It had been hanging in the closet since then, never touched. Now, he put this suit on. On the lapel of his jacket, he pinned a colorful rooster, a large, valuable pin that his grandfather had bought for him in Poland years before. He stuffed his pockets with various yo-yos.

"Just in case somebody needs one. You never know," he said. He didn't see that I was crying. He also put a regular baseball hat on his head, with some pins in it. He had dark sunglasses on with thick, red frames. He was eighteen but it would be hard to say only by looks how old he was. He looked like a kid dressed up for Halloween.

I couldn't find a parking space in front of the DES, and it surprised me. How did all these poor people get here? In their own cars? I found out soon that I was only partially right; right around the corner, I saw the people who probably had come by bus. Very few of them looked what could be considered normal. It was a group composed of either fat or too thin people, many of them using canes or walkers, most of them slightly sunburned, and at least half of them talking out loud, just like that, to themselves.

Inside, the line was long, even the one to the information window. Nobody was fast and some people were very impatient. The woman behind the glass at the information window had a slightly sleepy look. She repeated her answers to the customers, while looking at the computer screen. Sometimes, she would reach for the proper paperwork and slide it below the glass window. She gave instructions to the applicants:

"This needs to be filled out. Pay attention to the highlighted places. After filling it out you can go to window three to make an appointment with the DES representative."

Usually, the applicant would slowly turn around while already examining the highlighted places on the paper and almost always turned back to the window. Most of the time, the next person would already be talking to the lady behind the glass. The previous applicant would step aside, waiting for a moment when the window would be available, for the five seconds between applicants. The applicants waiting aside formed an additional, informal line, or actually two of them, since the customers would leave the window going either to the left or to the right. When the lady closed the window by putting up a big sign informing of the lunch break, a window to the left opened up. This created an immense commotion with all the lines. A wave went through them. They stabilized after a moment, taking the previous shape and look, only in a different place.

In all this crowd, Alex played with his yo-yo and it was impossible to stop him. Even in the DES crowd, he stood out. With his suit and a hat and the sunglasses that he didn't take off, even though we were inside, he looked more than different. Some people laughed at him and some were angry, mostly, because he needed space for his yo-yo tricks and he was so absorbed in doing them he didn't pay attention that he might hit somebody.

Some children came closer to him, obviously interested, and he immediately gave them the yo-yos from his pocket. Their mother waved in a friendly way from the chair she was sitting in, close to the main door. Me, too; I wanted to sit in a chair. I knew that only the people who already had an appointment with a ticketed number were sitting. The whole left side of the room was filled with rows of chairs. It looked like a movie theater but all the seats were taken.

It was extremely difficult to fill out the paperwork on site but I was determined to do it at once. There were examples of the forms on the side wall, filled in all possible languages, but the English example was missing. I had to go back to the line, all the time paying attention and talking to Alex. Suffice it to say that we did manage to make an appointment. It was scheduled at noon, three days later, at the same location.

When we left, I decided I would stop at one of the galleries which was hanging my work occasionally. I needed to pick up my small painting that hadn't sold during the last show. I had known the owners a long time, and for many years, they exclusively represented my work. This gallery was considered to be prestigious in town. Furthermore, the owners knew Alex and not only from my paintings, since I painted my children a lot. They knew him personally. When Alex worked for Earle's plastics company, he would also make deliveries. He would deliver plastic sheets for this gallery. We still had the plastics business, but obviously, Alex didn't work there any more. The owners loved him and they had told me that several times.

It looked though that their positive feelings towards Alex disappeared the moment we entered the gallery.

They let us inside their very large office where they also had a limited framing shop. When Alex walked in, playing with his yo-yo, the wife got angry, and even angrier at her husband, who tried to be nice to Alex. She yelled at her husband and he quickly changed his behavior. I got my small painting and we left immediately.

Two days later, we went back to the DES for the scheduled

appointment. I knew this time I would be sitting in a gray chair, but would Alex sit? I deeply doubted it. He got dressed nicely, again, but didn't put the suit on and I was grateful. It must have been Tessa working on him. All this time, they were still together. She really tried to help Alex and did her best to keep him focused and taking his meds. Well, Alex didn't put the suit on, but he didn't forget his yo-yo. Again, he had plenty of spare ones in his pockets, and one in his hand, that one he was constantly throwing. I knew we had to be on time in the DES, but not a minute earlier, because I didn't know how Alex would behave. Or rather, I knew how he would behave, and that was the reason not to get there too early. I parked the car, and we waited outside. When our appointment time came, I steered us inside. When I say 'steered', I mean it. Alex didn't really want to come in. The yo-yo he was playing with had more space outside. I sat in the closest chair, but Alex didn't want to sit down. That was a problem because we still had to wait inside for another twenty minutes. These were terrible minutes. I could see only the thick line in front of us, the very line we were standing in two days earlier. We were now in the theater; the people in the line were mostly new to the system. Keeping Alex at bay was very hard, that's all I can say.

When our number was called, I jumped up and we followed the man in a gray suit who opened the large wooden door for us. When the door slowly shut behind us, the man looked at Alex and pointed to his yo-yo. Alex was still playing with it.

"You can't come in with that thing," he said. He slightly squatted while trying to avoid Alex's yo-yo which was flying close to his chest. As a result, his name tag with the picture got caught on Alex's toy. The man got angry.

At this point of his life, Alex didn't expect anybody to be unhappy or mean.

"Which thing?" he asked, and looked around. We were standing by the large door leading to the DES interior space, where the cubicles were located

"Don't play games," the man said, rather impatiently. "That thing." He pointed to the yo-yo, again. He untangled his name tag.

"Oh!" Alex understood. "Do you want one?" From his pocket he pulled out a yo-yo. I wanted to say something but I kept my mouth shut. Luckily, the man gave up on Alex, and led us to a cubicle where a middle-aged lady was sitting at a computer. The lady was rather large. Her shirt was pink, and she was wearing a bright green necklace which looked as if was made out of plastic triangular shapes. She also had green earrings.

"Can you stop playing with that thing?" the lady immediately asked. "Are you Alex?"

"Yes, I am," Alex caught the yo-yo which was flying close to the lady's desk. He threw it again.

"Can he stop doing that?" she said.

Now the lady was looking at me I tried to show that I was concerned and asked Alex nicely to stop playing and sit down; we had to go over his paperwork. He did sit down, but only for fifteen seconds or so. He would sit and not even focus but jump up and play, again and again. It was very difficult to get through the appointment without making that lady angry. Well, on the other hand, her anger helped us, too. She definitely wanted to get rid of us so she quickly went through the paperwork that we had filled out and the form from COPE. She confirmed government insurance and the food stamps.

The Electronic Benefit Transfer card or 'EBT' was supposed to come in the mail.

"It will look like a regular debit card that people use in the store," the lady said.

#

After the appointment, we went back to Alex's house, where Tessa was waiting. I left Alex there and I drove away with a heavy heart. While dropping him off, I only glimpsed inside and was terrified at the number of yo-yos I could see just at the entrance. Tessa kept organizing them and that helped some. I told her something would need to be done with the yo-yos and I would let her know if I had any new idea. Throwing them away was out of question.

After sticking to his meds for about four weeks, Alex calmed down enough to see that the number of yo-yos was overwhelming. I was happy with that.

"Well, you bought them," I said. "So maybe you could sell them." Alex was having one of his better days and I figured it was a good time to plant that idea in his head.

"Wow, Mom, what a great idea!" he said. "Of course, we should sell them. We will make tons of money!"

Easier said than done. Try to sell plain plastic yo-yos, even for a dollar each. Where? How? These were my questions. After careful deliberations, we all agreed that the yo-yos needed to have more personality, so to speak, in order to get the attention of any potential buyer.

"We have to buy a pog puncher," Alex said. "And since I don't have any money, you will have to buy it. But Mom, think of it as of investment."

I already knew that pogs were these round cardboard pieces glued to the yo-yo's top and bottom. Now I found out what a pog puncher was. It was a tool to cut out pogs. It more or less looked like a hammer. There were many different ones online so I told Alex to choose.

The overall plan was about making the pogs in the yo-yos more attractive. I volunteered to put my artwork on them. Putting on paintings of famous and long-gone artists wasn't a good option, because of the legal implications; my artwork was safe.

And so was Earle's. His paintings had a modern look. My art was figurative. Alex called Earle and asked for permission to use his art on the yo-yos. I wondered if Earle registered that phone call. Of course he agreed, but I was glad he even picked up the phone. Being as stressed as he was at that time, I knew he didn't like to talk to Alex.

In addition to the artwork, I suggested pictures of local animals; coyotes, javelinas, snakes, etc. Alex agreed heartily but then he got scared, again, that we would use someone else's pictures, and there would be a liability.

"You have a camera," he told me. "Maybe you'll take pictures?"

I agreed.

I went to the Desert Museum and took lots of pictures. At home, I set myself to work on all the artwork for the pogs. I had to go to the print shop and print the properly formatted and cropped pictures on thick, glossy paper All this took me long time. It was a major designing project.

I felt very much alone with all of this. I couldn't share with Earle too much because he was getting more and more depressed since he knew the company was simply sinking.

And if the company was sinking, we were sinking too. He thought that only his work could save us and he was certainly right. The overwhelming amount of money though we had to pay for the gallery's mortgage every month was killing his spirit. The whole situation with the gallery looked like it would never end.

Often, I would wake up really early in the morning and drive to the gallery where I still had a studio. I wanted to paint before I went to work. My oil paints had a strong odor, so Earle even put a window in the wall, so I could get some ventilation. But I had to enter the building through the delivery door and usually a homeless person would be sleeping there, glued to that door. Once I called Earle about it. I knew he was up. He couldn't sleep either. He picked up the phone, and after I told him about my encounter with the sleeping homeless man by the door, he got very stressed out. He said that I could either step over this man or wait until he showed up but he wasn't sure when that would happen. I was quiet and then I said 'okay'. I didn't tell him the wall adjacent to the door was covered in human feces, again.

Besides all Earle's problems, he was still painting sometimes, and we used his art for the pogs, too. As my feelings of alienation and inadequacy were growing, I was seeking solitude in my art studio, but even there, the yo-yos wouldn't leave me. I was thinking about my beautiful, awesome son, my genius child, punching and gluing pogs to yo-yos in a small house, along with his fiancée, and two dogs who walked around in shoes that Alex and Lisa made for them, and sometimes, bow ties, too. I felt like crying all the time. I was painting large landscapes, trying to focus only on my technique. I didn't know how to live. The image of Alex's eighteen old body bent over the entangled yo-yos' strings, and his skillful fingers patiently working on untying them, was popping in my head all the time. It made me cry inside and out. Inside, all the time. Outside, only when I was alone.

After the first batch of yo-yos was done, I was supposed to take them on several sales calls. We picked the Desert Museum gift shop and the Tucson Museum of Art store to start.

I have to say that, in the past, when I used to try to get into a new gallery, I would do that kind of thing. I would walk in with the portfolio, being perfectly aware of the fact that I wasn't the first, or the last person waking in with a sales purpose that day. I tried to forget that and be as genuine as I thought was necessary, and totally ingenuine overall. It was tough.

I remembered that feeling when I was parking the car in front of the Desert Museum. *'What are you doing?'* I asked myself. *'Run!'* I heard myself say, talking to myself. I pushed the fear away and tried to look at the comical side of the whole situation. After all, I was going to sell yo-yos, or rather, try to sell yo-yos. A good salesperson would know how to sell a locomotive to an individual who would never think it was needed. The individual could even be convinced taking an expensive loan wouldn't hurt. I looked at the box with the yo-yos that was on the passenger seat. Unfortunately, I realized again I wasn't a good salesperson. I realized other things, too; I used to love the company of people, and talking to them, and this feeling was generally reciprocated. I realized, again I was going to go and try to sell the yo-yos, while being severely depressed, and that I was doing it for my beloved son whose life and health had gone haywire. *'Did it go haywire, or was it always like that?'* I wondered.

I wiped my tears, checked my face in the mirror and waited a few moments for the color of my eyes and face to go back to normal before I finally went to the gift shop.

Eventually, the yo-yos were taken into the two stores of our choice. The Desert Museum was harder to get in than the Tucson Museum of Art. The ladies at the Desert Museum were more cautious. I had to tell them I'd taken the pictures of the animals by myself. At the Art Museum, the manager of the store was way more open minded. He took fifteen yo-yos, if I remember well.

After a few years, maybe ten of them were sold. Once every few months a check would come in the mail, for five or six dollars. It made Alex very happy, every time.

About four years after these events, an email came to my inbox. The manager of the store in the Art Museum had retired and the new manager was going through the inventory. He stumbled upon the cardboard box with the yo-yos. Fortunately, my email address was printed on the inside of the cover. '*Are these yours?*' the email said. '*Would you want to pick them up?*'

Chapter 8
Great vacation

The summer was coming and my eldest son came to visit from Poland. He brought his fiancée along. Both of them were in Medical School in Warsaw, and they decided they wanted to come and get married in the United States. And of course, they decided to spend the whole summer in the USA, three months altogether. Alex was released from his second hospital stay and he too was happy when he learned about his brother's visit. He immediately told this to his new girlfriend, Beth. He'd met her a few weeks after he left the hospital at a radio station festival in Tucson Electric Park. Our Piedra Seca house was very spacious. I was more than happy about my eldest son and his fiancée's visit and decided to take them on vacation. Not only them, though. Alex would come, too, along with his new girlfriend. I also wanted to take Andrew. The whole last year of his middle school he'd spent in a boarding school in Poland. He invited his female friend to come and spend the summer in the USA, too. Her name was Elsa.

A few weeks after she came, Andrew and Elsa started to fight and not get along. In that case, I started to take care of all Elsa's needs all summer long. I didn't mind. I liked the girl. I found her talented, sensitive and unique. Earle wouldn't go with us on vacation. He had to stay and work. I didn't know how deeply in trouble we were by then; I didn't realize that the recession had already reached us, too. I was too busy taking care of other people to pay attention to his business. I didn't feel as if I was involved in it. I mean, obviously, I was involved as his wife, but I wasn't aware of how things were going since there was no history to my involvement. Andrew resigned from going on the trip. He had constant fights with Alex and felt ostracized, humiliated and laughed at. I distinctly remember how one afternoon he tried to take the car and go out. I don't know why Alex was opposed to the idea; all I saw was Alex standing in front of the car, pressing the hood with his body and widespread arms. Andrew was at the wheel and I knew how angry he was at Alex; I also knew how much Alex wanted to dare him to the very end. I ran out of the house and managed to interrupt that situation. Andrew wanted to run away from home that day. In fact, he left and sent me a bunch of text messages, all of them desperate. He was blaming me for all his misfortunes. In the evening, Earle went out to look for him and brought him home. They went out together and had a conversation. Earle always understood Andrew and would try to help him, no matter what. But to all go on vacation together with him? It just wouldn't work. Besides, Andrew was best friends with Tessa now, and it emotionally affected Alex. He was sad about Tessa. He missed her. He cried. And here was his seventeen-year-old brother hanging out with his former girlfriend.

Every day, I was either bringing, or someone else was bringing, Alex to our Piedra Seca house. He was depressed. He wanted to do well. He was taking a prescribed medicine called Depakote, for what he'd been told his ailment was, namely, bipolar disorder. He'd gained a little weight and he didn't like it. And he was sad. So when his new girlfriend showed up, I was relieved. Beth was very quiet and different from Tessa. She was a tall girl with blond hair, blue eyes and a square jaw. She was very soft spoken. I was also happy when she decided that she would go on a trip with us. We would take two cars. My eldest son and I would be the drivers. We would all fit, and the trip would last about two weeks.

It was a great trip. My eldest son and Alex were getting along really well. We went to Utah, Nevada and California. We spent time in the various canyons as well as on the beaches. I had so much hope, then. The thing that started to bother me more frequently was money. I called Earle every day, and I could sense that he was anxious, or out of sorts, or something else. I sensed it before we left, but as I said, the crowd of all those young people was just too big, with their goals and issues, to even stop and think.

We split our group on the way back. My eldest son and his fiancée continued to Las Vegas, where they got married. I brought the rest of the group home.

That summer, we didn't only go on a long vacation. We did many things together. We traveled around Tucson, always camping in the amazing wilderness. There were also hikes we could do from the house, like the one we did in July, to Finger Rock.

It was an awesome hike. Although July in Tucson isn't hike friendly because it's simply too hot, this hike was special. My eldest son, his wife, Alex and I went together. Finger Rock is a very difficult hike. Getting to the very summit on the big rock next to Finger Rock is possible without the ropes, although having them would be helpful. Before we reached the summit, there were a few places where the rocks weren't stable. Alex was in front of me and he stepped on one. He lost his balance but only slightly. He quickly turned around and stretched his hand out to me. I grabbed his hand and he pulled me up, so I wouldn't even have to step on the shaky rock.

Finger Rock is visible from almost every place in the central area of Tucson, wherever the Catalina Mountains are visible. I look at it every day. I see it from my street. I can't help but go back in my mind to that moment when I felt Alex was confident and helpful. I remember how good it felt to trust his hand, to be pulled up.

#

The last day of August, my eldest son and his newlywed wife went back to their Medical School in Poland. Andrew's friend, Elsa, went back to Poland, too. Alex went back to the Studio and the University of Arizona. I went back to Piedra Seca house, only to understand that the present situation wouldn't last much longer. The recession grabbed us by the throat and on first September my husband, Earle, decided that it would be helpful if I could come and help at his company. He had let go of his main salesperson already in May. It was obvious that things were going really badly. There was no money for the payroll and what about the bills?

I came to work the next day, not knowing anything about plastics, machining and fabrication, and having only Alex on my mind.

I truly had started to "re-raise" him, and these were Earle's words, not mine. This is why Alex and I became even closer. We were in touch every day; that wasn't new to us, but now, though, I felt loved. We communicated and I was helping. Also, Beth had a large family and they all loved Alex, and that was reciprocal. He even told Beth's mother that he was diagnosed with bipolar disorder and he has to take medication. She was fine with it and loved him all the same. Alex was spending Christmas with them, decorating ginger-bread houses and playing with the kids. He was showing them all his yo-yo tricks and teaching them, too. Sometime in January, Beth moved in with him, and again, it seemed that things were going well. I followed Alex's grades and they were good.

At this time, Alex told me that he was thinking about changing his major, becoming an Emergency Medical Technician and also a firefighter. We investigated the admission process, and since there was a physical ability exam, we started to go to LA Fitness together. I was picking up Alex after work and dropping him off at Desert house after the workout. Desert house was perfectly located for a student. The bus stop was within a minute walk from the house and the bus went straight to the University. The classes were still going okay. He was a business major at the time. Beth didn't go to university yet but she was planning to do so. Together, they lived in the Studio.

Then one day, Alex told me she wanted to move out.

"Really?" I said, surprised. "Something happened?"

"Nothing happened. We are friends. It's just, you know, the Studio is one big space, there's no bedroom or some kind of privacy for anybody. Practically speaking, it's a one-person space..."

Well, it could be enough space for two people, I thought. Beth had artistic inclinations. She painted and knitted and was making projects out of plastic grocery shopping bags. Alex, on the other hand, had his yo-yos and ever ending projects involving them. I guess both of them couldn't fit in the Studio, and she moved back in with her parents. She left lots of plastic bags behind.

Chapter 9
On my own

I remember how clean and organized the Studio was when Tessa lived there with Alex. They started to live in the Studio after the Flanwill house was robbed and Tessa was afraid to stay there. After the robbery we rented Flanwill house to some other people and Alex and Tessa moved to Desert Studio. We were planning to rent out the front house. They lived in the back, and before they broke up, things didn't go too well between them. I think now that Tessa felt bad because she could see clearly that Alex was doing things that he wasn't supposed to do.

He was growing marijuana in the Studio in the large closet and she must have felt she was part of it. I didn't know anything about his agricultural project. It wasn't a reason why they broke up or at least I don't think so. But the overall feeling of participating in things which were illegal didn't sit well with Tessa.

I wondered, sometimes, whether something suspicious was going on. When Tessa moved back to Flanwill house after she'd left Alex, they agreed Alex would buy her a new bed. A truck was needed to transport it, so of course, Earle lent Alex his van. We went to the mattress store and Tessa chose a bed. Alex then pulled out five hundred-dollar bills and paid for it. I was surprised. Where was this cash coming from?

Also, there was a car issue. When Alex was doing well, he told us he would like to buy a car. Not only did he want to use it in town, but also to go on snowboarding trips. Snowboarding had been Alex's passion since he was a child. He had good grades, he said. He didn't *'deserve'* a car, but he *'thought he deserved'* one. These were his own words. He only asked for help with the down payment. He calculated his payments and said he would be able to manage, provided we paid all the bills, and his father was still sending money for his school. We also paid for other miscellaneous things, like clothing, books, and such like. He had food stamps. How one can have food stamps and apply for a car loan? And get that loan? I still don't understand.

Alex needed a co-signatory and Earle or I weren't able to be considered. We were barely surviving and our names shouldn't appear on any new loans. So, Alex convinced Tessa to co-sign with him.

He got a loan and purchased a used Toyota Scion, a perfect car for his snowboarding trips, since he was able to sleep inside it. Even when Tessa moved out, she was still on the loan he'd got for his car. Alex lived by himself in Desert Studio. He had a car, plenty of yo-yos, food-stamps and marijuana in the closet. He was going to his classes. People got used to Alex's yo-yos. He always had one with him, and he always played with it. He went to all of his college classes with a yo-yo and the professors didn't mind.

The Desert front house was rented to a young couple. The man's name was Adrian and his pregnant girlfriend's, Angela. Alex got along with them just fine until Angela started to complain about Alex one day.

"His trash smells," she said. "He doesn't take it out to the bin. He just leaves it outside."

I told that to Alex.

"You need to take your trash around the house and throw it into the bin," I said. "Tucson isn't a place where trash can be left outside. If you do it once every two days, it would be enough. You are a college student. You should understand that."

It was true. All this time Alex was still a freshman in college. With all the problems, hospital stays, missed finals, it didn't seem he could progress.

Alex said that his trash didn't smell, that the bin is too far, that Adrian sucks and that they had a fight, because Adrian said that he was going to buy Desert house from me and evict Alex. I was amused. Adrian was barely making their own payments and I never wanted to sell Desert house. Anyway, those tenants didn't last long. After they didn't pay for two months and I went to talk to them, I saw the house was empty. They had just left. It was about the end of the Fall semester.

Alex wasn't doing well. It wasn't only about the trash.

He became rude and demanding. I didn't understand why. To me, it seemed that things should've improved, especially since I was convinced that Alex was taking his meds. I drove him once a month, I think, to the lab where his blood was taken. That was according to the hospital judge's verdict. I remembered his second hospitalization trial. I call it a trial, although there was nothing to be 'tried' for, per se. The psychiatric unit of Kino Hospital has its own courtroom, where a regular judge resides and conducts trials of people who are committed by a third party. The judge would also decide if a patient would be forced into having medication in cases where the patient didn't want to take it. The second hospitalization happened after Mr White committed Alex. At the end of his stay at the unit, the trial was called and I went. The whole session lasted only half an hour or so, and the judge laughed several times, especially when Alex made jokes about his very long and Polish last name.

"What is your name?" the judge asked.

"Alex Wojtkowski. It might be too long to remember, and I have a shortcut ready for you. Just "Watch-Your-House-Key." You will always remember my name. Can I have my yo-yo back?"

The judge's verdict for Alex was for him to take his meds but if he wouldn't, the State would have to force him to do that.

So, I thought that he was taking his meds. But what else was he taking? I didn't know. I knew that he had started to smoke pot again and probably enormous amounts. I assumed that he needed money for good marijuana and the yo-yos, and he started to buy expensive ones, made of titanium. I don't know if he managed to sell the marijuana he was growing in my closet, but he posted a picture of a new crop on Facebook. I didn't know that the fruit of his efforts was actually coming from the Studio closet. I only saw the electric bill going up, but then, the Studio's air conditioning unit wasn't very efficient, and if somebody wasn't careful with the thermostat, the bill could be high. I didn't know that the closet was furnished with high-class lamps and other marihuana growing equipment. I saw rubber seals on the edges of the closet one day when I visited but it didn't occur to me that these would have anything to do with a hydroponics closet's growing needs.

Our relationship started to deteriorate really quickly. We

fought about everything; money, behavior, etc. I felt Alex's hatred every single day. He was sending me the longest text messages, full of poison, and no matter how unreasonable he was, once in a while one or two sentences would go directly to my heart; especially when he blamed me for his current situation. He blamed me for his hospitalizations. He was saying that I locked him up simply because I must have hated him for some reason. Then, he would say, that 'no', he knew I didn't hate him, I was just plain stupid, according to him, and that was that.

One evening he came to our house. He brought Beth with him. Earle and I were sitting on the large porch. It was an evening visit. I don't remember exactly what brought him over, but when they sat with us Alex started to verbally abuse me, Earle told him to get out. Alex, though, continued talking to me.

"I remember going with you over to your boyfriend's house, where I had to sit and play video games, eat salad, while you and him were upstairs doing God knows what." Alex was referring to my relationship which started after Matthias was arrested for domestic violence. The relationship with that boyfriend lasted not quite three years and broke up right before I met Earle. Alex added a few ugly words, and this was when Earle told him to go. Alex grabbed Beth and ran out in anger. It wasn't unusual. He was angry all the time.

From his lengthy, super angry and abusive text messages, I could detect he was stressing out about money. But why? The food stamps were more than enough for his food, his father paid the tuition fees, I paid for all his books and supplies and all his bills. He had a beautiful studio to live in, close to his school. He even had a car. He was going on his snowboarding trips, once the snow showed up on Mt. Lemmon.

During his winter break in February, he even went in his car to Telluride, Colorado where he worked part-time to earn money for the ski pass. During this trip though, I got a very strange phone call from him. Alex called me from the highway; I don't know which one. As usual, he was very angry with me. He didn't hesitate to call me names; after that, though, he hung up, only to call me again and start over. During this conversation, I learned that Alex was on his way to the closest grocery store in Arizona, because *'the card, doesn't work in Colorado'*. He meant his EBT, food stamps card. I was bewildered. I didn't share this information with anybody. I had no strength.

I didn't want to share anything to do with Alex with Earle because Earle was totally beside himself as it was. Now we were in the midst of the Great Recession. The stress was immense. We had to let go of most of the employees. Once in a while Earle asked me to shoot him, after he had a few beers.

People were losing homes and lives when I decided to go back to school and finally get my elementary school teaching certificate. I felt very confident with small children, and I had lots of experience with my own children. I'm talking about teaching them basic things; reading, writing, art and music. I wrote lots of children's books, custom designed for my children. Alex got a fair share of them. In my books, he was always a hero.

I had to start from scratch. I was forty-nine when I signed up for classes at Pima Community College. I went full time because the classes were in the evening, so I could work during the day. I filled in the Free Application for Federal Student Aid (FAFSA) and got enough scholarship to be happy. Earle wasn't doing well. It was because of the financial situation, but also, his health started to fail. He started to cough. He was going through violent spasms of coughing which prevented him from doing work. He would hold onto the wall and become so red in his face that it truly worried me. I didn't know how to help him, short of scheduling his doctor's appointments and going with him. After a spasm, Earle would go back to work and say everything would be all right. He tried to be positive. He was so stressed out!

One day, a friend of mine called me. She was crying and complaining about her very difficult daughter, who was nineteen, I believe.

"Do you want another daughter?" she said. She was sad and angry.

I wouldn't take another child, but I understood how desperately my friend needed help. She wanted a summer job for her daughter. I talked to Earle about it, and of course, Earle wanted to help.

"Tell your friend to call me," he said.

My friend called the next day and asked for Earle. Earle was at his desk, his face buried in his hands. He had just found out a big order had been rejected.

"It's my friend. I told you yesterday, remember? It's about her daughter," I said. He didn't look at me.

"I can't talk to anybody," I heard him say.

I didn't know what to tell my friend. A few days later, she brought her daughter and the girl worked for us during the summer. Earle was very helpful and he taught her lots of things. Considering all this, I didn't want to share my troubles about Alex with Earle. I didn't want to add to his plate. There were days though when I felt extremely lonely with this baggage, like when we went to visit another friend of mine who lived close to our house, maybe a mile away. I don't remember why we went there together, maybe to pretend that things were normal. Earle didn't even want a cup of tea. While we were sitting there, Alex called my cellphone and he specifically asked for Earle. From Alex's voice I detected that he was in a good mood and I gave my phone to Earle. Already, as I was handing him the phone, he gave me a look charged with such anger t I almost felt my hand melting. He talked to Alex for maybe a few seconds. When finished, he gave me the phone back. He left my friend's house and went home, walking.

When it came to problems with Alex, I was on my own.

#

Even though Earle didn't want to deal with my problems with Alex, he agreed to use his help in clearing up around the gallery. Weeds were growing all over the parking lot and we were facing fines if we didn't pull them out.

I dropped Alex off in the morning, around ten, with a water bottle, a wide brimmed hat and sunscreen. Just when we pulled up on the parking lot closer to the gallery's delivery door, I saw that that door was all smeared with human waste. And the building was tagged, again. I told Alex to start on the opposite side of the parking lot and I would pick him up in two hours, for lunch. He also had a doctor's appointment that day. I drove to work and told Earle about the soiled door. I stayed at work, then left back to pick up Alex, because of his doctor's appointment. The doctor was on time so after the appointment we went back to the gallery, only to find Earle already there.

I don't remember what saddened me more, Earle's anger or his determination to overcome the difficulty.

"That's all he did?" Earle pointed at the small patch where Alex had actually removed the grass. "All? How's this going to help?"

Earle looked at me from under his crooked baseball hat. He was holding a shovel. I looked back at him.

"I will do it, by myself," he yelled. "The only thing that I know for sure in life is how to work. I know how to work and when I work, I know I'm doing something for the better." He was very angry. I looked at him in this huge parking lot, one man with the shovel, and really, I thought about the legend of Sisyphus and his never-ending jobs. I had only sadness, not tears.

Earle set himself to work immediately and was yelling while digging into this incredibly hard caliche. I could see it breaking under his shovel.

Slowly, I turned around and headed for the exit. I stopped before the street and checked the mirror. I saw Earle throwing the shovel to the side. He picked up the hose and turned on the water and started hosing down the soiled delivery door.

Alex looked into the side mirror and observed Earle for a moment.

"This is how people are shitting on Earle's dream," he said. He was sad. He took a sip of water from his water bottle. We drove away.

Chapter 10
How do birds do it?

When Alex was little, he was simply awesome. It was the time when I always called him 'Oles' because I was teaching him Polish and it was his Polish name. As a mother of five, I know very well that there are no children better than others or that we love more. That is, of course, to the contrary opinion of the very children whose opinions are driven by the need for love and attention, and more love and attention. But at the same time, as a parent, I would like to make two statements.

The first one is that we do have separate relationships with our different children. After all, they are different human beings and they shake the universe around them in their own, unique way. We like to spend time with them together and one-on-one. Some children though have a unique talent of building that one-on-one relationship. And Alex was in that very group.

One could say that I'm biased. But really? What I'm trying to say is that he was building our relationship on *his* end, very strongly, already as a child. It wasn't only a mother's love and effort. All children do that, but some do more than others.

I taught him how to read in Polish, which is my native language, when he was not quite three years old. I remember his baby cheeks moving up and down and this concentration in his forehead while he was deciphering the words. Slowly moving his big head, he not only looked cute, but almost funny. One day his father wanted to show off to his cousin that his son knew how to read in Polish. It happened in Poland, where we went on my children's father's sabbatical. I remember that whole situation. It was after some birthday party. Alex's father gave a book to Alex's uncle and said:

"Show it to him. You don't believe me so you need to see for yourself how a three-year-old can read."

The uncle showed it to Alex and Alex started to read as usual. Alex didn't even notice that the book was upside down, the way his uncle was holding it.

Alex was writing and drawing with his left hand, which would make him lefthanded, but he was eating with his right hand. For a while as a child, he played the cello, and I didn't change the order of strings, as it was strung for with left-handed student. He played as a right-handed person.

This isn't a book where I only want to write how great Alex was. One mother from his preschool called him 'Alexander the Great'. But it's hard to totally omit it. I said I wanted to make two statements, and I already made the one about our 'special one-on-one relationship'. I would like to make the second statement now, parallel to the first one and just as universal.

A parent loves all his/her children, but the child who needs help in the moment gets the parent's immediate attention. Did I love this child more? The word "love" might be not the right one. Let's put it differently. A parent cares and worries most for the child that is hurting and is in need at that particular moment.

Many years ago, when all my children were still very young, I was hanging washed diapers on a cloth line behind our house. I looked down and saw a small bird, a featherless chick, dead on the ground, covered in ants. I threw it away but I always remembered the sad impression it made on me. In the evening I called a friend of mine and told her about it.

"The mother must have thrown it away," she said. "That's what they do when the baby is weak or sick."

How do birds do it? Why are we different? Whenever any of my kids started limping in life, I felt as it were my only child. All the others were there, of course. They needed to be fed and clothed, but while I was taking care of them, my mind would constantly come back, as if pushed by magnetic force, to this one, limping child.

Is this what evolution did to us, and other species didn't progress in that direction? Were we, the people, ever like those birds in my backyard?

I don't know the answers to those questions, and to tell the truth, I'm not even interested. I can't imagine myself throwing away the weakest child, even if the science of evolution, ethics, philosophy and religion would instruct me otherwise. The point I'm trying to make here isn't only about help and responsibility. It's about love; earthly, primordial love. Not the love we are challenged with when we face the abyss of grief, when losing a child.

#

Alex tried pot for the first time when he was thirteen. I don't know where it happened. It is hard to know where and when your child tries to smoke marijuana for the first time. Usually, it is either after school in a friend's house or at some school party. There was no pot in our house. Neither Alex's father nor I had any interest in smoking pot. We didn't have friends who were using it either. Alex liked pot very much right from the start. At this time, Matthias and I were already separated and the divorce was on its way.

These were trying times. Actually, times were always trying in our family. Alex's father, Matthias, was a controlling and abusive person. Being extremely intelligent, well-educated and successful didn't make him emotionally intelligent. His position as a tenured University math professor kept him busy. He didn't want to realize that our family was a sinking ship.

Our family wasn't falling apart because of love affairs or illnesses. The reason was power and control. And lies, of course, all of them backed up by fears.

When I mention lies, I realize, of course, that one might think of affairs that spouses have when considering what is a bad marriage. Not in our case. Everybody was lying, including me, out of fear of the truth being discovered by a monster father or a monster husband.

What kind of truth? The list would be longer that this book, but let's sample it.

A left-over green onion, molding slightly, had to be thrown away. But wait! After coming back from work, Matthias might or might not check out the garbage. His seeing the wasted onion would end in yelling and criticism lasting weeks and it would be mentioned for years. It was easier just to take the onion to the garbage bin outside. But wait! Not *our* garbage. It wasn't unusual for Alex's father to check our garbage bin in the alley. Luckily, not far from our house was an apartment complex which had big garbage containers and there was no evidence of Matthias checking this one out. One had to be careful, though, and just in case, toss our small garbage bag really far in. All the kids knew that. They knew they had to lie, just to survive.

#

I think that Alex liked smoking pot because it relaxed him. Having strong OCD and an abusive father gave him too much stress.

Alex's father wasn't only verbally abusive. He was aggressive and violent. The kids were pushed and hit and kicked. It was always unexpected because it was hard to foresee what could trigger their father's anger. Generally, it was assumed it could be anything, so the children walked on eggshells. The story about the super soaker could demonstrate that situation.

When Alex was about ten years old, I got him a super soaker, a water gun, a big, colorful, plastic toy, with two water containers. He was running outside and playing with it, but when his father came home, the situation changed abruptly. Alex happened to run into the kitchen and ask for a drink. He put the super soaker on the tiled floor.

"I need more water for it," he said. "It's empty"

He started drinking his lemonade. In the meantime, his father took the super soaker and placed it on the doormat, outside. Alex choked on his drink.

"What are you doing, Dad?" he said, coughing. "Leave it here!"

"No. There're bacteria inside. Any water will have bacteria. It's a stupid toy. Only your mother could have bought you something like that. It can't be in the house!"

Alex put his glass on the countertop and immediately

103

brought the super soaker back to the kitchen. I tried to mediate.

"Alex, please take it to the bathroom. We can refill it there," I said.

"Bathroom?" Matthias said. "Bacteria in the bathroom is as destructive as it is in the kitchen!"

I started to lose patience.

"What bacteria?" I asked. "Don't be crazy. It's a brand-new toy, straight from the store. And it's tap water inside. What harm can this do?"

There was no joking with Matthias and no reasoning, either. After a few more tries on my part and a few points of resistance on his, his aggression grew exponentially. He looked at me.

"You will now say to Alex that the bacteria in the super soaker is dangerous," he said.

"I won't say that," I said.

I should have known better. Matthias walked around the countertop and hit me with his fist on my shoulder. Alex ran to him and kicked him in the leg, but his father pushed him against the wall.

Eventually, I admitted that the bacteria in the super soaker could cause harm and I went outside with Alex, to fill his toy with water from the hose. It was enough for my ex to calm down and sit and eat his dinner. My mother-in-law was visiting us, then, and she witnessed how her son hit me. She saw it through the window, from the porch. By shrugging her shoulders, she showed disapproval for her son's action, but she didn't say anything. The whole incident with the super soaker shows how abusive Alex's father was and what tensions Alex was going through. No wonder he wanted to relieve his stress later on in life and started to smoke pot!

One December night when Alex was twelve, his father was arrested for domestic violence. Our daughters, Mia and Lara, were playing cards in Mia's room. Their father claimed they were too loud. I objected. We had a fight and he pushed me against the wall. I hit my head and our daughters called the police. Mia was fourteen years old and Lara fifteen and a half. Matthias was issued a restraining order and couldn't come to the house. I stayed with the five kids, their ages ranging from roughly ten to eighteen. I remember our first confrontation that had to do with marijuana. One evening, he told me he was smoking pot and that he intended to smoke it regularly, every day. He told me that it made him feel great, that he could feel relaxed finally, that when he smoked it, he didn't feel any tension for the very first time in his life.

I didn't agree with his demands, and we had a terrible fight. I said '*no*' to pot, and '*no, no, no*', to coming home from school and comfortably smoking it in the living room, in the safety of the home, since pot was illegal. To my '*no's*', Alex said (or rather yelled) '*yes*', many times, after which he left the house, slamming the door behind him.

I made myself a cup of herbal tea and I sat down at the kitchen table. I was terrified. My eldest son was away in college and so were my two daughters. The youngest child, a boy of nine, had gone to spend the night over at his friend house. I felt very much alone. My boyfriend, whom I was dating after I divorced, was a nice man, but certainly not somebody I could lean on. I didn't even know that he was an avid pot smoker himself. He was high often but I simply didn't know about it. I didn't smoke pot. It didn't even occurr to me that a career man, which he was, would smoke pot. But this was irrelevant when it came to Alex. I desperately needed help but none was forthcoming. I thought I would manage.

I was trying to figure out what triggered his behavior. It was early Fall. That past summer, when Alex had turned thirteen, he'd taken a trip to Paris and Poland. My cousin, who lived in Paris, wanted to help me out and invited Alex over for a visit. After that, he was going to Poland to spend some time there. We arranged for the passport and Alex went. He went to Paris and later on to Poland. In Poland he went to visit his first cousin on his father's side, and he stayed for a couple of weeks with him in his auntie's mountain hut. After this trip, Alex came back to Tucson sad and aggressive. I wasn't sure why, but altogether, I thought it must be simply his age. His face was breaking out and I ordered the second treatment of Accutane, the anti-acne medication. Many years later, I found out what was the source of his depression, then. Alex, himself, told me. At the time though, I felt lonely with my problems.

My tea was getting cold. I wasn't even drinking it but only looking at the cup. The sound of the door being slammed still rang in my ears. I got up from the table and called Alex on his cell phone several times and he picked up the phone every time. Also, every time, he was extremely angry and yelled back at me. I begged him not to be stubborn. I asked him to come home and talk.

"Will you let me smoke pot in the house if I come back?" he would ask.

To this question I would always say 'no', and Alex would hang up.

I called two of my close friends, Bob and Mary. Alex had known them since he was little. They came over the next day to talk to him. Unfortunately, they didn't get any good results. We sat at the kitchen table, and after long explanations and arguing, my friends left. They hugged me by the door, told me to hang in there. They also told me they were sorry for me. I didn't need that. I was already sorry for myself but I certainly was grateful that they came promptly and tried to help.

There was only one person who I thought could help. His name was Kevin.

Chapter 11
Kevin

Kevin, was a man of about thirty-six or thirty-seven. At the time of starting his friendship with Alex, he owned a skate shop on a busy street, a walking distance form our house. Kevin was divorced. He had a young son and he shared a custody with the boy's mother. A twelve-year-old Alex, an avid skate boarder, visited the shop often and Kevin came to like him. Alex's father didn't like the skate shop at all, and the more he told Alex not to spend time there, the more Alex went. Very soon though, Matthias was arrested, left the house and I filed for divorce. By then, Alex was spending even more time at the shop. After a very short time, Alex was helping in the shop. He wasn't officially hired, but for a few hours of help, he would be given new skateboard wheels or other stuff. I was amazed when one day I came to the shop and found Alex running the store. Alex was still only twelve.

"Kevin is tired today," he said, after he finished helping the customer that was just leaving. Before shutting the drawer of the cash register, Alex lifted the drawer's top level, and moved a few hundred bills down after counting them. Then, he shut the drawer and looked at me.

"Kevin is tired today?" I mechanically repeated. I was watching my son in disbelief. When and where did he learn all these things? I wanted to say something, but somebody walked into the store, and Alex's attention shifted immediately. The customer was a young man looking for new wheels for his longboard. For a while, I didn't know what they were talking about but they certainly understood each other. The young man ended up by buying wheels and something else. I don't know what kind of attachment to his skateboard that was, but it was quite expensive. The young man left and new customers came in. This time it was a young boy with his mother. The boy must have been six or seven. They were looking for new skate boarding equipment and Alex took care of everything. He sold them a set of skateboarding gear, together with a helmet. I was amazed. I forgot about Kevin being tired. I just wanted to know where he was.

"Shh" Alex said. He put his finger on his lips and waved towards the office door.

"He's taking a nap. Attended a party, yesterday. Hangover, you know," he said.

"Ah," I whispered and sat down on a small bench, made of old skateboards. As I did that, the office door opened and Kevin walked out. He didn't look as if he had a hangover to me but I didn't know Kevin well, then. He only looked messy. Maybe he needed a haircut and a shave but that was all.

"Kevin, you remember my mom, don't you?" Alex said.

Kevin moved closer. He acted as if he wanted to iron his shirt with the two open palms of his hands.

"Sure. I remember. Your name is Monika, right?" He stopped "ironing" and shook my hand. "Congratulations on such an awesome son. Alex is simply fantastic. Do you know he can run the whole shop?"

I knew he could. I just witnessed it.

We sat down together. Kevin pulled out a twenty-dollar

bill and told Alex to go across the street and buy him a burger. "The biggest they have."

"And make sure you get some ketchup and mustard. And here," he added, pulling out another bill out of his pocket. "Get yourself something too, so you won't walk around hungry. May I offer you something?" Kevin looked at me now.

I thanked him and said "no". Alex left to buy food.

Alex loved Kevin and he loved him for years. Kevin became his father figure, and really, nobody could influence that situation. It seemed that the more I would try to keep Alex apart from the skate shop, the more time Alex would spend there. And Kevin? I didn't really know what to think of him. He seemed like a genuine guy to me, but I was always accused of being naïve, so maybe I had my eyes closed to all the shady business dealings He certainly knew what he was doing. He looked healthy and well. His bulky muscles were covered in many sophisticated tattoos. Of course, Alex's father despised this kind of influence on his son but the opposition from Alex was more than strong. Knowing this, I befriended Kevin. Not that I became his personal friend, no. But I accepted him and invited him to the house on various occasions when Matthias was already out of the house and the divorce that took two years was already on its way.

Kevin's late father used to be a policeman. Alex said that Kevin never had a good relationship with his father, and maybe that also had some kind of influence on his relationship with Kevin. Alex told me that Kevin organized a group of people who would fight, so-called "tweakers," meaning guys who used cocaine or heroin.

Kevin took Alex on snowboarding trips to the White Mountains where Alex would babysit Kevin's son, Cole. On one of those trips Alex tried snowboarding for the first time. He fell in love with it. From then on, he was impatiently waiting for winter to come, and when it came, he would observe the weather report every day, waiting for the snow to show up on our local Mt. Lemmon so he could go snowboarding. Alex's father was very much against this new love of Alex's (yes, it was 'love', it wasn't a hobby), saying that we lived in the desert and even thinking of snowboarding was simply stupid. Of course, there was a logic to his thinking but who said that Alex was reasonable? He loved snowboarding, period. He said that several times. I knew that it was easier to pick one's battles with Alex, and if he did fine everywhere else, I wouldn't mind snowboarding. Especially, because Kevin would provide Alex with equipment or at least facilitate it for him to make enough money to buy it. Alex worshipped Kevin. He didn't question him. He just loved him. He wanted to be like Kevin. And he wanted to have tattoos, too.

I was against tattoos. Personally, I never had one so, obviously, I didn't want my children to have any. It was clear to me that, at least until they became eighteen, none of them would be able to get one. Didn't children require parental consent? We talked a lot about it at home, especially after I was already separated from my first husband, Matthias. Everybody knew what I thought. It was a plain 'no' to tattoos.

My surprise was huge when it turned out that Alex not only got a tattoo, but also had his nipples pierced. He was thirteen when one day he simply walked into the kitchen, without his shirt on. His hair was messy, and he looked as if he had just woken up. His long pajama pants hung on his bony hips.

111

"I wanted to tell you that I have these two rings and a tattoo." He pointed to his nipples.

I was speechless.

"I wanted to tell you because my brothers and sisters told me that you wouldn't love me if I had a tattoo. So, here it is," he said. With his pointer he was showing me a small, red tattoo placed on his chest, on his left side. Alex was standing by the kitchen table a few feet away from me, but even from this distance, I could his tattoo. It looked like a keyhole.

"Are you crazy? Alex! How can you even say that?" I asked.

He looked at me, relieved.

"Okay, Mom. I was worried. Do you like my tattoo?"

I walked around the countertop and came closer to Alex and examined his tattoo. It was in color. It was on his upper chest, closer to the shoulder. It definitely looked like a red keyhole, outlined with a dark, blue line.

"It's unusual," I said. "But I don't want to say that I like it because I don't like tattoos in general. Many awesome people have them, though, so I want you to know that it has nothing to do with how I see and understand people."

We hugged. Right when he was going out to the backyard, one of the rings got caught on the edge of the sliding glass door handle. The door was in motion because Alex had pushed it. He screamed and so did I, as I saw his nipple almost being pulled out of his chest.

"It's all good, Mom! It's okay!" Alex said, after he freed the ring. "It didn't really hurt that much. It only looked scary."

I didn't know about that.

That agreeable attitude of mine wasn't something I came up with only then. I knew it from the past. I practiced patience for his passions and interests. Alex had displayed passionate behaviors since he was little. I will never forget his complete infatuation with, for example, Star Wars. One would say that any boy would like Star Wars, of course. Some would like it more, some less. But with Alex, it was never a question of liking more or less. It was love and passion and nothing counted any more. He must have been around eight years old when he told me that there were only three things that he loved in his life. I remember the day he told me, because we were hiking on Mt. Lemmon, our local mountain. Alex was walking in front of me, stopping often and talking.

"Luke Skywalker," he said. "I love the man." He stopped and squatted to tie his shoe. I pulled out my water bottle and waited for Alex to finish and offer him a sip. He wasn't getting up though but only looked up at me and continued.

"The next one is Jesus. I know we need to love Jesus, and I truly love him."

I was nodding my head waiting for Alex to get up. Once he saw my water bottle, he got up quickly.

"Then, there is a long space where nobody is important." He waved his hand in a wide, circular gesture. "And after this space come my parents. I love them too, of course. But they are far behind Luke and Jesus." Alex took my water but only started drinking after making sure that I understood my place in the Universe, at least when it came to his point of view.

When he was nine, there was Pokémon. I had to learn everything about them. Alex himself would prepare tests for me, with multiple choice checkboxes nicely highlighted and some hint questions, so I would be able to pass.

Another one was his love for his small rat, Milly. The story of having rats in a cage in the house was simple. My younger daughter, Mia, always wanted to have a cat, and her father, after long-time negotiations and bargaining, promised her one, only to break her heart and not fulfill the promise. He just ignored her, then was rude. Anyway, in a pet store I bought a rat and she had her pet. It wasn't long after this event that, in Alex's school, the snake needed to be fed. I was always questioning that scientific approach to education but it didn't change the fact that second graders did have a snake in the cage, in class, and the snake had to eat. Once in a while a rat was given to the snake, and the snake would devour it. The kids didn't need to look if they didn't want to. Some of them were curious though and looked.

That particular day, the rat was given to the snake and the snake ignored it. Supposedly, the teacher was trying to wake up the snake but the snake simply wasn't hungry or maybe it was just starting to hibernate since it was a late fall. Who knows? Anyway, the teacher pulled out the rat from the cage and announced to the class that "our rat presumably is not supposed to be food," and asked if anybody wanted it. Alex wanted it, of course. He brought it to the car, holding it with both his hands, and immediately started explaining the situation. We were already driving through the city and he still was talking.

"All this time when the rat was in the cage, I was praying for the snake not to eat it. I imagined that prayers would work, sometimes. Now, I know for sure," he said.

We went straight to the pet shop to buy more supplies for the two rats, now. It started the era of rats in our house. About two months later, Alex advertised on the internet an 'INTERNATIONAL RAT COMPETITION', in our house, of course. I was informed at the last moment. Alex' teacher was invited to be a judge. She came with her boyfriend. There were labyrinths made out of books, there were prizes and various categories in which the rats were supposed to compete. I prepared hot dogs and something sweet. One stranger who found our ad showed up with a cage and his own rat. It was a big one, with brown fur, I remember. We ate hot-dogs together. At this competition, my Mia's rat won the beauty contest and Alex's rat was declared the smartest one.

Anyway, I could write forever about Alex's passions and loves, but I just wanted to stress that he was serious about everything that he undertook. And snowboarding was now one of those things.

Besides snowboarding, Kevin would take Alex in the summer on wakeboarding trips, also for the reason of babysitting his son. Kevin probably felt the love and devotion on Alex's part and that made him like Alex even more.

Years later, Alex told me that it wasn't Kevin who showed him how to smoke pot.

"You can think what you want, but it wasn't Kevin. It was in school where I tried. And thank God, for that moment. It changed my life," he said.

Indeed, our lives were changed.

One day, I was supposed to pick up somebody from the airport in Phoenix. Alex had turned sixteen and already had a driver license. I let him drive my white Ford pick-up truck, which I'd recently exchanged for two paintings of mine. That was a lucky exchange. My friends had a spare car and I had plenty of paintings. I did that though only thinking about Alex's transportation. I had an old MR2, a small two-seater Toyota, for my needs, but it was too small to pick up my friend and her luggage from the airport. That day then, I took the Ford pick-up.

As I was driving towards Phoenix, there was a funny smell in the car. I didn't know where it was coming from. By Casa Grande I finally opened the ash tray and I saw burned stuff which looked like dead cockroaches. I stopped the car and emptied the ashtray onto the rest area. When I came back to Tucson after dropping off my friend in her house, I was still furious.

"Are you crazy? What did you do yesterday?" I yelled. I was ready to confront Alex. I was very angry, standing by Alex's bed, the evening I came back.

"What?" he said, turning to the other side. He was sleeping, although it wasn't late yet.

I walked out of his room and called Kevin. I told him what had happened, and he said he wanted to talk to Alex.

"Yeah, she found a few roaches," I heard Alex saying to the phone.

Roaches, I thought. I didn't know that marihuana butts were called roaches, but it was exactly my impression when I saw them first in the ashtray.

"He said he will come tomorrow at noon," Alex said. He was sitting on his bed, fully awake. I could see he was scared. "He said he will break my ass. See what you did?" He looked at me. He was almost crying. "You don't want to call him again? Do something about it. Kevin isn't joking. He never jokes when he says he will break somebody's ass."

I left Alex in his room. I was pleased that Kevin was coming, especially because it looked very much as if he was on my side.

Kevin came in the morning with a new girlfriend. The girlfriend was young and blond, and as I was told, pregnant, although she hadn't started showing. She sat at the kitchen table, and I asked her if she would like to eat some of the pierogis, a polish specialty which looked a little like Italian tortellinis, that I made. She said 'yes', but then she left them on the plate. She told me that she was pregnant and didn't feel well. Later on, it turned out that she wasn't pregnant at all. She only wanted Kevin's attention.

The girlfriend didn't distract me, though. I was listening to her with one ear. My whole attention was directed to the porch, where Kevin was having a conversation with Alex. Alex stood in front of him, red faced, with eyes full of tears. Kevin was talking to him, at first quietly, but then he raised his voice and started shouting. The more he yelled, the more scared Alex was becoming. I heard the words. There were plenty of 'f... k's and other swearing. At one point Kevin stood up and went to Alex's room. There, he spent a few minutes making an incredible noise. It sounded as if he was breaking furniture. It turned out though that he was only searching Alex's room. He found stuff. I saw it. He told Alex to carry everything to the porch; glass pipes and a bong and some other glass objects for which I couldn't imagine the purpose. But Kevin and Alex must have known. Kevin was taking one thing after another and throwing it against the concrete porch floor.

"Your mom gets you this nice truck and nice stuff and money, and you buy yourself this shit, right? Now look, look where your stuff is going. To the trash!" These were Kevin's words.

After all this breaking and smashing, Kevin walked into the kitchen, and gladly accepted pierogis that I offered. Alex was cleaning the porch. I could see that he was relieved. Well, his ass wasn't broken, only a few pipes and bongs. Marijuana buds were all over the porch and Alex was sweeping them up.

I must say that I, personally, wasn't giving Alex any money. If I was, it was only occasionally and a little. Alex always had a job. He trained himself as a bike mechanic at the local non-profit organization which was fixing old bicycles from all sorts of donated bike-related hardware. This non-profit also had classes for anybody who was interested in learning about bicycles. Ever since he was thirteen, Alex was very involved with Bicycle Inter-Community Art & Salvage also known as BICAS. By the time he was fourteen, Alex was hired as a bike mechanic at the local store. Because he was under age, my consent was needed. Of course, he only worked part time. The day after his sixteenth birthday, Alex got hired in a different shop, without my consent, since he didn't need it. He was also making more money. Again, he only worked part-time. He was giving lots of attention to Kevin and to his own projects.

Alex was also fixing computers for my boyfriend's business. Needless to say, Alex was doing an excellent job and he was very well paid. He could afford these glass pipes and who knows what that Kevin smashed to pieces on our porch. He could afford excellent pot, too

#

Kevin's presence in Alex's life didn't end with smashing bongs on the porch. But that day showed me something else about Alex, something I knew about but somehow didn't want to admit or, rather, just didn't know what to do about.

In the evening, as I was doing the dishes in the kitchen, I heard Alex on the phone with his friend, Dusty. Not that I wanted to listen, but the door to Alex' room was open, and I had just finished rinsing the plates, so I could hear at least Alex's end of the conversation.

"... and then, Kevin nicely explained to Mom everything, man. She's cool now. Isn't Kevin great?" Alex said.

I wondered about that, but not for long, since very soon Alex finished the conversation and came to the kitchen to get something to drink.

"So, isn't Kevin awesome?" Alex said.

"Yes, I guess," I said. "But what do you mean?"

"Mom, how he explained everything to you," he said.

I didn't want to confront Alex. I was happy that the stuff was gone and broken, and in the trash can. But I never stopped thinking about Alex saying what he said. Was he serious? He looked serious. Kevin didn't explain anything. It was the first time when I clearly saw Alex being delusional. Alex hadn't smoked enough pot yet to have this side effect. He simply was delusional by nature.

#

All these stories connected to Kevin happened when Alex was a teenager.

Now Alex was eighteen and going to his college classes. He was working and smoking pot every day, only I didn't know about it. I mean, I just didn't *think* about it. He was doing well. But it only could have lasted so long. I didn't know that Alex was helping himself by taking Adderall, which is a powerful stimulant of the nervous system. Adderall is mostly prescribed for attention deficit hyperactivity disorder, ADHD. All this world of pot, medications and drugs was new and unknown to me. I didn't even know what Adderall did. When Alex told me that his English teacher at the University was taking it, I didn't pay too much attention. One day though, when Alex and I were sitting at the Jamba Juice on Park Ave, close to the University of Arizona's main gate, Alex told me that he's selling Adderall to his teacher. Well, that got my attention. Not because of Adderall, but because Alex was selling something. That didn't sound good. A student passed us by on a bike. He waved to Alex, and Alex waved back.

"And that's Brian. He sells me larger quantities of Adderall," Alex said. "He's my Astronomy class buddy."

"I don't understand," I said. "Who's selling to whom and what? Are you okay?" I asked.

"I'm doing great, Mom. Don't worry. I have to go," he said and got up. He hugged me as usual, and left.

Chapter 12
Moving to the Studio

Earle and I obviously didn't know what life had prepared for us and we were doing what we thought was for the best every day. Earle was going to his plastics company every morning and I stayed in the studio painting. Alex was doing well after his second hospitalization. He and Tessa were still living together in Flanwill house. I was in touch with Alex every day, sometimes several times a day. Alex's younger brother, Andrew, came back from his school abroad and lived with us, but he was spending most of his time in Flanwill house, together with Alex and Tessa. Andrew even suggested once that he would like to move in with them but his wishes were quickly dismissed. He was a senior in high school. His school was far from our house. Earle simply bought him a car and the problem was resolved.

But he was still going every day to Alex's and spending time there. Then came the night that moved things in a different direction. Andrew went to visit his brother, as usual, in the evening. Alex and Tessa left to run an errand. They told Andrew they will be back in twenty minutes. Andrew stayed with the two dogs that belonged to Tessa and Alex. He was sitting on the couch, with his back to the door, when somebody walked in through the unlocked door, grabbed my son and pressed a cold hard object to the back of his head. It took my son only a few seconds to realize it was a gun. The dogs started barking and the intruder threw my son to the ground, face to the carpet, the gun still pressed to his head. He told him to calm down the dogs, warning him that, if they kept barking, he would shoot Andrew first and them later. He demanded money and he was given some small change. Then, he must have gotten scared or something, because he left.

Andrew was terrified. He only got up from the carpet when Alex and Tessa walked in. They called me on the phone and Earle and I immediately went there. So did the police but nothing substantial was found or discovered.

Tessa started crying. Alex hugged her. I proposed for them all to go to Desert house and not to stay at Flanwill house. They eagerly agreed.

I still don't understand that whole situation with the home invasion. I know they do happen and can be random. Was this one random?

I was trying to find out, and even after a few days passed by, I kept asking questions. Alex's replies didn't shine too much light on the event. He told me though that on the evening of the invasion, before he and Tessa left to run an errand and even before Andrew came, a man had knocked on the door and said he had a flat tire. He asked for help. Alex walked out with him but then it turned out that the car was gone.

"Gone? With a flat tire? Are you sure?" I kept asking.

"Mom, I know what I'm saying," Alex said. "I have to tell you though that all the way across the driveway, I thought that this dude would jump me. I almost felt him on my shoulders. Now I know he came to sniff what was inside…"

Well, I thought. *What did he sniff? Why did you say, sniff? Did it smell like something, like marijuana, for example? Or was 'sniff' only a figure of speech.* I didn't elaborate on it.

After the robbery Alex and Tessa moved to the Studio for good. The home invasion happened in the Fall, and by the Summer, I could clearly see that Alex's and Tessa's relationship was deteriorating. In the early Summer I took a trip to Sedona. It was a prize trip, two nights in a nice hotel. I never fall for these kinds of things, but this time, I was tempted. Especially because I found out Tessa had never been to the Grand Canyon. That was beyond my understanding. It was like an illustration of either total poverty or total neglect; to be born in Arizona, to literate parents, and never see the Grand Canyon, not even going on a school trip. I really was bewildered. I decided to make a trip to Sedona and the Grand Canyon. We would spend two nights in Sedona and one in Flagstaff. I took Alex, Tessa, and Andrew, the high school senior. Earle stayed at work. I was happy and proud to take those young people on a trip, and especially, to show Tessa places that she had never seen. But she was quiet and always a little subdued. Alex was displaying his overpowering personality. He told Andrew to do some dangerous jumps into the water at Slide Rock Canyon. But then, my youngest son was always doing dangerous things even without being told. There was no need for Alex to challenge him, but he did it anyway. As a result, Andrew was doing super dangerous things. Alex was the leader and his brother followed him as if Alex was God himself. On this trip to Sedona, though, their relationship was changing and outgrowing itself. What was good for them as boys wasn't necessarily good for the boys who had become men.

I saved a picture from this trip. Alex and Tessa are sitting on a low concrete wall, with the Grand Canyon behind them.

Tessa looks sad. Alex looks a little angry or preoccupied. That's how they look to me. I had no idea what was inside their heads. They are holding hands.

As I mentioned, after the home invasion and move to the Studio, their relationship deteriorated quickly. After we came back from our trip to Sedona, things sped up. I could see how difficult Alex was, but I didn't know how to help him more, or help Tessa, or help both of them. Tessa was always sad and quiet, at least when I showed up. She still didn't want to move back with her grandmother. I secretly wanted the problem to resolve itself but it just wasn't happening. After one of their huge fights, when Alex and Tessa contacted me separately, I came to the Studio to talk with Tessa. We sat down on two white plastic chairs in the Studio's backyard.

"Do you want to move back to Flanwill house?" I asked.

Her eyes were red and puffy. Her black hair looked even darker, contrasting the white chair. She was still crying after the last fight. Her blue shirt was wrinkled, very unlike her. Tessa was very clean and organized. I could hardly believe she would even consider moving back. After all, she was very stressed out after the home invasion. I was surprised when she eagerly agreed to my proposition and wanted to move back as soon as possible. The Flanwill house was for rent but Tessa wanted to pay. She had found a job at a restaurant and was making some money. I didn't charge her much and it looked like she was happy to move back, live by herself with her dogs, and be kind of on her own.

These events started a new era of Alex living in the Studio by himself.

Chapter 13
Third hospitalization

Alex lived in the Studio by himself but he wasn't happy about it. He didn't cry over Tessa, at least he didn't tell me about it, but his behavior was deteriorating every day. He was rude and demanding. He was also loud and sarcastic. Whenever he called, he yelled instead of talking. This was the start of my loneliest days.

Earle was in such bad shape that he forgot about my birthday. It wouldn't be such a big deal if it wasn't for the fact that, from the beginning of our relationship, he was the one who paid attention to special occasions.

For all those occasions, however small, he would always buy me flowers along with a card, and my favorite chocolate. Sometime he would buy them without an occasion. To forget about my birthday wasn't like him. Although I knew how depressed he was, it saddened me.

I knew that we would eventually have to foreclose on our Piedra Seca house. But so what? One place less for Earle to worry about. I had a son I had to help and no one to talk to. I wouldn't want to burden Earle, but once in a while I would slip by telling him how I felt and even cry. Every time his angry reaction told me I shouldn't do it. For example, he would leave the room and slam the door. He probably felt helpless and overwhelmed. I knew I should keep all Alex's problems to myself. But I needed somebody. One person I could talk to was my eldest son, the medical student. I called him almost every day, especially now that Alex was getting worse and worse. My eldest son was patient and truly supportive. In fact, he was the only one who understood how I felt when I said I was thinking about committing Alex for a third time.

Alex's school friends were calling me and complaining about Alex's behavior. I heard it all. Alex was driving high and hanging out with very shady people. Even Andrew's friends who knew Alex would call me and tell me they thought something needed to be done with Alex.

"But what? Do what?" I would ask.

He needs to take his meds or go to hospital again, was the standard answer.

The front house was rented to a young couple, Angela and Troy. Troy attended the local college and Angela worked in a hospital. She was a nurse aide. I wasn't happy with them because they were usually late with rent but eventually, they paid.

Angela kept complaining about the flies which supposedly were very happy with Alex's trash. He didn't pay attention to my pleas about throwing trash away. I thought I might need to lower Angela's rent so she wouldn't complain but she was adamant. The trash really stank. It wasn't her fancy. I talked to Alex several times about his trash but nothing changed. After one month of unpaid rent, Angela and Troy left the front house. They left at night and never picked up the phone calls from me. I had to look for new renters.

Tessa now was holding down two jobs. One was in the sushi restaurant and the second one in our plastics company, and once in a while, I would share my sadness with her. I was desperate for any kind of support. But these were all children. Couldn't I find an adult who would listen and understand? But such is solitude. It will simply squeeze your throat. And who wants to suffocate?

#

For me personally, Alex's text messages and emails were the worst. He sent them almost daily. They were terribly abusive and full of hatred. They were very long, too. Alex would describe in detail how he had been hurt by me and how I had destroyed him, mostly because I'd committed him to the hospital. These messages became unbearable.

Alex blamed me for all the medications that he had to take, even though I didn't know anything about the medications. I thought that they were supposed to help. There was one incident when firefighters were called to the Studio and I only found out about it the next day. Apparently, Alex took one of the meds that he was prescribed. It was an antipsychotic medication Fluphenazine. I don't know if he took too much. He swore he didn't and I was inclined to believe him. Alex tended to be extremely accurate. After he took this medication, he started to feel so bad that, in desperation, he called Lara, my elder daughter. They were close at the time and took several college classes together. After she came and saw him shaking, they decided to call nine-one-one. I don't remember if Alex was taken to the hospital that night but he called me the next day and insisted on me taking him to the Emergency Room. I showed up immediately and we went.

Truly, I didn't know how to help him, and he was telling

me very strange things.

"Mom, look, my leg is going somewhere, look, hold it!"

His leg looked all right to me, but his head was jerking to one side. And it looked like his hand was making some involuntary movements.

At the hospital, while we were waiting for the doctor to come in a small area with the curtains drawn for privacy, Alex was making noises and walking along beside the bed. He couldn't be still, even for a moment.

"Ants, Mom, ants are crawling all over me. I know there are no ants here. Can the doctor hurry up? Mom, do something!"

I stuck my head out but nobody was in a hurry. Finally, the doctor came, and after assessing the situation, he said that all these symptoms would go away soon. He also said that maybe Alex should stop taking fluphenazine because this was the drug that caused his dystonic movements. That's what he said, 'dystonic', meaning uncontrollable muscle movements.

I had no idea what all this meant. Alex was taking the drugs he was prescribed. After this incident, I couldn't stand his text messages any longer. He kind of tried to threaten me in his unique, funny way. He said he would take me to court for making him sell counterfeit software. I never did that and wondered where he got that idea from. Then I remembered that Alex used to help my ex-boyfriend fix computers and he was generously paid for this work. The software in Alex's head must have been a residue from that time.

Alex also ran into financial problems. He was spending too much money. He was growing his beloved yo-yo collection. His new titanium yo-yos had different colors, and looked really exquisite. But they weren't cheap. One time,

Alex couldn't help himself and showed off his latest purchase. He said he paid about four hundred dollars for one of those yo-yos. I remember how he broke that news to me.

"I paid four hundred dollars," he said. "For the body only."

I didn't know what the yo-yo's body meant. No string? Now what? 'Isn't a yo-yo a body only, in general?' I wanted to ask but I didn't. I was speechless.

Alex also bought two special cases for his collections. These were the two cases I knew of, maybe he had more. I wondered; who on Earth specializes in making storage cases for yo-yos? And special yo-yos, on top of it? The titanium ones were a bit smaller in diameter than the regular plastic ones. The cases he bought were portable with numerical coding locks. The big case was the size of a small travel suitcase. It was made out of metal. The cases were filled with custom sized foam layers, with appropriate holes, to hold the yo-yos. The big case had two layers of foam. I didn't know until later, that the lower layer holes were filled with plastic containers of different strands of marijuana.

The Studio didn't look anything even close to normal. To say that it was a mess would be a huge understatement. Trash was everywhere: empty paper bags from various fast-food restaurants, pizza boxes with leftovers, colorful previously frozen drinks with plastic straws still in them, yo-yo strings and Alex's dirty clothes everywhere on the floor. One might wonder why the clothes were not in the closet. The Studio was provided with a very large closet that stretched from wall to wall. It was always closed when I would come over so I didn't know what was in it. The Studio was a disaster. One couldn't open the door it was so messy. And although it reeked of marijuana, it also smelled like trash and spoiled food.

At first, I tried to motivate Alex and make him clean with me. But it didn't work. Alex became so abusive and mean that it was simply better not to be around him. Whenever he talked to me, he was either sarcastic or pretentious. With his deep voice and in actually a funny way, he would demand money, while looking at me and fumbling with his small, plastic earring. In one email after a long tirade of what I'd done and how I was, he said that every click of his mouse is worth at least one dollar, then he calculated approximately how much I owed him for writing to me.

Alex, the most creative person I have ever known, was creative even now. It would have been funny if it wasn't tragic.

I knew that maybe he was still going to school but thought nothing good would come from it.

I felt the terrible things coming to us and I knew that I would have to proceed. I was afraid. I had anxiety. I was waking up sweating in the middle of the night and immediately thinking about Alex. I would turn over but the sleep was gone.

I asked for help. One by one, I asked all the young people who were hanging out with Alex to help me commit him. I asked all the ones who had complained to me and were telling me terrible stories about him, how he was driving high, how abusive he was, how he was shopping and how many traffic violations he already had. I knew he had speeding tickets and I knew he wasn't paying them. I knew that Alex soon would be arrested and the whole story would become even worse. My eldest son supported me in thinking that way.

I didn't ask Earle for help this time. He needed help himself, hourly. He was sick with his cough, overworked and depressed. He was grieving the lost properties and feared the future.

Everybody that I asked for help denied me. They all did it differently, though.

Andrew just disappeared. Whenever there was a good moment to talk, he managed to get away. When he thought I finally got it that he wouldn't even listen to my problems with Alex, he stopped disappearing.

One of Alex's closest friends was so high when I called that I thought he simply fell asleep while talking to me. The words in his sentences were further and further apart, until I couldn't wait any longer for the next one and I hung up.

There was Tessa, too. She knew I needed help. I saw her daily, since she still worked for us. I understood she wouldn't help me, before I asked. I knew she was afraid of Alex's anger.

I didn't want to bother the church minister, Mr White. He already helped me enough. Nobody was left but me.

I didn't even know where to go. Call the police? But why? What for? There was an office where I was told Alex could be committed. It was somewhere on Dodge Street and I went there.

After filling in the given paperwork, I wrote a few sentences in a free comments box. I wrote about trash, driving high, anger and shopping. The free comments box was full and everything written was true.

A nice lady came out of her office and took the paperwork from me. She was younger than me but not by much. Her thick bifocal glasses made a dent in a middle of her nose. I only saw this dent when she adjusted her glasses in order to read the paperwork. When she finished reading, she looked straight at me and asked if I was sure I wanted to commit Alex.

"That's why I'm here," I said.

"I know," she said. She had a very soft voice. "The reason I'm asking though, is because it's a tremendous violation to oneself to be committed, to be forced to take medications."

"I know that, but again, should I do nothing?" I asked her.

"No," she said. "You can fill out the paperwork every day, if you think you need to. Even if your request is denied, you can reapply the next day." This is exactly what happened. My request was denied and I came back the next day. I checked the box "request denied in the past" and in the field "how many times," I put the number one. Every other field I filled pretty much the same way as I did in my first application.

I was told that Alex wouldn't know who filled out the papers; ever.

This request was approved.

I don't remember how I was put in touch or told what time the police would come to the Studio, where I knew Alex was, but I was there when they came. It was around noon and the weather was hot that day.

Two police officers, male and female, met me in front of the house. The policewoman was tall and skinny. Her slightly gray bangs were cut short, revealing a wide forehead. She was very sympathetic but professional at the same time. The policeman was shorter and pudgy. His face was wide and sweaty. He was wiping his cheeks with a Kleenex. I figured he was hot in his dark uniform. The policewoman asked if I had a spare key to the Studio. I did and I gave it to her.

"We will knock on the door first," the policewoman said. "We don't want to scare him. Does he have a gun?"

"Not that I know of," I said.

They drove in their police car around the back alley and drove into the backyard, since the old wire gate was wide open.

They parked and got out of the car leaving its doors open. The second police car came right after them but the driver never got out. It parked in the middle of the alley.

I was already standing between the two oleanders in the shade, behind Alex's car that was still parked in the backyard. I felt it was a good hiding spot. The oleanders were thick in this place. Plus, I was in the shade and anybody who was in the sunshine would have to focus hard in order to see me. With my right hand I was holding up one of the branches full of pink oleander flowers. They were obstructing my view. I was focusing on the Studio door but once in a while I was distracted by the flickering computer screen in the police car.

"Alex?" the policewoman shouted. She was standing behind the policeman while he knocked on the door. There was no reply.

"Alex, open up. Police!" The policeman said this time. They both had their guns drawn. They looked as if they knew what they were doing.

Did I know what I was doing? Even today, I would have to say that I'm not sure.

The officers called Alex several times, but when this didn't work, the policewoman gave the key to her companion and he stuck it in the keyhole. She grabbed her gun in two hands and lifted it up in the air, while he opened the now unlocked door. They ran in, while screaming; *"Hands up! Don't move!"*

My hands dropped and the pink flowers filled my vision. One of them was significantly bigger than the others. The noises from the Studio were fading away as I was now studying the inside of that flower, its yellow stamen, and what seemed to me, never-ending pink depth.

#

I only came out from my hiding place between the oleanders after I saw the alley's dust lifting into the air, as the car with Alex drove away. The policewoman was the only officer remaining on the scene after the action was over.

"It's a blessing that we didn't fire any shots," she told me while Alex was on his way to Kino Hospital. "He was calm, standing on his bed, but he was holding his cellphone in his hand, and that's always confusing. We see something in a suspect's hand and we fire. It would be too bad," the policewoman said.

Indeed, I thought. I thanked her. The policewoman gave me back the key and hugged me.

"Hang in there. It's over," she said.

With tears streaming down my face and blurring my vision, I entered the Studio. Only this part was over. A whole new one was about to start.

Once inside the Studio, I kicked away a few pieces of clothing and papers, and made room on the floor for me to sit down. I wasn't capable of cleaning, arranging, throwing trash away, or even thinking. I was only capable of crying. The image of Alex being dragged out from the Studio by the policeman didn't want to leave my head. With my eyes closed or opened, it was all I saw; his confused face half covered with his messy hair. Alex's whole body impersonated fear, and I felt it. In my own heart I felt his skipping or rushing heartbeat. In my muscles I felt the tension of all his muscles. I tried to live through his and my feelings simultaneously but it was an impossible task. Especially because I couldn't get rid of the feeling of his overall innocence. It was all killing me. The vision of how Alex was pushed into the second car that was waiting in the alley was very painful. The policeman kept his hand on Alex's head so he wouldn't hit the roof of the car while getting in, but he still hit it and he jerked his head back. The police pressed on Alex's shoulders, and only then, he bent over and got inside.

Now that it was over, I knew this event was only starting its cruel work in my memory, to continue to make me suffer, in its own, unique way of building guilt.

Me, the mom, had arranged for my beloved son to be taken to hospital for the third time. How was I going to be able to live with myself?

I couldn't understand what had happened, even though I was the one who had committed Alex.

But he was my Alex, by baby, my genius, my smart, spiritual son. He was the most spiritual of all my children. To say that he believed in God would be an understatement; he *knew* that God existed. Except for a short time during his early teens, when Alex thought that he knew better and he could laugh at the concept of God, he quickly came back to it. I am not talking about being religious. He didn't go to church for mass, only for his youth group meetings, and that was mainly a social event for him. I am talking about spirituality. Alex had a deep sense of God. Since he was a little kid, he prayed every day.

I remember one time when Alex was about seven years old, we had a visiting math professor with his wife staying with us for a month or so. One evening we were sitting in the kitchen, drinking tea. We talked about God and spirituality. The professor was the one who started that topic.

"Of course, there's nothing." The professor said. "We live because we live, there's no reason and that's the only reason. There's a nirvana, though, and you can attain it by meditating. It happened to me, I think, or at least I must have been close to it."

He continued talking about nirvana, and how wonderful it is. Alex was playing with a puzzle. Then, while holding a piece of puzzle in his hand, he looked at the professor.

"So, you don't know about God?" he asked.

"I know, of course," the professor said.

"But you say he isn't anywhere, right? You just said that." Alex said.

"Well, I know about the 'concept' of God," the professor said. "It doesn't mean that God exists."

"Okay, then. God might very well think that you don't exist. You are just a concept, too." Alex said, and went back to his puzzle. The professor's wife was a psychologist. She hid her smile inside her tea cup.

Alex was a kind of child who didn't do things for attention. He wasn't pretentious but as natural as one can be.

This was my son, the very same person from years ago who I was locking up in the psychiatric unit for the third time today, according to my own decision. I thought that my heart would burst into pieces.

Chapter 14
Accident

Alex remained in the hospital for two weeks, and when he got out, he started to do better. He was on medication (Depakote). He wasn't going crazy, like he did in the past. Overall, things started to improve, again. Most importantly, he was doing well in his classes.

I managed to rent the front House again. A young couple moved in. Alex met them the day they moved in. He was coming back from his classes when he saw the U-Haul truck in front of the house.

His name was Dominic and her name was Ashley. Dominic was short and very skinny. His black hair was cut short. When he smiled, he showed very white teeth. His eyes were as dark as his hair. Ashley was also short. She had a round face and blue eyes. Her blond hair was brushed and tied with a pink scrunchy in a ponytail. They had one baby and she was pregnant. Alex called me a few days after we signed the lease. He was ecstatic.

"Mom! I love my new neighbors. Awesome people!" he shouted.

"I'm glad. They look like decent people, don't they? We both liked them, Earle and me," I said.

Later on, I found out why there was such a liking, on both sides. They all enjoyed smoking pot. There were two major connections Alex had with Dominic; marijuana and snowboarding.

It started well. I forgot where Dominic was working, but he had a job. He and Ashely took care of their baby. They also had two big dogs, Great Danes, to Alex's delight. Alex loved dogs in general, but to have two of them in his own backyard, was a real treat.

Alex was busy attending classes, but he also spent a lot of time at home, hanging out with Dominic. I didn't know that Dominic had guns until Alex, occasionally, told me that Dominic had to gun-proof the house, because the baby was growing and the second one was going to be born soon.

"Guns?" I asked.

"Yeah, Mom, some people need them," Alex said.

"What does he need them for, then?" I asked.

"To defend himself, for instance," Alex said.

He started to sound annoyed, so I didn't say anything. But it made me wonder what Dominic needed the guns for. This question took me further. Where did Dominic get the money to buy his nice jeep? It was a nice jeep, with big tires. Was all its cost from his and Ashley's job? Then Alex told me Dominic was from a very wealthy family and his father had a huge house. He even said it was a mansion in the upscale part of town. I thought this explained it all.

As the winter was coming, together with the snowboarding season, Alex and Dominic decided to go on a snowboarding trip together. One afternoon Alex called me and told me they were going into the White Mountains. And off they went.

It was Thursday late afternoon when the text message came to my phone. I was at work, trying to figure out how to pay the current shop bills. I was surprised to receive a text from Dominic. I only had his phone number saved because he was our tenant. I read the text carefully.

It said that Alex had had in a snowboarding accident. It said that he was conscious, but hurt. It repeated that he was hurt. He was hurt to the point that a helicopter was coming to pick him up and take him to the trauma center at University Medical Center Tucson.

My head was spinning. Without closing the phone, I went straight to the warehouse and showed the text to Earle.

"We need to go," he said.

I went outside and waited for him. He had to leave the shop to our only other employee. Tessa had already gone home for the day. The spinning in my head didn't prevent me from thinking while I waited. As I was repeatedly reading the text message, I felt my heart pounding in my chest.

Now, it was obvious to me. I'm not a psychic, but the familiar feeling of certainty had happened to me before in life. At this moment, I knew that Alex was not *meant* to do well. I didn't know why, but I felt that all the efforts, the hospitalizations, the struggles, the therapies, were fruitless. I had been feeling that, at the end, we had succeeded, because Alex now was doing well. Yes, he had been hospitalized three times, but so what? It was in the past. We didn't even talk any more about his last hospital stay, which by any means was very traumatic. He asked me now and then how the police were able to open his door without having the key when they took him to the hospital. But he never pressed the matter. After the third hospitalization he was assigned to COPE agency again to be monitored for his bipolar medications. He was taking all his meds and going to the meetings. And now, he had plans. He was going to college. He was odd, strange, played with yo-yos in class, but the teachers loved him. He was extremely talented and helpful. He was coming to his business math class earlier, so he could help other people with the more difficult problems and equations. His chemistry professor thought very highly of Alex.

These successes bothered the devil, and it was only waiting to cancel them in one, quick fall. While standing on the parking lot and waiting for Earle to come out, I almost felt the devil sitting on my back and suffocating me. Once in a while, it would show me its ugly face, and whisper into my ear. *You were thinking that your precious boy was saved, right? Well, it's not the case. I can't let him do well. The plan is different, for him, and therefore, for you.*

Alex was doing too well. It couldn't go on.

#

We parked our car in front of the UMC and we waited maybe only thirty minutes or so for the helicopter to show up on the horizon.

Whatever was going on around me seemed to slow down. I was very anxious, of course. I didn't know what was going on inside that helicopter. I didn't know how badly Alex was hurt. But I figured that, if the helicopter had to be sent, then things were not good. I was going out of my mind, but I must have looked normal, since Earle made a comment.

"You know that they don't give him this kind of ride for no reason, don't you?"

I nodded my head.

As I watched the helicopter landing on the roof of the

hospital building, we walked inside the Emergency Unit, and I explained the situation to the receptionist.

She contacted several people via phone and we were rushed towards the trauma center. I walked fast to wherever I was shown I needed to go. I wanted to run.

When we walked into a room where Alex already was, still on the stretcher, he looked at me and I had an overpowering urge to hug him, or even only touch him. I was afraid though; there were many people around the stretcher. They all were preparing Alex for moving him to the hospital bed. I moved away and stayed behind all these working people, who were doing their best in order not to hurt him. There were several doctors around him, and I didn't know who was who. The nurses were all very busy doing various things and asking Alex questions. Alex' body was immobilized, including his neck. One of the doctors told him to try to move his fingers. He moved them, and with every motion, I felt a relief: Alex could move his fingers. I wiped sweat off my forehead. The doctor lifted a blanket from Alex' feet, and told him to move his toes. One foot was okay, but the other not so much. Alex couldn't move all his toes. But he had feeling in his foot. Not all of it, but some.

From the questions and answers I learned what had happened. While doing his last snowboard round of the day, Alex slipped on fresh ice that had just started to form, since the slope was in the shade, and it was a very late afternoon. Going full speed, he hit a tree.

#

In the next hour, all the necessary tests and MRIs were done on Alex. As I was waiting in the hallway for him to be wheeled back, my mind was racing and I was hot and cold at the same time. He could move his hands and feel his legs; one of them seemed to be okay. Things couldn't be *that* bad. I wasn't praying. In fact, I don't know what I was doing.

When his bed was brought back to the room, I could finally approach my son. Without being able to move his head, he rolled his eyes to where I stood.

"Don't worry, Mom," he said. "It will all be okay. I will be fine, soon."

I wanted so much to hug him, but I was afraid that I might cause him even more pain. Once in a while a terrible twist would pass through his face, and I could see he was in pain.

The doctor came in, with the X-ray results. The doctor was young and tall, maybe in his thirties. His hair was blond, almost yellow. His glasses had golden frames.

"You broke your back," he said, standing at the foot of the bed. Alex lowered his eyes, to see better. I stepped a little away from the bed.

"You will need surgery, this we know for sure. Several surgeries. The orthopedic surgeon will be here early in the morning to revise all the images and assess the situation. You might need several surgeries, as I said. Do you have any questions?"

Alex was quick to ask.

"Will I ever be able to snowboard, again?"

The doctor wasn't surprised.

"Right now, buddy, we need to figure out if you will be able to walk. I cannot answer your question." The doctor checked the hour on his watch. "Are you in pain? On a scale of one to ten…"

The doctor's voice trailed away. A moment later, I saw a nurse coming in with pills and a new IV bag, with stronger painkillers.

#

After Earle and I left the hospital, we drove home. We still lived in Piedra Seca house. It was already late, and Earle was told by our employee he had locked up the shop.

At home, Earle took out a bottle of wine from the fridge and poured us two generous glasses. I drank some with him, but then he started coughing and pretty soon went to bed. I remember making a remark about his cough. I thought t Earle was coughing too often and for no reason. It bothered me. I didn't like it. I had even mentioned this to him a few times, that maybe he should go and see a doctor, but Earle didn't have the time and didn't feel like it.

I took my wine to the garage and sat on the concrete step which led to the laundry room. The images of the devil mocking me came back. I poured another glass and I went to get the phone. I carefully counted the hours and I figured that it must be about eleven in the morning in Poland. I had to call Alex's father.

To my surprise, he picked up the phone immediately. He just happened to be in his office.

"What happened?" he asked. We hadn't talked for five years.

I told him. I heard a long silence. I was quiet, too. Then, I heard a click and a busy signal came on. I got up and turned around, knocking down my glass. I forgot I had put it by my feet. It didn't break but the wine spilled on the concrete floor.

PART TWO

Chapter 15
The surgeon

The next morning, I received a phone call from the orthopedic surgeon's office. I was called about Alex's surgery. An appointment was made for me to come the very same day, in the afternoon. I started to count the hours. In the meantime, I went to work and did some paperwork in the office. I left early and went to the hospital. While I was waiting for an elevator to come, my thoughts were racing. The main thought was that I missed Alex and I just wanted to see him. I peeked into his room and saw that he was asleep. His slightly sweaty forehead was covered with blond hair. I looked at his face and marveled at how peaceful his sleep was, not even one wrinkle or grimace which would indicate he was dreaming. I left him and started pacing the hallway, back and forth, thinking that maybe he would wake up before his appointment. But since the hour was approaching and he wasn't waking up, I went to the elevators and started to look at the list of departments displayed on the wall. I was scanning the floor numbers, the last names of the doctors and the departments. Alex's orthopedic surgeon's office was only a floor above me. I took the stairs.

I found the proper door and entered. I approached the counter and was told to sit and wait. The nice young lady with hair made into a several dozens of braids and the brightest smile told me that she would call me as soon as the doctor was ready. I sat down and listened to the conversation of two young women sitting in the corner. Their blue scrubs suggested they were nurses. They were talking about Alex's surgeon. It was a pleasure to listen to them, really. It's rare to see so much reverence and respect toward the boss, anywhere nowadays. The surgeon was obviously the boss here, and very well respected.

When my name was called, I came close to the desk. An older woman in a blue outfit came out from another office and told me to follow her.

The orthopedic surgeon was waiting for me. He was a man in his fifties, small and pudgy. I saw him standing in front of his office, at the end of the hallway. We shook hands and introduced ourselves. After the first spoken words I could recognize his strong personality. His passion for his work was overpowering. I immediately liked the man. I also respected him, just like all his staff.

He asked me to sit down on a tall stool. He sat on the one closer to the computer which he quickly started to navigate while talking.

"This is close to a miracle. Your son broke his lower spine in half. You can see it here," he said.

On the screen he brought up some more pictures so I could see what he was talking about. I'm not a doctor and I don't easily recognize broken bones and such on pictures, but after a moment, I saw Alex's spine.

It was broken. Just like a wooden stick. The piece on top of the picture was totally detached form the piece at the bottom. My heart stopped.

"I will show you where I think the miracle is, unless you already saw it?" the surgeon said. He looked at me.

I shook my head 'no'. He touched the computer screen and pointed out the image to me. "Here. Do you see it?"

Again, I didn't. The surgeon zoomed into the area he was pointing to. From the blurry pixels I could see something that looked like a rope or a string.

"Now, you see. These are nerves. They didn't break. That's why Alex can move his toes. There's a chance he will walk."

I truly appreciated the surgeon's effort and him using words like nerves and bones, instead of their medical descriptions. I was crying, too. While talking, he pushed a box of Kleenex towards me. My tears were abundant, but quiet.

"The surgery is scheduled for tomorrow. We will take the two parts of the spine, press them together and reinforce that place with plate and screws. Alex is young. If everything goes well, he will walk. But not any time soon," he said.

He paused and looked at the pictures again. I think that, for a moment, he forgot about my presence. I could see him analyzing images, again and again. He kept zooming in and out of them several times.

"We have to be careful and not do more damage. It's tricky. It can be done," he finally said.

I wiped my eyes with another Kleenex and looked around his office. I saw several framed thank-you letters along with gifts placed behind the glass in a wooden cabinet. There were also pictures of former patients, taken before and after the surgery and recovery. The pictures were mostly taken outside. One very big picture was from the football field and another one from the basketball court. I even saw one skier, but not a snowboarder. I looked again at this small man and I admired the skill and talent of his hands combined with technology. He had changed so many lives.

I left his office feeling hopeful and went to see Alex.

#

Alex was awake and I could finally touch him. I touched the blankets and thought about sitting down on the edge of his bed, just to be closer. Then I was afraid I might move him or something, and I looked around for a chair. I found a stool and sat down and I looked at Alex. His forehead was slightly sweaty. With patches of his blond hair sticking to it and his slightly watery blue eyes, he looked miserable.

"Don't worry, Mom." Alex said. "After the surgery I will be like new."

I could see that he was under the influence of pain medication, and I was grateful.

For once, Alex's practical side didn't leave him. He started to talk about school and making plans. He wanted to finish the semester. I wasn't sure about anything any more but I followed his thoughts. Maybe it was me who wanted him to finish the semester and he was following my lead. It was probable since I had invested so much into his college education. It wasn't even about the money. I'm talking about hospitalizations times three, all my doing. Now, when Alex was doing well, he was in a hospital again, only in a different unit. And this time I had nothing to do with it. Or did I?

Alex's father was always against snowboarding. He opposed the idea of any sport, except hiking and cycling, which he considered suitable for Tucson. I didn't like snowboarding either, but I went along with it. I'd never snowboarded and I only skied until I was fourteen. A bad fall that broke my leg prevented me from skiing ever again. I didn't miss it. But I knew one thing. The more I opposed my younger boys' ideas about snowboarding or skateboarding, the more they would do it. So yes, I bought the helmets and elbow and knee pads, several tickets and memberships to the YMCAs and other skate parks. Our California trips were highlighted by us going to the various skate parks.

In Tucson, I would drive my boys to all the possible places where they could ride their skateboards. Often, I was waiting for them at the parking lot and looking through the fence. I would close my eyes when Andrew would jump over the stacked trash-bins and look away when Alex, with the wind in his eyes, would throw himself into the concrete hole. In the winter, I would sometimes take the boys to our local Mt. Lemmon, where they would show me their snowboarding tricks. Was this encouraging?

All those thoughts were going through my head as I was looking at Alex's immobilized neck. I heard him talking to me. He was describing, again, what had happened.

"The tree had a right to be there, Mom. I slipped. I was going really fast. You know what I felt? A thud, that's how I would call it. 'A thud'. I don't know what happened next. The pain wasn't normal and I couldn't move."

I was listening. I didn't ask Alex to tell me how it happened. I didn't ask anything.

"It will take you a while to recover," I finally said. "For at least a semester you won't be able to do much." I decided that I would present the situation as it was presented to me, that Alex might walk again.

"I know," Alex said. "The thing is, that I've already done so much in school. I would hate to waste it."

"Many things can be done on the computer, nowadays. And if your teachers cooperate, at least some of your work wouldn't be wasted. Maybe I should buy you a good laptop," I said.

"That would be helpful," he immediately agreed.

The next day I came to the hospital with a new laptop. I was making very little money and Earle and I were in a deep financial trouble, but I was saving almost everything I made. For emergencies... This was an emergency.

The surgery was scheduled for eight in the morning. I came much earlier. It was still dark when I left the house.

When I walked into Alex's room, he was already awake. A nurse was filling in a chart on the wall. She told me that Alex was going to the surgery unit in half an hour. It sounded very close, this half hour. It seemed to me there was almost no time left.

"Look," I said. I showed Alex his new laptop.

"Awesome, Mom. Now I will try to log on into my U of A account and see what are the deadlines. I will also email my professors."

Alex didn't mind how little time he had. He opened the box and turned on the computer. He was able to go online and log into his University of Arizona account. Two male nurses came in but Alex didn't mind that his bed was being detached from the wall and rolled out of the room. He was still furiously typing while being wheeled towards the surgery unit. I was walking alongside. Alex only closed his laptop in front of the wooden double doors leading to the surgery unit.

"I emailed my chemistry teacher, "Alex said. "Don't worry, Mom."

The nurse took the laptop from him and handed it over to

me. Her eyes were cold. I could read her face. *'What kind of mother are you? Your son might never walk again, and you bring him a computer so he can do his homework?'*

#

The surgery went well. We met the surgeon in the hall and he told us all about it. Screws and plates were installed in Alex's back. They were supposed to stay there for a year or two; he couldn't tell exactly. He couldn't tell us either how fast the recovery would go, or if Alex would be able to walk. He told me to come back tomorrow for a longer conversation. Right now, he was too tired.

I came back the next day. We met in his office. We started to talk about Alex's health options.

"Do you think he will walk?" I asked.

"Possibly, yes." That was all he said and I clung to that even though he repeated the word 'possibly', and told me that he couldn't promise anything. It was noon on a sunny day but the dark film on the office windows made it look cloudy, or at least gave the impression of an evening light. I had come there with big hopes and all I got was this "possibly, yes" answer. The only thing I had was hope.

After two days of lying flat in bed Alex was supposed to use a wheelchair. One day when I came to the hospital after work, Alex said that he would like to go for a walk.

"For a walk?" I said.

"In a wheelchair, Mom. Let's call a nurse. The hospital is supposed to have a wheelchair ready for me."

I called a nurse, and with her help, we placed Alex in a wheelchair. Slowly, I pushed the it through the door and into the hallway. I asked the nurse first if we could go outside.

"Of course, you can. But be careful and don't go far," the nurse said.

It's hard to get far from the University Medical Center hospital while pushing a wheelchair for the first time. Alex really wanted to get on the street, so we ended up by the traffic lights where a crosswalk is right in front of the hospital. Alex was constantly talking. He was in very high spirits and full of hope. I didn't know then that this was still a result of the medications he was on. I only understood that when I showed up the next morning and Alex's mood resembled a deflated balloon.

"I felt great yesterday," he said.

I remembered. During the whole first wheelchair ride to the crosswalk Alex was animated and happy. It was hard to believe now. His positive energy was so contagious that I even thought it was helping me to push the wheelchair faster when we were crossing the street.

"I'm so glad it's only my back. It's not a big deal. Before we know it I will be walking and back in school. You bought me an awesome laptop, Mom. I didn't check if I got any emails from my professors but I will do as soon as possible."

I knew that Alex's sister had informed his teachers about the accident so I didn't have to go to the University.

But all this good mood was yesterday. Today was different.

"They must have changed my meds," Alex said.

He didn't even want to sit in his wheelchair. We were planning his discharge. The surgeon told him that under no circumstances should Alex try to stand up. He only could lie down and use the wheelchair with somebody's help. During the day or waking hours, he should be using the long plastic brace which completely enclosed and immobilized his torso. The brace was hard to put on. I had to put it flat on Alex's bed, then he had to kind of roll into it and I would secure the Velcro tapes. He needed to have the dressing of the surgery wound changed daily. I was going to do that. And of course, he must take all the prescribed medications. There were many bottles and prescriptions we took with us.

I had prepared the Studio for Alex's return. Alex didn't want to go to Piedra Seca house as his friends wouldn't visit him there. Earle made a wooden floor outside the Studio with little ramps so the wheelchair wouldn't get stuck. I got all the appropriate equipment for Alex's toilet and shower. I remember when I saw the stitches on his back for the first time. I was afraid I would hurt him. I was happy Alex couldn't see my face. His eyes were closed and buried in a pillow. I was terrified and worked hard to pretend that things looked great. But the stiches gave me chills. They were black and the skin around them was red and swollen. I contacted the nurse about it but she said it was normal, that stiches are only pretty when they are gone.

Chapter 16
Coming home

For Alex's coming home, the front house renters, Ashley and Dominic, prepared a party. Ashley made steaks and invited some friends. Alex's best friend, Joe, was invited along with Chris and other people from Alex's college. I didn't know most of them, personally. I had only heard about them from Alex. After dinner, though, the guests left early because Alex was tired. I came a little after dinner and was staying till later just to make sure that Alex would have everything he needed.

"It's all good, Mom. If I need anything, Dominic and Ashley are here," he said.

I knew that but still felt anxious. I helped clean up. We agreed that I would stop by in the morning before work and would come after work. Then I changed his dressing.

While driving to Piedra Seca house I felt numb from being tired and stressed. I knew that I would only become more stressed at home. Earle was depressed. Life was becoming harder and harder. The work situation didn't seem to improve and Earle's cough seemed to worsen. He went to various doctors but they all said that his lungs were just fine and there was no need to worry. Since our insurance wasn't very good, we even drove to the Mexican town across the border called Nogales, where we paid cash for all the necessary tests. We even saw the specialist there. I was pretty sure Earle's cough was getting worse every time he was drinking alcohol. When I called my eldest son, the medical student, and told him that, he listened carefully.

"It's possible that the cough is an allergic reaction," he said. "Are you suggesting an allergy to alcohol?"

"I don't know," I said. "I just know what I see."

"It wouldn't pass in Poland," he said. That was a joke. Polish people are famous for drinking alcohol. One could say that to be drunk is Polish second nature.

This phone conversation took place early in the morning, so I was still able to appreciate the joke. We tried to laugh but it didn't work. Alex had a broken back. Earle had a cough and was depressed. We were on the verge of bankruptcy and the stress was accumulating.

I was driving home after work and thinking that the road to the house seemed longer than usual. How were we going to proceed with all the difficulties? With Alex in a wheelchair, me working and being in school and with Earle desperately trying to keep afloat? We'd already put Piedra Seca house up for sale, as initially planned, even though the renovation wasn't finished. But nobody was buying anything. And the gallery building wasn't selling either.

There was no other way. We had to continue living and pulling through every day. After Alex's accident many of my friends got in touch with us. They showed their goodwill and empathy. One friend brought us lunch at work, the other two went to see Alex in the Studio. As much as I appreciated all this, their actions didn't take off the weight of the situation. During all this time I wouldn't even say I lived one life. I felt as if I lived at least three lives now.

In the first life I was a mother. That's always there, right?

The situation required my physical presence and actions. I had to be with Alex. And I was. We became closer than ever, or so I thought. I knew that Alex hated me for putting him in a 'mental hospital' and I knew he loved me very much at the same time. Sometimes, he expressed his conflict, although after the third hospital stay it was less often. Probably because of his pain and how dependent he was, the internal conflict was almost forgotten.

One day when I was changing his dressing, I was particularly careful. I didn't feel confident that day. Maybe because Earle was coughing all night and even though I slept in a different room now, covering my head with my blanket, I heard his struggle with breathing. I had bad dreams too. All these things affected my mood and the sight of Alex's wound scared me again.

"Go ahead, Mom, it's not a big deal," he mumbled to his pillow.

I peeled off a big, rectangular rubberlike material and gauze, then threw the gauze into the garbage. I unpacked a fresh pack of gauze and carefully placed it on Alex's wound. I secured it with the rubberlike material provided in the package.

"Done," I said. I threw away the empty package and went to the sink to wash my hands.

Then I heard sounds coming from Alex's bed area. They almost didn't seem human. The whines and yelps I heard didn't have time to remind me anything particular, although the image of a slaughtered pig I saw in a small Polish town when I was a child flashed in my memory. The pig was going to be slaughtered right behind the fence where I was standing with the empty milk bottle, waiting for the cow to be milked.

It happened during my summer vacation. Grandma sent me to buy milk and cheese. I will never forget that pig pleading for its life. And I will never forget Alex's scream. I guess Alex was trying to turn and his back didn't fully agree with his intention. He was moaning and this was what I heard initially. Then he screamed.

I panicked. I ran to his bed. Alex's face was twisted in a grimace but he didn't scream any more.

"It's all good, Mom," he whispered, looking at me. His lips were dry and his eyes blue and empty. His forehead was covered with sweat. "I moved in a wrong way. I should have been more careful."

I was trying not to cry but the tears were silently flowing down my cheeks. I kept wiping them away but the new ones were coming and it looked like as if nothing could be done to stop that flow.

"Don't cry, Mom," Alex said.

I tried to smile through my tears.

"What's tomorrow? What day of the week?" Alex said.

I had to check the calendar on the wall.

"Friday," I said.

"We could do something? Like, go somewhere?" Alex said.

"Of course. Wherever you want," I said.

I finished cleaning and emptied the temporary toilet Alex was using. I stayed a while longer. Alex was falling asleep. I decided it was time to take off his brace. We both did our best in doing it. I only was helping Alex to turn a little bit, so I wouldn't hurt him by a stronger move. I put his brace on the chair close to his bed. I fixed myself tea and waited for him to fall asleep. Then I left.

I was back in the morning. On Fridays, I wasn't going to the office so Alex and I had a whole day to ourselves.

It was that time of my life when my physical strength was truly needed and I was glad I was in good shape. Right after Alex's surgery, I started to fold and lift his wheelchair several times a day. Placing the wheelchair in the trunk of my car required strength. After doing this for a week I developed a significant pain in my back. I was going to the gym and carefully choosing the machines I thought would strengthen the required muscles and trying to apply good lifting techniques wherever Alex and I went places.

And we went out quite a lot.

About a week after the surgery, we went to the shopping mall. I wanted to buy a small TV for Alex.

First, we went to Sears. There we chose a stiff support for his bed so when he was in a sitting position, he had something to lean on. I also bought a soft red blanket. I traveled back and forth to the car with the wheelchair, using the elevators. The last item we brought to the car was a TV.

After this trip we started to go outside. Even going around the neighborhood for twenty minutes or so was a great pleasure to Alex. On the days when I didn't go to work, we would go even further from home, like to Randolph Park. There is a large lake there and I would push the wheelchair as close to its edge as I could. Then I would put the wheelchair on brakes and we would feed the ducks bread we brought with us. Alex always reminded me to take some bread. He liked to feed the ducks and look at the turtles which would occasionally show up.

We went grocery shopping together. We went to the mall more often and I would buy Alex new clothes, mostly sweatpants, shirts and lose garments, in general. We chose things that would be easy to put on considering his brace and very limited ability to move. We went to his doctors' appointments and to his COPE appointments. I must say that COPE was the only place where nobody was surprised by Alex showing up in a wheelchair. A new counselor indifferently asked what had happened and didn't even seem to listen to Alex's answer. She must have been in her early thirties, small, pudgy, with lots of makeup on her round face. Her perfume was very strong. I could barely stand it.

"Aha, fast snowboarding," she said, finally. She shook her head and brushed her black hair away from her cheek.

I guess COPE is just that kind of place. It's hard to surprise them. Because Alex was in a wheelchair, his counselor applied for additional monetary assistance, not just the food stamps. She made all the necessary DES appointments. We only had to show up, which we did.

I don't know how much pot Alex was smoking at this time. I presume a lot. Almost always when I went to the Studio he had those squinting eyes, as if he was about to fall asleep. Also, now Alex was taking pain medications, so it was hard to say which substance had a stronger effect.

Chapter 17
Life in the wheelchair

For the first three months after the surgery, Alex was in a wheelchair. Life in the Studio was busy. People were visiting Alex and I was there every day. During the first month, the surgical wound needed daily attention, but after that, the tension loosened up a little. The prognosis for Alex was optimistic. The doctor said that, after three months or so, Alex might try to stand up.

For now, though, he was still in a wheelchair and staying in the Studio watching movies. It bothered him that he couldn't throw his yo-yo far enough because his wheelchair was too low. He played with the yo-yos anyway, only more in a 'parallel' manner, versus the 'vertical' one.

Alex was taking painkillers. He had many prescriptions for them.

During the first three months nobody even asked him what happened to the previous prescription. Why did it go so fast? Nobody asked if his pain was the same or different. He also had financial assistance from DES and the food stamps and we paid all the bills. The house didn't cost him any money. I couldn't understand why he never had any money. Well, while in a wheelchair at least it didn't matter since Alex was going out only with me.

Alex had lots of friends who he constantly talked to on the

phone but I didn't know most of them. These were the ones that I called 'new' friends. They were new to me. I didn't know their stories and families. Some of them were his college friends, some must have been what I called 'pot' connections. He would tell me about some of them once in a while, when he was in a good mood, like about this girl who was trying to quit using drugs. Somebody stole a small radio from the Studio and Alex assumed it was her.

"It's very hard to quit, Mom. A person like that will steal anything, just to get some money," he said. I was supposed to show understanding.

All these 'new' friends were back. They actually never left. It was Alex who was leaving, occasionally, to spend time in hospital. Now they were visiting him all the time.

From his 'old' friends only Joe remained. And Joe was Alex's best friend; ever. I loved Joe. I knew him from elementary school. He was in constant touch with Alex.

Alex and Andrew still didn't fix their relationship. Their conflict persisted and it was hard on both of them. Tessa broke up with Alex before his third hospitalization but she remained friends with Andrew. This friendship wasn't really the only source of the conflict but it didn't help. Strangely enough, Alex got even more power over Andrew just by the fact that he was wheelchair bound. Andrew had a really hard time with the wheelchair situation. He was angry and conflicted. I encouraged both of them not to hang out with each other as much, but they were adults now and did as they pleased. Their conflict was out of my control.

Alex was under the influence of his pain medications most of the time. I was at a loss. I knew he was in pain but I wasn't him. I didn't know how often and how much his back or foot or something was making his life unbearable. Questioning his need for pain medication seemed unethical, at least at this point. I was trying to find some activities for Alex. The TV and computer were already there. I thought of taking Alex with me to my drawing sessions. The group of artists met in the gallery building once a week. We would ask our friends to model for us if we couldn't book a professional model. I asked Alex if he could model for us, occasionally.

"I will," he said. "So many people did nice things for me. Maybe that would be a way to repay, at least a little."

He did it once. It wasn't long after his accident. Alex was in pain but he really wanted to attend. I brought him over to my studio and parked his wheelchair close to the podium. I still have that portrait of Alex which I made with dry pastels. His head is shaved, almost bald. His cheeks are sunken, emphasizing his square jaw. In my drawing Alex is very skinny and that makes his eyes look too big. They have grey swollen circles under them. The eyelids are slightly puffy which adds to Alex's 'sleepy' look. I remember somebody's comment after seeing this portrait. It was a stranger who had never seen Alex and didn't even know it was my son. She called Alex a 'special needs' person.

Sometimes, I look at it, and he looks back at me from that large piece of paper. It breaks my heart every time. No picture or any photograph has the power of that drawing.

Alex was artistically talented, so about a month after his surgery we kind of went back to his childhood projects and made a trip to a Hobby Shop. For once, I didn't try to save money. We bought a big model of a ship to be put together and painted. Alex started to work on it the next day. We came back to the Hobby Shop several times to buy a small brush, or a special paint for his project.

Another thing that I thought of was to take Alex over to some of my friends, for a change. We would go to drink a cup of tea or eat lunch. I wanted to make his life less boring and keep him interested in something other than mere existence. Alex wasn't very thrilled with this idea but I thought it wouldn't hurt him to hang out with other people too, not only his college friends who maybe were looking for drugs.

I had a friend who particularly came to my mind since he was always helpful. His name was Brad. He was older than me. I had known him for years. He was a physicist and worked as such on very complicated projects. He eagerly agreed to have Alex over for two hours or so and talk to him about physics.

I drove Alex to his house and pushed the wheelchair through the driveway and then through the door. I was surprised to see packing paper all over the grey carpet.

"I wanted to protect the carpet. It's new," Brad said.

I had a strange feeling in my stomach but I quickly dismissed it as being oversensitive. Brad had a right to keep his house clean. I rolled the wheelchair in. I left Alex in Brad's house and drove away. An hour and half later, I got a text message from Alex. He was ready for a pick up. I drove to Brad's house, and after the short goodbyes and thank yous, I took Alex home. He immediately fell asleep.

The next day I called Brad and asked how it went.

"He's worthless. This guy is going nowhere. He's not interested in anything. He's a total zero, I'm telling you," Brad said.

I felt my jaws tightening. I was quiet but he continued.

"I tried to show him things in math, or physics, anything. He just didn't want to focus even a little. He's worthless," Brad repeated.

I tried to apply a famous phrase of Jesus: "Father, forgive them, for they do not know what they are doing," and that was the only reason why I didn't hang up. I politely finished the conversation. After I put my phone away and went to the kitchen to make myself tea, I cried. While squeezing lemon with my shaky hands, I was trying to understand how was it possible to be so insensitive. I was questioning myself. Did I hear him right? Did Brad really say "worthless" to me, about my beloved wheelchair bound son? This friend was the one who had come to two hearings in the psychiatric hospital to support me when I was committing Alex. Did he really want to support me? Who in the whole world really wanted to support me? How many people do things only out of curiosity? Did this particular friend understand the extent of my love for Alex? He had children of his own whom he loved. Then what was wrong? Lack of imagination? But then, how can one be a physicist without imagination? I didn't have the answers but I was so terribly shaken I wanted to share it with somebody. But with whom? Earle? Not only was he buried in his own financial problems but he didn't like Brad too much. I didn't want to add fuel to his feelings. Should I share it with my other children? Which one and what for? To put more burden on them?

The visit over to Brad's happened only two months after Alex's accident. I thought things would improve. I didn't tell anybody. I kept my thoughts to myself.

Chapter 18
Standing up and drinking versus drugs

I was at work when my phone rang. I saw Alex's name and I quickly picked up.

"Mom! Guess what I'm doing?" He was shouting.

"I have no idea," I said.

"I'm standing, Mom!"

"Sit down!" I shouted back. I panicked. The doctor wouldn't allow Alex to stand up yet.

"Why?" he said. "If I can stand up, I will."

"What about if you would hurt yourself and all this hard work will go to nothing?" I said.

He said he would only sit down when he got tired of standing and that was actually pretty soon. I drove to see him right after my evening class. I could barely sit through the class. I was very anxious to see what Alex was doing. We had a doctor's appointment the next day so I figured that at least Alex wouldn't have too much time to hurt himself.

It turned out though there was no need to worry. The doctor was happy with Alex.

"Just don't keep standing for a long time," he said when we saw him the next day. "Keep it short, like a few seconds at a time. You are supporting yourself with your arms, right? Show me."

Alex showed the doctor how he was standing up. He was in his plastic brace, of course, and visibly making an effort. His face was beaming with joy.

"Good job," the doctor said. "In about a week we could think about crutches."

Crutches! I thoughts. *My son will be walking.* I held back my tears and excused myself, saying that I needed to go to the bathroom. My eyelids were swollen with tears and I was afraid to blink. I knew if I did that, they would roll down my cheeks showing my weakness. I got up without lifting my gaze and moved to the door with my eyes following the design on the carpet. Once in the hallway I put my arm over my face and rushed to the restroom.

There, I could cry.

#

Exactly a week later, we picked up the crutches. It didn't mean that we got rid of the wheelchair. It was still easier to transport Alex from place to place while using it. The crutches were at home for him to practise standing up.

I was there when he made his first step. I cried again and Alex laughed. His face showed fear, pride and excitement at the same time. Most of all though, it showed childish happiness.

Every day various friends were visiting Alex in the Studio. His best friend, Joe, and his older sister were the regulars. But there were also many other friends of Alex who were passing by. While I was happy he had visitors, I didn't necessarily like them.

I still don't know how "normal" it is for young people to

use drugs. I don't know much about drugs altogether. I grew up in communist Poland where most of society drank alcohol and smoked cigarettes. Illegal drugs were considered a foreign idea. To be precise, it was a capitalist idea, something that communist propaganda tried to associate only with the West.

As a child, when I was coming back from school, it was normal for me to see drunk men sound asleep across the sidewalk. Usually, they were somewhere in the vicinity of a small kiosk selling beer. Nobody was surprised. The drunk person lying on the ground wasn't dangerous. I remember stepping over drunk men while getting to the main door of the apartment building in which my family lived. I wasn't afraid. The talking drunks were a little worse because they would try to get one's attention and expected certain answers to their questions. The younger drunks were more aggressive than the older ones so I learned to cross the street when I would see one or a group of them, which was even worse.

My father was very critical of the street drunks but he was drinking too except that, after getting drunk, he wouldn't lie down on a sidewalk but in his bed. Also, the quality of the alcohol my father was consuming couldn't even be compared to that consumed by the street drunks. While my father could purchase high end bottles of scotch, foreign vodkas and cognacs, the regular Polish drunk was left with a bottle of pure alcohol, which was a simple solvent solution or fuel for small camping stoves. This product could have been purchased in a cleaning supply store. It came in a clear glass bottle with a skull and crossbones tag printed on it. The solution was purple in color. Several times I have seen drunks filtering it through a slice of white bread before drinking it. This filtering was changing the strong purple color into a lighter one. The drunks believed it also was getting rid of the poison.

When my father didn't have any expensive alcohol at home and didn't want to bother to go anywhere to purchase it, he would give me some money and send me downstairs to the small store which carried alcohol and cigarettes. I was supposed to buy his cigarettes, too.

Nobody cared that I was only eleven or twelve at the time. The lady in the store would give me a bottle and a pack of cigarettes with the matches.

"I know you are a good girl and this is for you parents," she would say.

She was right. It was for my parents, not only my father. If my mother was home, they would drink together.

Young people started drinking early in life and it was culturally accepted. I remember how I got terribly drunk the first time. I was fourteen. It was at a party my mother held in our apartment. My father had already moved out by that time. The divorced followed later. There were many people at the party and I kept drinking vodka, one shot after another. Nobody paid attention. The next morning, the urge to vomit woke me up. I didn't remember anything. My mother came into my room with a cup of hot tea. I could tell she felt very guilty.

I got drunk plenty of times when I lived in Poland but I never smoked pot. I didn't even know what pot was. Sometimes, while watching a foreign movie, I saw strange behavior from people who used drugs. While discussing these movies with my friends, I heard that these movie characters were drug users, junkies, sick people, and that they all should be put in jail because they were damaging a healthy society.

Well, okay, there were not many drug users in Poland, but

even so, how could a society like a Polish one, ever have been called healthy while drinking so much? Alcohol is like a weapon of mass destruction. It will eventually destroy any society.

Even the Polish community in Tucson is more tolerant towards drinking at a young age. I remember when Alex was still a Junior in high-school and I was invited to a party over at a close friend's house. I went with Alex and he got drunk. He kept drinking regardless of my protests. I remember him drunk and even aggressive. When I demanded his car key and told him he wouldn't be able to drive, he yelled at me. I was very distressed. My friends tried to calm me down.

"Look, it's better like that," they would say, "if he gets drunk with adults you know, not somewhere else without you knowing. That way you still have control. He's a good boy. It will all be good, you will see. It's part of growing up."

I wasn't convinced.

Chapter 19
Pot and pills

One day, about four months after the surgery, I came to the Studio. It was a hot day, about eleven in the morning. I was going to pull in from the back alley. As usual, the gate was wide open. With Alex in the wheelchair, nobody was closing it any more. One time when I did that, Alex asked me to leave it open in case one of his friends might need a place to park a car. As I was pulling into the backyard, I saw Alex. He was slowly moving with the aid of his crutches.

"Hey, what are you doing?" I asked.

"Nothing, just walking." He smiled.

It was true. He used his crutches more and more. Again, we didn't get rid of the wheelchair but it was always in my trunk, just in case.

About three weeks after using the crutches, Alex's walking skills improved immensely. He asked me to put away the wheelchair for good. Not only he was moving around by himself with the help of crutches, but he started to talk about dropping these, too.

"I could walk with a cane only," he said.

After consulting with the doctor, we bought a cane of his choice.

During that consultation though, Alex asked for more pain-killers. The doctor looked at him.

"How much pain are you in?" he said.

"It comes and goes," Alex replied. "But it's there, every day. I can't sit for more than fifteen or twenty minutes."

Alex kept talking but I only observed the doctor's face. He believed everything Alex was saying and didn't hesitate to write him a prescription.

On the way home, we stopped at the pharmacy to drop off the prescription forms. I was supposed to pick up his medications later.

Alex took his pills and played with yo-yos. He had a significant social life too. Many people, friends, and friends of friends were coming to the Studio. I knew some of them but many I didn't. Sometimes, I would come to the Studio when somebody was visiting, or coming, or leaving. Some of those friends were his college buddies. They still talked about their classes. Other people didn't go to any schools and they promptly left when I showed up. One day when I walked in, I heard Alex talking on the phone with Matthias. It turned out that his father had got in touch with Alex and they were in regular contact. They talked about how Alex was doing. They also talked about Alex's relationship with Andrew. Matthias invited both of them to Poland for the summer vacations. Alex readily agreed, and after a consultation with the doctor about the trip, was impatiently waiting for his father to buy his airplane ticket.

His father bought it promptly, and in May, Alex and Andrew boarded a plane to Warsaw. I drove them to the airport. I could see that Andrew was happy to go to Poland. It meant an adventure to him. He was excited about flying on a plane and going across the ocean again. I pulled him aside and asked him to take care of Alex, to lift his luggage and try to make Alex's life easier in general. He readily agreed. I could see that he wanted me not to stress out about their trip and I appreciated that. Alex was equipped with a certificate stating that he had metal pieces in his back. He could only walk with a cane. I got him a very small and light backpack he could hang on one shoulder. It was more like a large pocket, not a backpack.

It was a long, three-month trip and it was mostly good. The only bad thing about it was that the boys' relationship didn't improve. If anything, it worsened. In Tucson they could avoid each other, but on the trip, they were together all the time. The old issues were always present. Otherwise, Alex had a great time. It looked like he really reconnected with his father. Matthias was generous. He wanted for Alex to have the best vacation. He even paid for Alex's trip to Amsterdam, the Netherlands, where Alex could meet and spend time with his half-sister who lived there.

Alex emailed me a picture from his trip to Amsterdam. I could see him sitting in either a pub or a coffee shop. It actually didn't matter where it was. What mattered to me was how high he was. It was visible on the picture; his puffy eyes, relaxed face, and that smile which usually was accompanied by a laughter I will never forget. One could say it was always coming straight from his belly, and while laughing, Alex could barely catch his breath. By this time though I would be happy if Alex only smoked pot and didn't use any other drugs, legal or illegal. I preferred weed to the opioids Alex had access to. So, the picture didn't bother me too much. I knew, though, that Alex had his medications with him.

On this trip Alex went with his father to the mountains where they did light hiking on small hills. Alex posted a picture on Facebook where he was leaning on his cane, with the mountains in the background. He also publicly commented with a laughing emoji face inserted into the text about what a 'welfare system user' he used to be.

I was relieved and hopeful. I thought that we had conquered the devil himself. When I picked up Alex and Andrew from Tucson International three months after I dropped them off, Alex immediately asked to stop by a locally owned restaurant called Egees for me to buy him a frozen fruit drink. There was one right on our way so we stopped and placed an order for the drinks and sandwiches.

"There's no place like Tucson," he said, after we had already pulled out from the Egees ordering bay. "Did you hear this lady at the window? It's ten in the evening and she's not complaining. She's happy and she says 'please' and 'thank you'. In Poland everybody is offended at all times for some reason. I love Tucson," he said it one more time, before he took another bite of his sandwich. His brother didn't have any comments but he was busy eating too.

At home I helped Alex unpack his luggage. In it I found a huge crystal vase with a letter from Alex's father to the orthopedic surgeon who did the surgery. The letter was long and full of gratitude. We took it along with the gift to the doctor's office when we went to Alex's next appointment.

The following week, after the appointment, Alex asked me for help signing up for the University of Arizona, again. The help mostly had to do with driving him around so he wouldn't have to walk too much between buildings. During one of those rides, Alex told me he will have to get a bicycle. He wanted the low kind, with small wheels.

"I think I can do it, Mom," he said.

Again, we confirmed with the doctor.

"You can try riding it if you feel confident and strong," the doctor said. But he still gave him a prescription for Alex's back pain.

Chapter 20
Being twenty-one

Alex's twenty-first birthday was coming. It would happen on August eleventh, right before the college classes started.

I called him on his birthday and we decided we would celebrate on the weekend. It was only Wednesday. On Thursday morning as I came to work, I wanted to call him to talk about the details. I sat at my desk, and as I reached for my cellphone, it rang. The flashing number wasn't familiar. Nevertheless, I picked up.

"Do you know Alexander Wojtkowski?" the male's voice asked.

"I do. It's my son," I said. Ugh, how much I hated those phone calls.

"We found his backpack, his clothes and his wallet close to the fountain next to our shop," the man said. "Do you know where he is or how to contact him? We also have his phone." Obviously, they had his phone because that's how they were able to contact me.

"I… I don't know right now. I mean, thank you for saving his stuff. I will be right there to pick it up," I said.

I was told where to go, and in a moment, I was driving toward University Boulevard to pick up Alex's stuff and maybe find out about what had happened.

Unfortunately, the nice people from a beauty salon who

had saved Alex's belongings didn't know anything.

The man whom I already knew from the phone conversation told me, "We don't know what happened."

I took Alex's things and went back to work. I immediately set myself to find him. I called all the hospitals in town and was relieved to find out that he hadn't been admitted to any of them. Then, I called all the jails that I could think of but to no avail, either. That also felt like a relief.

The last thing I could think of was going to his house to see what was going on there. As I was standing in traffic on my way to the Studio, I wondered why I didn't look for him at home in the first place. I guess, subconsciously, I wanted to exclude the worse possible events. I finally made it there and I knocked on Alex's door. Silence... After several tries, I actually pushed the door. Alex was in his bed, asleep.

I looked around for a place to sit but all the flat surfaces were taken by Alex's clothes, various folders, boxes, papers, and of course, yo-yos. Eventually, I found an empty chair. It was closely stuck under the table. I sat down.

"Alex?" I called his name several times.

He finally moved and mumbled something.

"I brought you your stuff," I said.

"What stuff?" Suddenly, Alex got curious and sat up on his bed. He had enough sense to cover himself since he was still naked.

"Your backpack and your cellphone. And here, your pants, shirt and underwear," I said. "I wonder how on Earth you got home without your pants? And what actually has happened to you?"

"Jeez, Mom, it's not hard to figure out. It was my birthday. I'm twenty-one. Of course, I went to a bar and got drunk. So what? Don't you tell me that you didn't do anything stupid in your life, okay?" he said. "In fact, I know you did. You told me yourself."

For a moment I wanted to remind him that I knew they were not-so-smart life choices, but I dropped these thoughts quickly. Of course, we talk to our children about what we did in our youth. We do it without expecting them to turn our experiences against us.

"I called all the hospitals and the jails, too. I was worried," I said.

"I'm sorry, Mom. You always worry. It's not my fault. And guess what? The police were actually nice this one time; cool guys who saw a distressed, naked twenty-one-year-old in the fountain and decided to take me home," he said.

"It was nice of them, indeed," I said.

"I already said it was nice. Because, you know, police aren't nice, in general. They can screw you really quickly. But this time, Mom, they even brought my bike home!"

I didn't offer any special help to Alex with his hangover. I still had work to do. I had to go back to the shop.

"I will see you tomorrow," I said and left.

The main feeling of mine was a relief that nothing had happened to Alex. I recalled the similar phone calls from the past which usually were leading to hospitalizations. This time, Alex just got drunk and went swimming in the fountain. It wasn't a big deal. But the fear that the phone call created in me was still in my stomach, confusing my gratitude. All this confusion led to me asking myself one big question. *'Why is it always Alex?'*

Chapter 21
Decline

A little after his birthday, Alex started to be unbelievably rude and demanding. The symptoms he displayed before going to the psychiatric hospital for the first time doubled. He was delusional again, especially when he talked about money. He was also extremely rude. To make things more confusing, some of the symptoms didn't come back. For example, Alex took care of his trash and the Studio wasn't as messy.

He was going to school but I didn't know how he was doing. DES was still giving him food stamps and financial assistance. Alex was eligible for help because of his psychiatric history and his broken back.

Alex was very attached to me, but at the same time, he didn't want me around. I could only say t he was rude and abusive to me, though not always.

He started to ride a bike to his classes. I thought he felt okay and that his pain was gone for the most part. He even shared some stories from school with me. He chose a different major although it didn't matter much at this point. His new major had to do with chemistry and materials. I thought Alex was excited. But whenever he didn't feel well, he would send me a text message demanding money and blaming me for putting him into the psychiatric hospital. He wanted me to apologize to him for his arrest when he was eleven years old.

His constant financial issues didn't have an end and didn't make any sense.

It turned out that Alex was also opening a new business although it was hard for me to understand what kind of business it was. He told me he wanted to get rich. And when he finally got rich, he would share his money. And in order to get rich one doesn't need to work like crazy. One just needs to be smart. He said he felt he was smart enough to get rich.

His new business had to do with some strange website called 'therichjerk' or something. The website was a scam but Alex fell for it. At least he couldn't lose too much money because he didn't have a lot. But he could get another credit card.

Here is another thing that I couldn't quite understand. How could a young person, a student without any means except his parents' support, get as many credit cards as he wanted? Alex couldn't even work. He was on food stamps and financial assistance. Nobody answered that question because I didn't even know who to ask.

Where's that one person who would take responsibility for this total stupidity?

Alex had many credit cards. All of them were maxed out. I knew the limits on them weren't very big, but hey, it's relative. Two thousand dollars for Alex was lots of money. And for me, too.

Alex also was making money on his pain pills. He never told me and I never asked. He was selling them. And what was he buying with the money he earned that way? Better marijuana and other drugs, I suppose. Maybe cocaine? He wasn't selling all his pills. He needed at least some of them for himself. I was dreading his second back surgery, the one that was required to remove the plates and screws from his back. I knew that the cycle of Alex's opioids wouldn't end any time soon.

Strangely enough, Alex was doing okay in school or so it seemed. He was very helpful to his classmates in math class and tried to help people who didn't understand the math problems as well as he did. Alex was a teacher's pet in his chemistry class, although I was told that he often fell asleep during lectures.

But his old paranoia started to creep up on Alex again. He claimed that people were trying to "get him."

The front house on Desert Avenue, so called Desert house, was still rented to Ashley and Dominic. But their relationship was not going well. They stopped getting along. They were fighting in the front house every day and Alex took Ashley's side. He told me that Dominic was a jerk because he walked away with another woman, leaving Ashley with two babies without even marrying her. The fights were constant. This situation lasted about two months. Eventually Dominic left, taking the dogs with him. This actually hurt Alex more than Ashley's moving out. a few weeks after. Alex loved the dogs. One of the dogs slept with Alex on his bed, often.

Now the front house was empty again.

I didn't even try to advertise the front house for rent. I knew that Piedra Seca house Earle and I lived in would soon be foreclosed and we would have to live somewhere. It was logical t we would have to move to Desert house, because where else? Earle didn't admit it or he just didn't want to talk about it. He didn't want to talk about anything. He just wanted to survive the next day. We didn't fight, but during one of Earle's outbursts of anger, he stomped his foot and looked straight into my face and shouted.

"I will never live in Desert house. Even if Alex won't be there!"

I wasn't sure why Desert house wasn't good enough for him to live in. Or maybe it would constantly remind him of his financial failure? I didn't feel like asking. I knew he wouldn't give me any reasonable answer.

But where would we go? The gallery building wasn't selling and Earle said he was thinking about putting in a shower to live there. I knew I wouldn't live there. It was insane.

Alex wasn't cooperating, and if his behavior continued to decline, I knew I would have to show him the door, finally. I wasn't ready to do that. Every day, though, Alex was trying my patience.

Chapter 22
Pain pills and Pain clinic

During the Fall semester Alex's decline continued. I was taking him to his regular doctors' appointments. I could see he was looking for pain medications. Finally, his orthopedic surgeon cut Alex's opiates. That's why Alex found a so-called pain clinic. I wasn't familiar with that kind of clinic until Alex asked me to take him there.

"Do you need more pain medication?" I asked. "Isn't your doctor prescribing it for you?"

We were in the car driving to the pain clinic. Alex gave me the address.

"Not enough. It hurts. My back hurts. I need meds," he said. "Plus, my surgeon is very busy. It's hard to get an appointment. When I am closer to my second surgery, I will talk to him."

I parked the car and we entered the clinic. Alex went to the counter and signed in. I sat down and looked around.

The waiting room was large. It had many low tables and chairs. The corner table lamps had round shades. The lamps were turned on and they looked like big, shining planets. The chairs were covered with a geometrical printed pattern of green, blue and orange.

There was an old lady sitting in a chair across from me reading a book. Diagonally from the entrance, there was a man, maybe in his fifties. He was scrolling the screen on his phone. A middle-aged couple sitting a little further had their heads up. They were watching a TV screen. I followed their gaze and watched an advertisement promising a painless life, if only the white pills shown at the bottom of the screen were taken.

Nobody looked like a drug addict.

This thought quickly brought another one. How do they look? Those addicts, how do they actually *look*? Are they any different than us "normal people?" Obviously, they are. We can see them sometimes. They are incredibly skinny and their teeth are bad. I recalled the "before and after" poster I saw on a city bus stop showing a meth addicted woman. In the picture on the right, it was hard to recognize the person portrayed on the left. It was the same woman though.

But these people here, they weren't meth users. The meth users were more like a COPE crowd, not like the people here, in the doctor's office.

All these thoughts were going through my head as I was trying to get away from thinking about painkillers and other addictions.

Alex's visit was short. We left the doctor's office maybe fifteen minutes after he was called in. In the car he asked me to take him to a pharmacy to drop off his prescription. We stopped at Walgreens close to the house.

"No need to wait," he said, coming out from Walgreens. "Just please drop me off at home. I will pick up my meds later or maybe even tomorrow on my way to school."

#

I took Alex to a pain clinic only that one time.

I was confused about the whole issue of pain, but at the same time, didn't want Alex to be in pain. The confusion helped me refuse to take him to the clinic the next time he asked me. His appointment was during one of my classes.

"I can't," I said. "I have a class and I can't miss it. We are preparing for a test."

"I'll change the hour," Alex said. "I'll call you back."

But when he called back, he had not only changed the hour of the appointment but the day as well.

"Oops," I said. "I can't do that either. I have a chemistry class. I can't miss it."

Two days later Alex called me from the Emergency Room at St. Joseph's Hospital. He told me that while coming out of the library at the University of Arizona he had to stop and push the emergency button. Several emergency poles are placed throughout the campus with buttons linked to the Emergency Services. Alex said he was in a terrible pain and pushing the button was the only thing that occurred to him since the emergency pole with its purple light was right there. The paramedics came immediately and took him to St. Joseph's Hospital.

When he called, I was at work. I shared the news with Tessa. She had left Alex a long time ago but still was working for us at the plastic company. She was also working her second job in a sushi restaurant. I was always pleased to be in her company. I think I loved her.

"I will go and visit him, too," she volunteered.

We left work early and went to the hospital. After about an hour we were in his room.

"What are you getting?" Tessa asked, while pointing at the

IV.

"Dilaudid." Alex said. He wouldn't conceal his contentment. I shivered. Dilaudid is a very powerful painkiller.

Alex remained in the hospital all the next day with a needle stuck in his arm for the quicker delivery of painkillers.

Chapter 23
In need of a gun

I traveled to Poland every year. Sometimes my trip would last only ten days if I couldn't afford a longer vacation. All my family still live there since I was the only one who had left the country. There, I still have a father and two dear sisters. Spending time with them is very important to me.

I had lots of "miles" saved up on our maxed-out credit cards but I wanted to stretch them as much as I could. This is why I decided to travel in the winter, between the Fall and Spring semesters. I would spend Christmas in Poland. Also, I would be using less "miles" in the off-season. To make sure I would be granted my award travel ticket, I booked it early, in the summer.

When fall came and my trip was approaching, I knew I had to square things away with Alex. I was only going for two weeks but wanted to make sure he had everything he needed. At the end of September, I told him that I would be gone in December and that Earle had agreed to help him with any of his needs. Alex told me not to worry. He was doing okay in school and promised me that, if he needed anything, he would call Earle. I was always worried about Alex but this time I tried to push my worries away.

In August I found out that Alex was meeting with the Freemasons One could say that this new interest of his came out of nowhere. Alex helped an older man carry groceries out of the store to a car and the man turned out to be a Mason. They chatted in the parking lot and the man invited Alex to a meeting. Alex developed a close relationship with the Masons. The Chapter he was close to was from Oracle, not Tucson. Oracle is a town about forty miles from Tucson. It was a group of older men who adored Alex and were willing to drive him back and forth to their meetings. Alex was anxious in getting through all the Masonic degrees or whatever the process was called. He told me that he was making progress.

One day at the beginning of October, Alex called me at work and asked me to come to his house in the afternoon. He wanted to read me something about the Masonic Credo. I call it a Credo because this is how it sounded. I know it had a different name. It was some kind of a document. I said I would come right after my class.

It was about five o'clock when I parked the car and went straight to the Studio, walking through the now empty front house. Alex opened the door for me and immediately showed me his new acquisition.

It was a gun; a big gun, the kind I only saw at the movies or on the news.

"You can't have that," I said. "What do you need it for?"

"What do you mean, I can't? Of course I can. I legally bought it in the gun shop," he said.

"Show me the receipt," I said.

He did. I carefully examined the yellow copy. He wasn't lying. The gun shop in Tucson, not even two miles away from Desert house, sold Alex an AK47. It was made in Romania in 1974. Alex paid cash.

"Alex, what do you need it for?" I repeated.

"To defend myself, Mom," he said. "Dominic had plenty of guns. Long ones, too. Everybody should have a gun for self-defense."

"Against whom?"

"Anybody that would want to mess with me."

"Why would anybody want to mess with you?"

"Nobody knows. Besides, don't you have a gun?"

#

It was one of those situations when your own good words and actions are turned against you. How could I defend the fact that I had a gun? But how dare Alex compare his imagined dangerous situations to my life, where bad things had really happened?

He told the truth. I did have a gun then and I still have it today. It never occurred to me that I would want to have one until I got raped with a knife on my neck, with my firstborn baby sleeping beside me. I remember it as if it was today.

It happened in February, early in the morning, about thirty years ago, when Matthias and I first moved to Tucson. That morning Matthias went skiing and somebody broke in while I was still asleep. I was tired from my sleep being interrupted by feeding my firstborn son so I didn't hear the French door glass breaking. The intruder placed a pillow on my head and a knife on my neck. He told me to be quiet because, if I yelled, he would kill the baby first, then me. I couldn't yell anyway. The pillow was suffocating me. He raped me, but the baby slept all the way through. The perpetrator never let me see his face. I only saw his hands and hair. And of course, I heard his voice.

Matthias came back in the evening, and after picking up

the police note from our door, he went to look for me at our friends' house. There were no cellphones then. I was there with our baby and a folder full of documents from the hospital and the police.

"We will have to buy a gun." Matthias said after he learned of what had happened. Just hearing his words made me feel protected. With my firstborn baby by my side, I felt very vulnerable.

Although the idea of a gun was as foreign to me as western movies, I liked it. I was from a communist country. In Poland, only police called militia and the military had guns. My father used to have a gun when he was a judge. The government allowed certain professionals to have guns. All my knowledge about guns came from Polish and Russian movies. Our communist television constantly showed movies about WW2 where a gun battle was a common thing. I also saw some foreign movies but not as many. Rarely watched American westerns also contributed to my gun related knowledge.

I remember the rape and the trauma it brought to my life. I also remember how much I counted on Matthias to protect me, especially because he started to talk about buying a gun.

That terrible day I was feeding the baby in my friends' house. I was also looking over the paperwork the police left me. When Matthias walked in I pushed the folder away and started crying. Matthias hugged me and went to the kitchen to talk to my friends. He sat on a couch. The door was open and I could enjoy the sight of people I knew. All I wanted was safety for my baby and for me. I clung to the idea of having a gun.

The conversation was about guns. Neither my friends nor Matthias knew much about them so it was established that we would go to the gun shop and find out.

Like most of my Matthias's promises, it was only a promise. After that conversation he didn't even want to talk about guns or about any kind of protection for the house either.

The next day after the rape, my other friend picked me up from the house and told Matthias she was taking me to her house for at least a week. I was relieved I wouldn't stay in my house by myself, since Mathias was always at work. He didn't think any protection for the house was necessary but I was terrified. I asked him to install an alarm.

He called an alarm shop, found out it would cost about twenty dollars per month and said no.

I begged. I cried. Nothing helped. Not only the twenty dollars expense bothered him but other things as well. Like, for example, the fact that the alarm would have to be on or off. I was looking at him when he was talking about it and knew the man had no clue what I went through. I thought I was talking to an insane person. Of course, the alarm would be either *on* or *off*. I was only asking for twenty dollars per month, for everybody's safety. Again, he said no. The victim witness program found therapy for me and I went about six times. Matthias didn't like that idea either. I didn't like the therapy sessions either but I guess for different reasons. I didn't know how and what to talk about during the sessions. I thought I said it all during the first session but then my doctor told me the therapist told him I didn't want to talk about some important things. I felt obligated to talk during the sessions because I felt very strange being silent and having the therapist in front of me. I certainly didn't want to talk about Matthias, the gun and the alarm, so I quit my therapy.

Our lease for the house was expiring soon, and because of

my constant fear, Matthias decided that I could go on a road trip with our baby. I would also take Matthias's mother who had just come to visit. We would drive through Northern Arizona. I agreed and off we went.

I was terrified all the time. To this day I have a hard time standing in an open space not knowing what's behind my back. But then, I was barely functional.

I was constantly thinking about a gun. It didn't matter to me that most probably I wouldn't have shot the criminal who raped me, provided I had a gun at that time. Maybe he would have shot me if I had the gun by my bed? I was asleep when he came in. The doors should have been secured. But I was still afraid.

The summer was coming. Matthias and I together with our baby went to Pasadena for the three whole months, where Matthias could collaborate with other professors on a new paper he was writing.

A few years later, when we finally bought a house of our own, I begged for an alarm one more time but to no avail.

After my mother- in-law and I came back to Tucson from the trip, I signed up for a self-defense class. It didn't help my fear. Since the attack we had moved many times and I was dragging the fear around with me.

Then I had a problem. We had three children then and the house was big. It had many windows and doors and Matthias traveled often to various conferences. When he was gone, I usually stayed up into the night as long as I could, until I would finally drop to my pillow and sleep for a few hours. But even this sleep, which should have been deep due to me being very tired, was interrupted by my nightmares. I was constantly waking up suffocating because in my dream somebody would cover my face with my pillow. As much as I was relieved to wake up, it only made me more alert and cautious. I didn't want to put my head on the pillow, because I was afraid I wouldn't hear a potential perpetrator breaking in. I would lie down on my back with my eyes open, piercing the thick blackness of the night and listening to the silence. I finally had an idea of securing the doors and windows in my own creative way. I did it only when Matthias was gone.

The laundry room door leading out to the backyard was the weakest one, so after dinner I would build a pyramid consisting of metal kitchen utensils. Two metal colanders were especially useful but so were frying pans and other pots. The pyramid leaned against the door so, if anybody opened it, all the falling pots and pans would make an incredible noise. I thought I would hear it. For the front door which was much heavier, I would just place a cast iron Dutch oven, with a few forks inside, in front of it.

I secured every window, and in my mind, went through all the possible scenarios while also thinking about Matthias's nature. It wasn't easy.

The idea of having a personal gun never left me, just like the fear. After I told my story to my second husband, Earle, he insisted on buying a gun for me. He personally had a revolver.

I also chose a revolver and I signed up for a Carrying Concealed Weapon class. The class came with training at an indoor shooting range.

I do have a gun, and as much as I never would like to use it, I know how to operate it. And when Earle is out of town, I make sure my gun is within my reach all night.

#

I was still standing on the porch and looking at Alex holding his AK47. I thought I was dreaming a bad dream. All my story went through my mind fast like lightning. But this was my story. What kind of story would Alex possibly have? Nothing that I knew of, at least not at this point. Yes, Andrew was assaulted in Flanwill house, but then again, Alex said that there was something fishy about the guy who came in and asked for help with the tire. And Dominic? What did he have guns for? I knew he had them. After Dominic and Ashley moved out, Alex showed me the place where they stored the guns so the baby wouldn't get to them.

I don't know why Alex bought his AK 47. The only thing which comes to my mind is that he was afraid of the very people he was hanging out with, or their friends, or the friends of their friends. Alex had lots of expensive medications in the Studio and to say he was protective of his possessions would be an understatement. Unfortunately, I was thinking that Alex had a strong propensity to paranoia. Now though, I think this was a harsh judgement. Who wouldn't be afraid of thugs and other drug users? I know I would. That's why it's better to stay away from shady people in the first place.

As I was looking at Alex holding a rifle, I replied to his question. I told him that he was right, I did have a revolver and that I was a responsible gun owner. I also told him I strongly recommended to him to sell his gun back to the store. I didn't want to fight with him because I knew he wouldn't even react to my suggestions if I made him angry. So, when Alex said he had called me to show me something else, I asked him what it was.

It was some Masonic document that he wanted to read to me. We sat down on the tiny porch of the front house. Alex had his AK on his shoulder. I made sure it wasn't loaded. He read me the Masonic document It had to do with God and existence altogether. I could see Alex was moved. He almost cried. Once in a while he petted his gun and he was calling it 'his baby.'

We ate food I brought with me although Alex didn't eat enough. I hugged him and went home.

Chapter 24
Get rid of the gun

For once, Matthias and I were on the same page. Alex had to get rid of his gun. Matthias and I didn't talk about it, but we both did what we could in that matter. Matthias was threatening Alex with withdrawing financial aid and I tried bribes and blackmails, too. I also tried regular, reasonable talk but that didn't work at all.

Alex's paternal grandmother, who lived in Poland, told him she was praying for him to give the gun away.

Nothing was helping. Day after day, the struggle about the gun continued.

One of these days I was drawing at the Drawing Studio and Alex called me. I picked up hoping that maybe he had changed his mind about the gun, got bored with it or something. It wasn't the case. He wanted to talk about something else, and when I brought up the gun situation, he got annoyed.

"No. No. No," he said. "I told you, Mom. I'm not getting rid of my baby."

"I will pay you well," I said. I still had money saved up for emergencies.

"No money can buy my baby," Alex said. "People don't sell their babies, do they?"

This conversation was going nowhere and I hung up.

Before I even spread another paper on my easel, he called me again, and when I picked up, he told me there was one, and only one, possibility for him to get rid of the gun. I was curious and prepared myself for full cooperation.

"I could exchange it for a bad ass motorcycle, Mom. It would have to be really awesome, though," he said.

"Okay," I said. "I will look into it."

I immediately walked around the easels, and without waiting for break time, asked my artist friend, Zach, to step outside with me. Zach left his paints and we went out toward the restrooms, where we couldn't be heard. I had known Zach for years. He knew all my kids. Alex was his favorite. If anybody would know about an available motorcycle, it would be Zach. We made sure that there were no people in the restroom, and whispering, I explained the situation.

"I know somebody who could help you," he said.

I was happy, but not for long. Alex called me about half an hour later and said that he had changed his mind. The motorcycle deal was off.

He started to go to shooting ranges. Most often though, he went to Reddington Pass where people go to shoot their guns even though it's not a regular range.

After going there to shoot he would post the pictures on Facebook. In all those pictures, Alex was standing and holding his gun. The pictures were showing him in different positions; Alex bending on one knee, Alex aiming, Alex with his gun pointing to the sky, Alex standing sideways or up front. He was skinny and I wondered where his cane was. It wasn't visible in the pictures and I knew for sure he needed it if he had to walk for a while.

Alex's father was completely beside himself and I think

Alex actually started to be afraid that his father would stop sending him money. Alex told Matthias he would get rid of the gun. At the same time, I was threatening him with eviction.

About two weeks after the failed motorcycle/gun exchange Alex called me and told me he needed money immediately. I wasn't surprised. Alex usually needed money. This time though, he told me, the issue was very urgent.

"What is it for?" I asked.

"My baby is at the police station," he said. "I need to buy it out."

When I heard the word "baby" I was confused, but it took only a short moment to realize that he was talking about his gun.

"Really?" I said. It was an early evening and I'd just opened a new bottle of wine. I'd done all my homework and even finished doing the dishes after dinner. Earle, of course, was still at work.

Alex's gun had been impounded by the police. As I was listening to the story, I started to have hope. I even poured myself a little more wine than usual. I was almost celebrating. It turned out that Alex had been stopped by the police but it had nothing to do with the gun. It had to do with a traffic violation and Alex wasn't even driving. He couldn't drive. One of his friends was driving from Reddington Pass. Alex was sitting in the passenger seat and the guns were in the car on the back seat. Alex couldn't tell me why the police confiscated the guns, but they did. The officer told Alex he could get his gun back after three days at the police station.

"It's my baby and those fuckers are keeping it at the station. They have no right," he yelled.

Right or not, they did have his gun and I was relieved; not

for long though.

And here came my other question. If the gun was already at the police station, why didn't it remain there rather than being released back to the owner? Alex was the legal owner of his gun but he shouldn't have been allowed to purchase it in the first place. The transaction was a mistake. If a young man or woman was treated for any mental condition and hospitalized three times in a row, he shouldn't have been able to buy a gun. With the gun being locked up at the police station I thought the system had a second chance and could fix its own error.

None of that happened. About a week after the impound of the gun, Alex got it back. He called me and told me that he finally had 'his baby' back.

"Okay," I said. "That means that it's still on the market. I want to buy it."

"Not today." Alex said. "But we can talk about it next week."

I thought he must have been very low on cash or simply in a good mood. I took it for whatever it was and kept repeating my offer every day. In between the offers I was bringing up the eviction plan. Something had to give.

#

I was very tired of Alex's gun situation. I felt powerless. None of my techniques worked; not he negotiations, not the bribing. I decided to try something new and I told Earle that I would like to go to New Mexico for the weekend. It would be my road trip with Alex. We would go and visit one of our properties that still wasn't foreclosed on. It was a piece of land by the San Francisco river. Although I knew that foreclosure was near, deep inside me I still hoped that maybe we would be able to keep that property, or at least part of it. Alex liked that place and was familiar with it, since it was there where Earle and I got married. When I invited Alex to go on a trip with me, he was happy.

"Of course I will go," he said.

I packed a tent and a small stove and off we went.

It took us five hours in my car to get to the place. For the whole length of the trip Alex kept a small, leather, fanny pack attached to his waist. Once in a while he would pull out something from it and eat it. I knew he had his marijuana pipe there and matches, but I didn't know about anything else.

The first evening I pitched our tent at a campsite. Alex helped me a little. He was heavily relying on his cane and couldn't bend. Then we drove from the campsite to town and went to the local restaurant for dinner. He ordered the tri-tip, his favorite beef cut, but couldn't eat even half of it. During dinner he got up twice and went out to do what? Smoke pot, I guess, or what? I wanted to talk to him about drugs and his use of them and I was afraid. When I finally overcame my fear and started the conversation Alex quickly interrupted me.

"You don't understand, Mom," he said. "By now, my brain probably looks like a sponge."

I was terrified and hopeful at the same time.

"Look," I said. "You can smoke your marijuana if you need to, but leave all the other drugs behind. The painkillers, too. Do you still need them every day?"

Alex wiped his mouth with the napkin, and when he started to talk, his lips were still red from the hot sauce.

"Finally, the day has come when you tell me I can smoke

pot. 'Please Alex, do smoke pot'" he said, half mocking me. "Too bad it's too late. I told you, my brain looks like a colander."

"It's never too late," I said. "This is not a cliché. The brain is an amazing thing. Don't say what you don't know," I said.

Alex crumpled his napkin and threw it on his plate. Then got up and limped around the table.

"You don't know," he said. "I will be back."

He grabbed his cane and started to walk towards the door. I took a long sip of my beer.

The next day we went for a hike to the Catwalk, which is a local path leading to an old mine. The path has a concrete sidewalk hanging over several waterfalls. The birds there are amazing. The path is wheelchair accessible, so Alex could walk there with his cane. After the walk we came back to the picnic table and turned on my small stove. We prepared our ramen soup. When the soup cooled down a little, we both enjoyed its salty flavor while listening to the birds and sometimes even looking at them if they sat close to us. It seemed that all our problems had gone away and all that counted in life was the soup, the birds, the trees and the amazingly fresh air.

Nothing changed during this trip. But we still had good moments.

Chapter 25
Intervention

The end of the year was lurking. I started to pack my clothes for my trip to Poland. I would be leaving right before Christmas.

At the beginning of December, I received an email from my elder daughter, Lara. She lived in town.

"Alex is a full-blown addict and you better plan an intervention. He should be put in a treatment facility."

The message was longer but this was its essence. I showed the message to Earle and we planned to go to Alex's Studio together with his sister and with Alex's dearest friend, Joe, who he had known since elementary school. I tried to contact as many people as I could. I kept saying this would be an intervention because Alex was hurting himself. Nobody wanted to come. I couldn't understand that. Where were his friends? I didn't have many phone numbers but I had some. I asked my daughter to call whoever she knew from Alex's circle. Nobody was available, which simply meant to me that nobody wanted to confront Alex.

The evening of the day I'd received the email the four of us showed up in Alex's Studio; Earle and me, Alex's sister, and his friend Joe. We arrived at slightly different times, but we waited for each other on the street, so we would be able to show up together in the Studio. We walked around the front house. It was getting dark. I turned on my cellphone to make some light and see where were we walking. I knocked on the glass window of the French Doors. A moment later, Alex showed up.

He was surprised and that was good. I could tell he wasn't happy about our visit.

"What is this visit about?" he said.

"We want to talk to you about drugs," Lara said. "You have a problem, Alex. You are doing drugs."

"You can leave then," Alex said. "I didn't ask you to come."

We all walked in and made ourselves comfortable. It showed Alex that the matter was serious and we wouldn't obey him. The light in the Studio was dim. The blue shades were drawn down. They always were.

"Did you tell them to come?" Alex said. He was talking to his sister. He pointed to us.

"Yes, I did," she said. "You are a drug user. Is this the person you want to be?"

"Insane! You are all insane!" Alex yelled. "And you," he pointed to Joe. "What are you doing here? Are you with them, too?"

Joe got up and nodded his head. His black hair fell on his forehead. He moved it away with his hand. Joe was very tall, too. All of us had to slightly look up in order to see his face. In the dim light of the Studio we could see the sadness on Joe's face.

"How can this be?" Alex was getting even more angry. "I don't do anything wrong! No more or worse than other people, dude? Don't tell me you want to be a traitor. You're my best friend!"

Joe looked Alex straight in the eyes.

"That's why I'm here," Joe said. "The other night I was worried. I worried for you, Alex. I worry all the time, now."

"For me?" Alex got up and started to walk around with the help of his cane. He was skinny. His movements were jerky. His unbuttoned shirt got caught on the chair and Alex pulled it back. It tore and the chair moved away from the table with a screeching sound.

"Yes, for you," Joe confirmed.

Now it was my turn. I shifted in my chair and looked Alex straight in the eyes.

"I think you don't understand how fortunate you are. You can study and have a place to live. Everything is paid for. You are even walking after breaking your back. Alex, why are you doing what you are doing?"

I got up and turned on the light in the bathroom, then I came back to my chair. I left the door open so we could see each other better. Alex liked it dark. I remembered how one night a few weeks after we came back from our trip to New Mexico, I couldn't sleep and left Piedra Seca house with the idea of going to my studio and working on my latest painting. The gallery building where my art studio currently was about ten minutes' drive to the Alex's Studio. It was about three in the morning. Certainly, too early to go to work. I had lots of time and I drove through Alex's neighborhood. I thought about how Alex really hated me and blamed me for everything, all his misfortunes. From the street I could see the blue light of the drawn shades. *'Three o'clock in the morning, and he isn't asleep?'* I thought. I felt an almost irresistible urge to go inside and hug Alex. I visualized myself knocking on his door. But then, I was afraid to do it. I was afraid of his anger and the depth of his depression, of the abyss that felt almost unbearable. The fear of being hurt even more prevented me from taking a risk.

I took this night drive only a few months before the intervention we were doing now.

Now, Alex was standing by the table and showing all of us the door while yelling at us. Then, he focused on his sister.

"You, cunt, cunt, cunt!" he yelled. He was also trying to spit on her.

Earle jumped up from his chair and quickly walked towards Alex.

"Stop it *now*," he said. "Never, *ever*, talk to a woman like that. Did you hear me?"

I knew that in a more normal situation and in Earle's case a punch might have followed. But Alex was skinny and had a broken back. It was a miracle he was walking at all even with the cane, so, of course Earle didn't touch him. Alex stopped calling Lara names, but now was even more adamant about us leaving him alone.

"Out! All of you!" he yelled. Nobody moved.

"Alex, we want some consensus," I said. "Some understanding. What are you going to do about your problem? Let's figure out how we can help you. And you, on your part, what you are willing to do to help yourself."

"Look again," Lara said. "And think again. Do you really want to be the person you are now?"

She'd already said that at the beginning of our meeting. There must have been some truth to it because it seemed that this sentence especially bothered Alex. He didn't try to spit on her or call her names this time.

"You can stay if you like," he said. "I'm leaving."

He grabbed his cane and left, slamming the door behind him.

Chapter 26
My trip to Poland

On December twenty third I got up very early in the morning and loaded my luggage into Earle's van. We drove to the airport.

After checking in and picking up my boarding pass, we sat down by the big glass windows overseeing the parking lot. Behind the row of hotels, we could see Tucson's downtown and the mountains on the horizon. I was drinking my coffee and reminding Earle about the things I'd asked him to do while I was gone. There weren't many. Earle almost lived at work. For the whole two weeks of my absence Earle told me he would take Alex to his appointments and help him in general, if he needed anything. I appreciated Earle's help.

I told Alex he could call me any time. I had an account with an inexpensive international calling plan and I left it with Alex.

He started to contact me on the third day of my stay in Poland. He also sent me emails. They mostly had to do with his father and the problems they had. Being his father, Matthias was very serious about Alex's possession of a gun. Matthias told Alex to get rid of his AK47 and Alex didn't want to do it. Matthias put it flat and plainly: either Alex would get rid of his gun or the money for college wouldn't be sent.

I understood this strategy and I was doing a similar thing

at my end with the threats of eviction. But then, I also thought that I didn't want Alex to be desperate. I wanted him to make a more conscientious decision about the gun, not act only out of fear and because of being blackmailed.

Nothing worked. At one point I even told Alex to give the gun to Earle for storage purposes only, and then email his father about it.

"We won't even sell it," I said. "It will still be yours, only in our house."

I knew that, if only Earle had it, he could lock it in the shop. It would be safe, there. Alex didn't like the idea. He wrote me the following email:

'You obviously don't get it. I feel like calling you the worst names, ever, and starting to scream. I'm keeping the rifle and I will be sending my father the pictures of me holding it. I AM NOT GETTING RID OF MY RIFLE. IT IS MORE IMPORTANT TO ME THAN SCHOOL, AND THAT IS THE TRUTH. I HATE MY FATHER WITH A TREMENDOUS PASSION. NOW EVERYBODY, FUCK OFF UNLESS YOU HAVE A GN'UINE IDEA THAT MIGHT ACTUALLY HELP ME'.

I sent him an email setting out his options. He only re-sent me the email above. I replied that he would have to move out, and oddly enough, he said that he had some other house in his mind. He said he would rent it. I told him then he wouldn't have any money to pay rent and maybe it would be a good idea to reconsider all the options. All he had to do was to sell me that gun or sell it back to the store. Alex told me then that, if I were him, I would probably have cracked under the pressure by now or would have been finished the moment I hit a tree on a snowboard. I didn't see any comparison or relevance. He only got annoyed when I asked for clarification.

"The difference is that, for some reason, I just keep going whether I want to or not," he said. He almost sounded as if he had nothing to do with his behavior, as if some higher power was leading him and he couldn't resist or didn't even care any more.

These conversations were taking place in December. I'd spent Christmas with my elder sister and was planning on spending New Year's Eve over at my younger sister's house.

The New Year brought a nice surprise. Alex called and said he would stay in the Studio and he agreed to sell me the gun. It looked like things were getting better. I told him that Earle and I were happy he would stay, but that there were some strings attached; no illegal drugs on our property but marijuana was excluded.

There was still another issue. Alex got a dog. It was a young female blue nose Pit Bull Terrier. Her name was Breezy. Earle was terrified. He didn't want Alex to have that dog but I was torn. One of Alex's shady friends had owned that dog to make money since Breezy was a purebred Pit Bull. This terrible person had Breezy have puppies before she was a year old, just to sell them and make more cash. Then this idiot abandoned her and left her in the backyard while running away from his rental house and moving to apartments where dogs weren't allowed. He told Alex he didn't have enough money to stay in the house and that the apartment was cheaper. He also said he had a family to look after since he and his girlfriend had just had a baby. It's a scary thought people like that even have children.

Anyway, this man had abandoned Breezy.

Alex was hiding the dog from us for a while, but after he

realized one of his siblings had spread the news about it, he confirmed it.

Two days after the intervention, when I came to say goodbye to Alex, he introduced me to the dog. I fell in love with that dog immediately. I didn't want to talk too much about it with Earle because I didn't want to upset him. Earle knew about the dog but he didn't accept it. He made sure everybody knew that, in his own words, *'he didn't trust that dog'.* After all, it was Alex's dog. Although initially I said that animals weren't allowed in the Studio, now I just stopped talking about it altogether.

The man Alex rescued Breezy from kept in touch with Alex. After some time, he even came back and proposed that Breezy have puppies again. He told Alex they would share the profits from the puppies' sale. To Alex's credit, he didn't agree. When I met Alex's sister for coffee, she told me the story.

"He didn't agree?" I said.

I was waiting for my cappuccino. The espresso machine was loud, and initially, I didn't hear her answer. After we finally found a quiet corner away from the other tables, we picked up our conversation.

"He didn't. I explained to him how wrong it was and he immediately understood. He doesn't want Breezy to be used, or any dog to suffer," she said.

I was happy that my children loved the dog and was proud Alex could resign from the money Breezy could make him from the puppies she would have to give birth to. I imagined it wasn't easy for him to refuse the previous owner a deal. Alex actually had to lie. He said that he'd had Breezy spayed. It wasn't true. At the time I was only thinking about it. I knew that, no matter what, eventually, I would have to have her spayed.

I was catching myself on the word "eventually." Eventually, what? What if Earle said that Breezy couldn't stay? How would I be able to resist? I couldn't think about all those things that in my head were titled: what about? I knew that Piedra Seca was going into foreclosure. I knew the problems with Alex were enormous. I knew we might still go bankrupt because the gallery building wasn't selling.

I was trotting through life like a horse with blinders. I couldn't look around. Everything was wrong. I had to block my vision. I was focusing on school, work, and painting. This was saving me from falling into an even deeper abyss of depression. I only wanted to see a few hours into the future, not even a whole day. Breezy was a good dog and she was bringing Alex lots of happiness. That was one thing. The other one was that I wanted everybody to be safe. I thought about the gate at Alex's Studio. It was always wide open. And all of Alex's friends or semi-friends passing through the Studio didn't make it safer for the dog.

Well, for now, I was in Poland and Alex wrote me an email in which he said that Breezy, at present, had it good. She was safe and had a good owner, him. And she slept in his bed.

Chapter 27
New Year 2011

On New Year's Day, I called Earle to wish us a better year. I also told him about Alex's decisions about staying in the Studio and selling his rifle. I didn't mention the dog. Earle said Alex was doing okay and that he was driving him to several doctor appointments.

"Several?" I asked.

"Yes, he had a bunch of them. But no problem, everything is taken care of," Earle said.

A few weeks later he explained to me that, while I was away, Alex had shown him a yellow pad with different doctors' offices listed. Alex would ask Earle to drive him to one of them, and after a visit, he would make a checkmark in his pad, as if he wanted to remember that he'd already 'used' this particular doctor. I'm saying 'used', because this is exactly what it was. He was going to all these doctors to get more pain medications, and he didn't want to get caught. It dawned on Earle only later that this was what was happening.

#

On January 8, 2011, while I was still in Poland, Earle was driving home from work. He turned on his radio and news about a shooting at a Safeway Plaza in Tucson came on.

Gabrielle Gifford was wounded and some people had died, including a child. As Earle was listening, his hands froze on the steering wheel. He pulled over to listen to the entire broadcast. His mind was racing. Young white male? College student? Had a weapon?

Earle's life was far from what we consider normal. He was under lots of stress every day. In his mind, he jumped to the conclusion that the shooter might have been Alex. Earle actually thought that it was Alex and he almost had a heart attack. His anxiety exploded. He couldn't drive or move. He was looking at a bunch of creosote bushes growing by the street. The green street sign reminded him he was parked on the side of River Road. He told me later all he was able to think of was how was he going to tell me the news.

Earle got home but he wasn't even capable of calling Alex just to check on him. So, when Alex called him a few minutes later and asked for another ride, Earle almost fainted. They agreed on a pick-up time for the next day. Alex wasn't stressed out about the shooting. He had his own problems, and simply didn't listen to the news.

#

In the meantime, I was still in Poland and Alex continued emailing me about his financial problems. His father told him he wouldn't send him any more money. Then there was an issue of a couch. In his emails Alex wrote me that his back was hurting and he needed a comfortable couch. He said it was a shame that a person with a broken back wasn't able to afford a couch. Supposedly, he even went to the furniture store and sat on one of the couches for a long time, crying. The emails from that time would have been amusing if they weren't tragic. In the last exchange we kind of established that the lack of a good couch prevented Alex from succeeding in anything.

Luckily, the problem got resolved because Earle promised to give Alex our red couch.

Then next email was again about the fight that Alex had had with his father. Alex wrote:

'My father cheated me. Can you call him and tell him that I need the money to survive?'

I knew that Alex had taken out several loans to pay for his tuition. He didn't need to do it because his father was paying for his tuition. Now though, Alex demanded money from his father to be deposited to his Bursar's account. To put it in short, his father didn't want to give him cash. In our next phone conversation, I asked Alex what he needed cash for.

"For everything, including pizza," he said.

Then he sent me an email explaining that his father had withheld cash from him already three times this past semester, and that he couldn't go on like that. He wanted to quit his relationship with his father. The ending of the email looked as if Alex had fallen asleep with his head on the keyboard since only straight lines were typed, a whole page worth of them, then many blank pages.

The whole issue was about one thousand dollars. Alex said that his father had given one thousand dollars to Alex's sister but didn't want to give it to him, even though initially he said he would. Alex also said that out of anger he had demolished his room, only sparing his yo-yos.

He posed a question, too. He was asking why his father was funding good education and helping all his other children, but left him on his own so he would be forced to make his spending money on campus by selling drugs. The last email in this exchange ended with capitalized 'FUCK MY LIFE', immediately followed by the next email, where Alex was asking me not to share the above sentence because those were his personal sentiments.

Alex was constantly calling me. Due to time difference between Poland and Arizona, sometimes we had conversations at very odd hours. I had to whisper in the middle of the night, not to wake up anybody. Our fights continued. A new idea was forming in Alex's mind. He was thinking about going to Costa Rica right after his second surgery. He said he would rest there. He explained to me that Kevin had moved there, and he was either managing a resort or even owned it. In some way Kevin, the former skate shop owner, remained Alex's hero.

"What resort?" I asked.

"Some kind of rehab," Alex said.

"Rehab? Wow," I said.

"I'm not sure. It might be some religious thing, too," Alex said.

Rehab? Religious? With Kevin, nobody knew. I was suspicious but also hopeful. Both things, rehab and religion, sounded good to me under the circumstances. I knew that Alex and Kevin were in touch. Alex said Kevin had reached out to him and invited him to Costa Rica. I didn't know the conditions of their agreement and I was getting mixed messages. First of all, the religious part of it was quickly denied.

"But you said yourself that this might be some religious thing," I said later in the week while talking to Alex.

I was still thinking about Kevin and his facility. I knew I didn't make it up. I remembered what Alex had said before.

Anyway, rehab was all that was left.

"Will you work there, or what?" I asked during our next conversation. "If everything is included, there's probably some way you would need to pay for it."

Again, the answers were unclear. One thing was clear though. After every fight Alex had with his father, he would say that he needed to go to Costa Rica.

"How long would you stay there?" I asked one day after listening to Alex's desperate cries about his life and repetitive statements about Costa Rica. I had one more week left in Poland. I wanted to spend quality time with my family but Alex's problems were constantly on my mind.

"I'm getting the fuck out of here. Forever," he said.

But on other days he would say he only needed to rest there and come back to school. Then, if we would fight about something, he would say:

"I thought I would go to Costa Rica to rest only, but now I'm convinced that I have to move away for good."

He told me that after I refused to lend him a car. A small sedan Earle had bought for Andrew was still in our possession. Andrew was away in college. Sometimes we still used that small car. But I wouldn't let Alex drive it and I asked Earle not to let Alex drive it either.

I told Alex that registering for the University of Arizona for next semester wasn't worth it if he really had a plan to go away. Also, that he wouldn't need a couch. He agreed.

"The beach will be my couch," he said.

My trip to Poland was getting closer to the end. Alex was happy about it. He said he would host a party for my homecoming.

Chapter 28
Coming back to Tucson

I came back to Tucson in the second week of January. Two days later, Alexander sold me his AK47. I paid him with the money I was saving from my paycheck. Earle took the gun to the shop and locked it in a closet. This ended the era of all the troubles connected with Alex's gun possession. Other troubles remained.

Alex was being rude, again. He was going to school but he wasn't doing well. He was blaming me for all his misfortunes. He had decided he would go to Costa Rica, right after he recovered from the second surgery. He also mentioned that he might go to Poland, to college over there.

I liked the idea. I thought changing the environment would be best for him. For now, though, he was calling several times a day only to blame me, or when he needed something. My elder daughter, Lara, was in constant touch with him and was going almost every day to the Studio. She really liked Breezy and wanted to spend time with the dog, too.

Alex didn't want to talk to me. Once in a while, he would send an ugly text message, telling me how little he thought of me. By that time, it was obvious that our Piedra Seca house would be foreclosed on. We'd stopped making payments. It was hard to be at work and around Earle in general. He was extremely depressed. He had also called the broker of our New

Mexico property and said he couldn't keep paying for it. We were done. We were still paying for the huge, empty gallery building every month though, because it was a loan guaranteed by our building on Huachuca Drive where the plastic company was.

All of it was a disaster.

I was working and going to school. I wanted to get my degree and start working with children.

Sometimes, Alex would call me and want something more than just to blame me. I would call it a practical favor.

Like a time when he called and asked if I wanted to buy his bicycle.

"I don't need it and I don't have the money," I said. "Why do you want to sell it? You do use your bike."

"I have the little one. I don't need the big one. Plus, I'm going to Costa Rica, and then to Poland. I need to get rid of my stuff. I'm selling up"

I didn't know how to help him with his bike, but I agreed to go with him and ask around if any shop with used furniture might want his table and chairs that he also wanted to sell. It was still our family table from the house sold after the divorce. The table was large and heavy.

One afternoon we got into my car and Alex directed me to several used furniture shops. He had them listed on a small piece of paper. I could see them numbered in his neat writing. The first store was close to Desert house. We got out of the car and walked in. It had a strong smell of old wood. The lady behind the counter was pretty old herself. She was skinny with a very wrinkled face. She wore glasses. We told her the purpose of our trip. No, we didn't have our stuff in the car. We were only asking, for now. She said she wasn't interested. We walked out and went inside the store next door, because it was also selling used furniture. Alex didn't have it on the list. There, the young man showed us around but said that he wasn't interested in getting in more stuff.

"Look," he said. "The store is full. I just don't have enough space to take anything."

He was maybe in his late twenties. He told us it was his father's store and he was only watching it several times a week. When we were walking out, he patted Alex on the back.

"Hang in there, man," he said. Alex didn't say anything. We drove to three more stores with the same results. Nobody wanted the table, with or without chairs. Nobody wanted the bike, either. Nobody wanted anything.

After getting out of the last store from Alex's list we came back to the car. I started driving. I was thinking about one more store that we could visit. Alex didn't have it on the list.

Alex was sitting in the passenger seat next to me. Suddenly, he started to cry. I turned right into the first small street and stopped the car. I started to cry too.

"I'm sorry, Alex. I'm so sorry," I wept.

"Mom, I'm sorry. I miss sitting at this table at home. I miss having Thanksgiving dinner with all of us. Mom!" Alex wept. His face was red and twisted in terrible sadness. He used his sleeve to wipe his cheeks. I didn't bother to look for a tissue. There were way too many tears for thin Kleenexes. "I want things to go back. I don't want to be big. I want to be little, again. I want to sit in our kitchen and I want you to give me dinner. At that table, Mom. At our table." Now he coughed into his elbow and wiped his mouth. The tears kept flowing.

I looked at the street ahead. I was parked in front of a yellow sign. It showed a black shape of a child with a balloon in hand. A little further I saw a red stop sign. Both yellow and red colors melted under my tears. I had trouble seeing anything. I felt pain on my forehead as my skin was crumpling in sadness. I felt tears dripping from my nose and wiped them with the palm of my hand.

"I'm sorry things are the way they are now," I cried. "I'm sorry I had to arrest you when you were little."

Now the floodgates opened. We both cried as if we were insane. I don't think I've cried like that in my whole life. It was a true attack of grief without anybody dead. We were both grieving lost hopes, for they were truly lost. I reached out to him and we hugged. I felt his neck and his body, shaking in the rhythm of his sobs. We both bellowed. The strangest sounds filled the car and I could almost smell the grief. It seemed as if the patched-up wounds had swelled and ripped the stiches, and blood with pus oozed out.

I wiped my mouth and face with a sleeve and sat back in my seat. I was still crying but at least regained my voice. I could speak without hiccups.

"Alex, it's not too late for anything," I said. "You can do it all." Now, I had faith.

"It's so important that you apologized for arresting me, Mom," Alex said still sobbing. His hair was a mess. It was sticking to his forehead. His lips were red and shaking. His nose was dripping with fluids. Only his eyes retained their blue color.

I looked at him through my tears. I did say I was sorry, but didn't apologize. I knew I didn't have any other choice then. I wiped my face again thinking that he still didn't get it. His grief, though, was the same and about the same as mine. I felt my faith going away, but I desperately didn't want to let it go.

I held on to it.

A pigeon sat on the hood right in front of us, and for a short moment, got all our attention. I turned on the engine and it flew away. We followed it with our gaze but lost it in the trees.

"Egees for dinner?" I said. My voice was almost calm. Alex nodded his head. He still couldn't talk. The closest Egees was only a few minutes away. We drove in silence, but Alex put his hand over my shoulder and kept it there till we parked in front of the restaurant.

After Alex ate his sandwich and I ate my fries, he asked me to drop him off at the Studio.

The next day things went back to normal. Alex continued sending me hateful text messages, blaming me. I told him that I would like to know when his surgery was going to happen and when he was going to go to Costa Rica and Poland. He told me that I would be the last one on this Earth to know anything whatsoever about his plans.

I stopped asking. I wanted to move out of Piedra Seca house as soon as possible. I couldn't stand looking at Earle being so terribly depressed, walking around the house and looking at all the improvements that we'd made. At the beginning of March, we bumped onto each other in Piedra Seca kitchen. Earle was putting his six pack into the fridge. I was busy packing in my bedroom and hadn't heard him coming home. It was an early evening and I was surprised to see Earle in the house. He literally almost lived at work. We sat on the couch, each of us holding a beer. Outside the large window, we could see the approaching night. Earle told me then that he was planning to stay in Piedra Seca house.

"Where would I go? Gallery? To the shop on Huachuca?"

he said.

"There's Desert house," I said.

Earle didn't even shrug his shoulders. He got up, opened the fridge and pulled out another beer. He popped it open and started to cough. I went outside. That was another thing, that cough of his.

Chapter 29
Kevin again

I knew Earle and I would eventually have to move to Desert house but I didn't press the issue. I didn't see the reason to rub it in, but I was packing my stuff, little by little. I was putting a few new boxes with my clothes into my car when my phone rang. I didn't recognize the number but decided to answer. I had a new phone and the contact list hadn't been updated. It was probable I knew the caller.

"Hi, Monika," the voice said.

"Who's this?" I said.

"Kevin," he said.

"Oh, Kevin," I said, after a brief silence.

I was very surprised. I didn't even know he had my phone number.

Kevin knew the date of Alex's surgery. I was surprised it was already scheduled, and not even for May, but for March. He also told me that Alex was going to come to Kevin's place in Costa Rica.

"Did he tell you when?" I asked.

"He said he would tell me when he buys the ticket. But in general, in March," he said.

"But Kevin, he would have to recover! It's still back surgery," I said. "You do know he's planning to go to Poland to college. He told you that, right?"

"He did. We will see how it goes. He's welcome to stay here as long as he wants." Kevin said.

Right after the conversation with Kevin, I called Alex. I stopped packing my clothes and went to the kitchen to make myself tea. With the phone between my ear and shoulder, I poured water into the tea kettle. Alex picked up the phone.

"Mom? he said. "Why are you calling me? Something happened?"

He was half mocking me. He sounded a little congested as if he had a cold. He was sarcastic, too.

I told him about my conversation with Kevin.

"You didn't tell me that you have the surgery already scheduled," I said.

"It's because you don't need to know. It's none of your business. It isn't your back, is it?" he said. I decided to ignore his sarcasm.

"Tell me," I said. "When are you planning to go to Costa Rica? Are you coming back or you are going to Poland straight from there?

"I can tell you exactly when I'm going to Costa Rica because I just bought the ticket. Literally, I clicked the mouse when you called. Since you already know about my plans there is no need to hide."

"You bought the ticket?" I said. "But you haven't had your surgery yet. How do you know how you will be feeling? What if the doctor tells you to stay?" I asked.

"I don't care. And you don't care. You just say you do. I'm going and I'm not coming back."

We spent some more time on the phone. We agreed that I would take him to the hospital for the surgery. It was coming up in four weeks.

I also told Alex that no matter what, he couldn't come back to the Studio. It was my final decision. He said that he would either stay in Costa Rica or go to Poland from there, and he would talk to his father about it. He certainly didn't want to come back to Tucson.

"In that case, please go through your stuff and choose what you want to keep. Put it in one pile. I will store your stuff. Everything else I will dispose of. So make a selection," I said. I also said that I would take care of Breezy.

I was coming to Desert house whenever I could. Knowing we were going to move in soon, I was painting the front house. I also finished building a so-called small studio. It used to be a simple open shed without any doors. I closed it up and put two windows and a door in. I hired a person to insulate it and put on a good roof with a skylight. Alex hated me for all this construction.

"Walls? A door? Did you ever think about me? Where will I sit and smoke a joint? The shed used to be a perfect place," he said. I ignored him. I reminded him he was leaving anyway.

In general, I was focusing on making the house livable for Earle and me. It was a good house, and although there was a mortgage on it, it was ours and empty. The mortgage was affordable and one has to live somewhere. I was spending my savings on paints and shopping on craigslist for sidewalk stones, bricks, and such like. Earle was extremely depressed but I decided I wouldn't think about it because, if I did, life would be unbearable. It already was, without his depression. But I was working with him eight hours a day.

One of these days, when I was in Desert house painting the small studio, Alex came in and introduced me to his new girlfriend. She was taking chemistry class with him. She was small and skinny, with wavy blond hair and blue eyes. I waved down to her with my brush from the ladder.

"Hi," I said. "It's nice to meet you. I will get down after I finish this wall. Five more minutes."

As I kept painting, Alex asked me if I could take him to the doctor and drop off his girlfriend at the dorm.

"Are you sick?" I asked him.

"Yeah. Don't you see?" he said.

I looked. He was pointing to his nose. It was running and red. I was thinking about his upcoming surgery and how the cold wouldn't be a good thing to have.

"Okay, I will take you. Where to? Urgent care?" I said.

"Yes, there's one by the campus," he said.

We left the house promptly. The new girlfriend in the back was quiet and politely answered my questions about school, etc. After I dropped her off, I drove to Urgent Care but, by the time I parked the car, Alex had changed his mind. He didn't want to go to the doctor any more.

"What about your cold?" I asked.

"It will be fine. Just take me home."

We drove back to the Studio. The next day, when I came after work, Alex gave me a yellow wrist watch which he said he'd purchased on eBay.

"I bought it for you," he said. "I have one for Earle, too. Please give it to him."

I was touched.

A few days later, I was talking to my elder daughter, Lara. She told me that the new girlfriend had left Alex. I called him and told him I was sorry.

"It's okay. I couldn't make her stay. She didn't even want a watch from me. She said she didn't like the color yellow.

How could I have known?"

That resolved the watch gift mystery to me. I also found out about what happened with the new girlfriend. Lara told me Alex was using cocaine all night long in front of this girl. The next morning, she called him and broke up with him.

"Oh," I said. I was so glad she had left him promptly before things had become more complicated. I was somewhat happy for her. I was sorry for Alex but then, I was sorry for him all the time.

Chapter 30
Second surgery and Costa Rica

On the day of Alex's surgery, I picked him up at around five in the morning and drove him to the hospital. Alex's best friend, Joe, was already there waiting for us.

Alex was very nervous. Once he buckled the seatbelt, he held tightly to the sides of his seat. His forehead was covered with sweat. He genuinely considered the possibility of dying during the surgery. I didn't know that he was so afraid of anesthesia and death in general. After a short car ride, I parked at the Admissions parking lot. We walked in and Alex reported himself to the lady at the front desk. She immediately directed him to the side office where we met the nurse who was in charge of admissions. The nurse was a middle-aged woman dressed in white, a little plump and with a good demeanor. She was guiding Alex through the mandatory questionnaire, and when she got to the fields with the living will options, Alex got especially angry.

"Everything I have goes to Joe," he said. "She," he pointed at me, "gets nothing." He didn't object when I paid the copay of one hundred dollars, the fee requested by his insurance though. It looked as if it was the only reason for me to come.

Contrary to his fears, Alex didn't die during the surgery. He woke up in the recovery room and was moved to the general floor, where he remained for the next three days. The surgeon gave him all the hardware that he'd taken out of Alex's back. The screws and the plate looked like a kit from Home Depot, only the color of the metal was somewhat special, iridescent blue and green. I took a picture of the whole set.

When Alex got signed out of the hospital, he didn't have to use the wheelchair. He walked out using crutches. He used them only for a few days. His eyes were set on the day of his departure to Costa Rica. The day of his trip was approaching fast. I reminded Alex several times about going through his stuff that he kept in the Studio. I told him to choose the things he would like me to keep for him and made sure he understood the rest of his stuff would be disposed of.

"I heard you the first time," he said when he decided that I was becoming boring.

About ten days after the surgery Alex was all packed and ready to go. He didn't want me to take him to the airport. He said that his friend, Chris, would do it.

"Okay, I'm still coming over," I said. "You need to show me the "to keep" pile. I would like to see how the house looks in general. Since you aren't coming back to the Studio, I would like to see how it looks before you leave"

His flight was leaving around noon. I came over to the Studio to say goodbye. The Studio was extremely messy. A small pile of his stuff consisting of a few books and documents was put aside in the corner. Alex was excited. We hugged.

"Good luck, son," I said.

"Oh, yeah. Wish me luck. I'll need it," he said. There was no sarcasm in his voice. He hugged the dog and hopped in the car. I could see him waving until the car disappeared around the corner.

#

After Alex's departure I had a breakdown. It was instantly after he left. In fact, I don't believe the car he was traveling in had made it to a major street yet, when I yelled, stomped my feet, and hit myself with my fists. I banged my head against the Studio wall and scratched my face. All the tension that was growing until now reached a summit, or this was what I thought. I didn't know then how many summits were ahead. When I finally stopped bellowing, I found myself on the floor, my cheek against the cool tile. Breezy was standing close to me and sniffing my hair. She was the only being that knew my state of mind. This dog was my savior and a big problem at the same time.

Technically, I still lived in Piedra Seca house with Earle but I knew I was only doing it for him. I also knew that I needed to permanently move to Desert house. I had to prepare that house for us, whether Earle wanted it or not, and I had to stay with the dog. There was no way this energetic Pit Bull could live with us in Piedra Seca house. Not only would we be moving very soon but we also had a cat. It was Mia's cat, but it had lived with us since she left for college, already several years ago. Also, the property in Piedra Seca house was big and not fenced. It was virtually a piece of desert without any backyard per se.

Earle liked the cat and the cat liked Earle and here I was with the Pit Bull.

The dog constantly missed me. When Alex was in the hospital after the surgery, I came to the Studio, sometimes even at three a clock in the morning just to spend time with the dog.

Then I had to go to work. After work, I had school which often lasted till nine in the evening. I would still go home because I didn't want severely depressed Earle to feel abandoned. The situation wasn't sustainable. And after Alex left for Costa Rica, the dog lived by itself with me only visiting.

I knew that now was the moment I needed to tell Earle I would be moving to Desert house. My nervous breakdown after Alex's departure made me feel that I had nothing to lose in life any more, and I wanted to be with Breezy.

"It's just becoming very difficult. Plus, I'm working on the house there. And the dog…" I said one evening when I came to see him after class.

Earle hated the idea of the dog. He gave me a terrible look but I still proceeded with packing my clothes. I was taking a few things at a time to Desert house every couple of days. About a week after Alex's departure, as I was focusing on school, work, and moving, my cellphone rang. It was Alex.

"I hate it. It sucks. Kevin's an asshole. I'm coming back," he said.

I was immediately very disturbed. I was packing the teacups into a box and I dropped one. Its handle broke off.

"What happened?" I asked.

"Nothing. It's over. I'm not staying there. I'm coming back to Tucson. I will go to Poland from Tucson. Dad is buying me the ticket," he said.

"Where are you now?" I asked.

"In a hotel. In California," he said.

"California? "I said. "How come?"

When he told me that he was in Yuma, the border town of Arizona, California and Mexico, I was even more puzzled. Alex didn't leave me time for questioning him. I only asked him once how he ended up in California.

"It doesn't matter. Yuma is the place. That's where I've ended up and it doesn't matter how," he said.

I never really found out what happened on Alex's way to Kevin's place in Costa Rica. I think he was there one day only but not even at Kevin's place. Supposedly, they had a terrible fight while talking on the phone and Alex changed his mind about his trip. He stayed in some hotel in Yuma and never went back to Costa Rica. Kevin called me about a month after the events. He said he just couldn't recognize Alex.

I didn't say anything. I didn't even ask questions about the details. I was beyond that. Many months later I received an email from Kevin. *'Whatever happens to Alex, I hope he's doing well'*, he wrote.

Chapter 31
Breezy

Alex's stay in Yuma was still puzzling me. I knew he wasn't doing well while staying in some hotel and planning his prompt comeback. I lived at Desert house now and Earle stayed at Piedra Seca house waiting for the foreclosure.

I wondered why Earle stayed there. Years later, he told me that he was afraid of vandalism. He thought that if the house was vandalized, the bank might make him accountable. I didn't know everything that was going through Earle's head but some things were clear to me. Primarily, he was depressed. The second thing was that he was totally done with Alex. Alex's name alone would only trigger Earle's anger. Also, the dog issue wasn't resolved.

I called all my friends and told them wonders about Breezy. I didn't want to give her away but thought that, if a good friend wanted her, I might. I truly loved the dog but Earle was against her staying with us. He was so depressed I had a hard time even thinking about having any conversation with him, especially about the future of the dog.

Sometimes, though, I felt sad and angry at the same time. I felt that Breezy and I belonged together. Lara supported me emotionally. She really wanted the dog to stay. I talked to Lara daily and I cried a lot, too. In those days, I went to Desert house late after my classes. Every time, the dog was insane with joy.

Breezy jumped and ran around and wiggled her tail, making it dance in the air like a whip. Her jaws were open in a big pit bull smile, and her tongue would hang out ready to lick me at any moment. Often, out of excitement, she would bring her blanket or any other thing she would spot, like a shopping bag or my shoe, and just lay by my feet as if it was her gift to me. I hadn't felt this kind of joy for years, if ever. To me, it was pure love. Every evening, after pouring a glass of red wine, I would sit on the dog's bed on the floor and go through albums full of photographs of my children. I was remembering their births, and toys, and dresses, and places we went. I was remembering their birthdays and holidays and special events. And I was also remembering our normal life. I was looking at the pictures of Alex, second guessing and doubting myself as a mother. What did I do wrong and when? Which turn was an evil one? I cried, and the dog's head along with the plastic sleeves of the album would become wet with my tears. Sometimes, I would read one or two of Alex's evil text messages and this would make me cry even more. The dog kept looking at me and licking my salty tears from my hands. Often, I would wake up in the early morning still in the dog's bed, Breezy snoring at my side.

I took her for a walk very early. At this time of year, the mornings were still dark and sometimes I took a flashlight. I was concerned about the coyote recently seen in the neighborhood. Lara texted me often, asking about Breezy and about her prospects of staying with me. The dialogue would be like this:

"I can't agree by myself to Breezy staying. Earle would have to agree too," I would say through tears. "How could I possibly keep the dog that Earle hates so much?"

"Mom, what about you? Do you count at all?" Lara would ask. After that, she would usually get angry and hang up. It couldn't last. A decision had to be made, and I could barely live dreading the moment when I would have to give Breezy away. I was angry at Earle for not agreeing on keeping her. I didn't know how to talk to him. But I felt tired and weak, too. I could only cry.

One morning when I was walking Breezy, my phone beeped and a text message showed up. Thinking it was from Lara, I stopped to read it. To my surprise it wasn't from her but from Earle. *'Fine, you can keep your dog'*, he wrote.

I immediately called Lara and told her the news.

"Awesome!" she said.

"I can't imagine why he changed his mind," I said.

"Why does it matter? What matters is that Breezy found a real home," she said. "Just thank him profusely."

I was overjoyed. I dropped to my knees on the still dark street and hugged and kissed the dog, which only made her happier and jumpier. I felt the roughness of asphalt imprinting into my skin but it still didn't make me get up. I only wanted to hug Breezy. My heart was light when I was leaving her in the house with a bunch of treats and going to work. I didn't even mind her whining too much, knowing I would see her in the evening and that she would stay with me.

When I got to work and saw Earle for the first time that day, I hugged him and thanked him. I could tell he was serious and angry but I decided to ignore it. Hey, he'd just agreed to the dog!

A few months later, he told me that Lara not only texted him several times about the dog, but also called. She did it the day he sent me the text message, early in the morning. She didn't care that it was before six in the morning. She presumed he wasn't asleep anyway and she was right. Earle received the first message from her at about five thirty. She called him at six. Earle was convinced Lara and I collaborated on this. We didn't. I had no idea about her actions and I told him so. At this point I didn't even care if he believed me, for I was telling the truth.

When I found out about all her actions, I called Lara after work to thank her.

"Mom, my pleasure," she said. "If you want to know what I told him, here it is. I told him I didn't think it was right to forbid you from having the little joy the dog was giving you. After everything you went through with Alex and the financial situation, you needed a break. I told him…"

"That's enough," I said. She wanted to continue but I interrupted her. My eyes were filling up with tears. "Thank you from my heart. And you are right. Breezy will have a good home."

#

I immediately bought Breezy a larger bed and scheduled an appointment at the Humane Society. I wanted to have her spayed as soon as possible. In the midst of a depression and great stress I was overjoyed. In the evenings I couldn't wait for the classes to end because I wanted to be home and hug the dog. She was waiting for me in the backyard no matter what time of day or night. Always hopeful, always happy, and giving me so much love.

Alex kept calling, first from Yuma, then from wherever he was on his way back to Tucson. I didn't know what to tell him. Not that he was waiting for my wisdom. On the contrary… he was calling to vent and complain. He was happy, though, that I was taking care of the dog. He asked about Breezy, and when I told him what was going on with her, he was relieved.

Alex was still out of town when one evening Earle and I went to our friends' house for tea. My friend, Ella, and her husband, Jim, both former music teachers of some of my children, sat at the table with cookies, different kind of cheeses, and fruit. It looked awesome. Ella and Jim were in their late forties and we had known each other for many years. Ella was small, with thick black hair and Chinese eyes after her parents. Jim was even smaller than her. He wore glasses with a shiny frame. His white, thick hair was neatly combed. I always admired their love for each other and the way they were raising their two daughters. Their house was modest and full of love. Their numerous cats would sleep in open violin cases during music lessons and nobody every chased them away. This family was sensitive, gentle and always helpful. About an hour into our evening, Earle's phone rang. On his screen we saw the land line number from Desert house. The problem was that we were not there, but at my friends' house. So, who was calling? Earle picked up the phone but the connection was disrupted.

The only logical person who came to my mind was Alex. I was terrified. Had he come back and broken into Desert house? Why? Why would he do that? I already told him I was taking over the place. His stuff wasn't there any more. I told him that too.

Similar thoughts must have gone through Earle's mind because I saw the anger on his face.

"Call the police," he said. "Nobody has the right to be there. I locked the door."

I called the police, crying. I explained what happened and

said that nobody was in danger. I also told the dispatcher that my husband and Jim were heading to the house right now. They wanted to know who was there.

"We will send an officer," the dispatcher said.

Earle and Jim left. I stayed, crying and worrying.

"What about if they arrest him?" I asked Ella. "They will arrest him, of course. Earle has had enough. If Alex finally ends up in jail, it would only be worse. I don't know what to do!" I said.

Ella made me more tea. Through my tears I could see the cookies and strawberries multiplying on the small plates. I took a Kleenex and wiped my face. I looked around to the familiar walls of Ella's living room. Her collection of angel statues rested on the table by the door. The orange cat was sitting by the book shelf. Everything was warm and friendly, but my soul was in a very dark place. I could see Ella was concerned and tried her best to be supportive. I appreciated her company. Desert house wasn't far, and pretty soon, Earle called me.

"The house is dark. But the officer just came and he has a big flashlight. We are going in. I will let you know," he said.

"Earle," I started talking, but he already hung up. I had so many things I wanted to say, to ask for. '*Be gentle*', I thought, '*be nice. Please, please, I don't want anything bad to happen*'. Maybe it was better that Earle had hung up and I didn't have a chance to weep into the receiver. How would I have put all those feelings into words? I didn't know.

Since Earle forgot the key, the officer had to jump over the fence. Earle followed him. Jim was covering the front of the house by staying on the street. Carefully, Earle and the officer walked through the side alley to the backyard. The house was dark and so was the Studio. Suddenly, from the darkness of the backyard Breezy appeared. She was running. In joyful jumps she passed by Earle and the officer. In the flood of light coming out of the officer's flashlight, they saw the house phone stuck in her huge jaws. The batteries had got loose and were dangling off the receiver as she was running around the backyard.

"Here it is," the officer said. "Case resolved. Not many of them are resolved so quickly in the city of Tucson."

Earle was astounded and so was Jim. They took the phone away from Breezy, and after petting her and filling her water bowl, they jumped in the car and drove back. They told us the whole story. I couldn't believe my ears. I constantly kept thanking God in my thoughts.

Once again, we sat down at the table. Ella made more tea. I also got a glass of wine.

My thoughts were racing. I knew I hadn't set a speed dial on the land line at Desert house. The phone was new and I hadn't had time to mess with it yet. I was feverishly searching in my memory if I even had called Earle from that line. I was pretty sure I hadn't. I told everybody about my doubts. Nobody laughed at me. Earle grew even more somber. Finally, Ella started talking.

"I don't know about all the facts. I mean whatever was happening before tonight's events. But I deeply feel that there's a special connection between Breezy and Monika," she said. She also asked me if I wanted another glass of wine. I didn't refuse. After the first glass I said that either Breezy knew how to dial the phone or a higher power helped her to do that. I wanted to say something on a lighter note. It was supposed to be a joke and Ella together with Jim gladly commented and laughed. Earle didn't laugh. He smiled a little, as if he didn't want to hurt anybody's feelings. And I knew I wasn't joking.

Chapter 32
Cleaning the Studio

I didn't know where Alex was but at least my status quo was established. I lived in Desert house. I started to clean the Studio immediately. I was cleaning and crying, especially in the evenings while going through the Alex's leftover stuff. It was mostly junk. But everything made me cry. Little things, like his plastic earrings he started to wear all over again, his multiple pairs of colorful sunglasses, his worn-out flip flops, and most of all, his yo-yos. These last items had a special talent of showing up in the most unexpected places, like the shower in the front house or the dirt in the backyard. There were some big things too, mainly furniture. Some of it I kept. The table and chairs were mine to begin with. But there was one piece I had a problem with. It was a very heavy, wooden workbench table that Matthias and I purchased for Alex one Christmas when he was eight years old. It was good only for the purpose for which it was made, meaning woodworking and bench working. I didn't need it in the Studio and didn't want it in the house. I was thinking about taking it to the shop but hesitated. I didn't want to have Alex's stuff in the shop. It was Earle's space. I put it on craigslist, classified advertisement website, but nobody was interested. Finally, I asked the man I hired to do the concrete sidewalks if he needed the workbench. He seemed like a handy person and I really wanted to put the workbench to use.

I remember how Alex worked on it. I remember how he made jewelry. It started in an odd way. Alex was about ten years old when my eldest son was in a car accident. The accident happened close to a place in the desert where people were shooting guns. When we went to the site the next day Alex picked up lots of empty shells. Out of these shells he made many necklaces. I still have a couple of them. I was so proud of his skill and imagination. I remember wearing one necklace to an art opening. With that necklace on my neck and chest I almost looked like Queen Cleopatra. I remembered people being attracted by it and asking who made it. After they found out about the empty shells they would step away. They almost looked offended and I couldn't understand that.

Later, Alex started to make jewelry out of small bicycle parts. His art was amazing. Out of this batch I also have a necklace and a few bracelets. I don't wear jewelry but would wear all the things made by Alex if the occasion would arise. I remembered all these things while looking at the workbench I was trying to get rid of now. I called the construction man again and made sure he was truly interested in the workbench.

"You will use the bench, right?" I asked cautiously when the construction man said that he really wanted the bench. "You are not going to sell it, are you?"

"I will use it, of course," he said. I trusted him. I told him a little bit about Alex and he seemed understanding.

It took me months to understand I gave the workbench to somebody who didn't care for it at all and probably sold it cheap. I only realized that after the construction man showed me his house. He was working on a new bathroom when I showed up one day to make a partial payment for the concrete sidewalks he had laid. He probably completely forgot about the workbench, but I was only looking for it and it was nowhere to be found. It was then when a powerful feeling flooded my soul. The feeling of hate in my very self. It was hate for my actions, ignorance and stupidity. It was hate and denial, at the same time. As I was hating myself, I was justifying my actions at the same time. Like, for example, the divorce from Matthias. I knew I should have left him earlier but I didn't do it. Then I was thinking totally ridiculous thoughts that I shouldn't have left him at all or at least let him have custody of all my children because then, maybe none of this would have happened with Alex. But then, I would remember the abuse Matthias was giving my other children, especially my eldest son and Lara. *'What if they murdered Matthias one day?'* I thought. *'What if I finally murdered him?'*, and on top of this, was the overpowering feeling of guilt. I felt guilty for causing Alex's misfortunes.

The cleaning of the Studio wasn't a happy process. I came home every evening and went through Alex's stuff. First, I kept the 'to keep' pile, of course. Then I continued with everything else and I must say that it felt as if I were cleaning after somebody who had died. That's how I felt. How little did I know?

I cried over Alex's drawings, the ones he did in elementary school. I collected as many of his art projects as I could. I put aside an enormous number of yo-yos, with special care for the boxes he had prepared for soldiers. I never made it to the place in town where the items for the soldiers were collected. Finally, I set what was left of Alex's stuff on the curb in front of the house, and pretty soon, a non-profit organization Big Brothers and Sisters collected everything.

Now the Studio was empty and freshly painted, too. I was waiting for the smell of paint to subside a little so I could unpack some of my things. In the meantime, I slept in the small middle studio together with the dog. I called it a middle studio because eventually this is what it became. I used it later for painting with oils, so no one could sleep there because of the smell. For now, though, I installed a big doggie door so Breezy could get out whenever she wanted. I also decided to spend the very rest of my savings on a block wall in front of the house, laying a concrete sidewalk between the Studio and the front house so Earle and I wouldn't have to walk in dust and mud. I hired a different workman for the wall project. I wanted Earle to be happy with the house after he moved in. And Alex?

Alex showed up in town after his Costa Rica trip and rented an apartment. His father was paying the rent. It was only a month until Alex was going to Poland anyway. Interestingly enough, a new girlfriend moved in with him. Lara told me they were in love.

"In love?" I was surprised. "Where did he meet her? What's she doing?"

Lara wasn't able to give me all the answers but she said that the new girlfriend was very pretty and smart. She attended Pima College and wanted to major in theater. Yes, she moved in with Alex because they figured they couldn't live without each other.

"But Alex is going to Poland, isn't he?" I asked.

"He is," Lara said.

"So… there's something I don't understand. Is she going with him? What's the deal?" I asked.

"I don't know, Mom," Lara said. "It's their deal. Why would you worry?"

I still couldn't understand these young people. While trying to explain Alex's and his new girlfriend's behavior, I searched in my memory for similar situations from my own youth. I still couldn't find any similarities and I certainly wasn't an exemplary teenager.

Right after Alex moved into his apartment, he started to send me horrible text messages again. He was asking for his stuff.

Unfortunately, there was no stuff left except his 'to keep' pile, which was already in storage. I was willing to give all these things to him any time. I told him this when he called me about two days after he came back to Tucson.

"I don't want any of that what you call 'to keep' shit," he said. "I want everything else. I want my towels, sheets, backpacks, papers, paper clips, pencils, my toothbrush with the toothpaste, the shampoo and conditioner. Thank God I took the good yo-yos with me but the rest of them wouldn't hurt, either. Where are the yo-yos?" The list of items and questions was long. I felt the sweat moisten my ear. I pulled the phone away from my head and looked at it. The screen was wet.

"I don't have all these things. You told me not to keep it. Besides, you are going to Poland, aren't you?" I asked.

"I need everything. It's none of your business where I'm going," he said and hung up.

Chapter 33
Anger

A few days after his return, Alex came to Desert house to pick up his electric toothbrush which I had put away for him. He came on a bicycle and he was fuming with anger. He wasn't drunk but certainly was under the influence of I don't know what. He almost couldn't walk straight, and to tell the truth, I have no idea how he could even ride a bike.

"It's your fault. All of this," he said, and with a wide gesture he kind of showed the world around. "If it weren't for you, I would be already finishing my major in business. I was in business school and I was doing great! Then you ruined everything."

He hopped on his bike and rode away in a wavy line leaving me at the curbside. I -knew he had a problem but I didn't understand the extent of it. I believed what he said, not all of it, but even a part made me feel like the guiltiest person. I didn't know how to live with myself. Sometimes this feeling comes back.

A few days later, Alex came to pick up something else. I forget what it was but I remember that time because of Breezy. She and I were standing at the window in the front house looking out at the street. Alex just came and got off his bike. He was there with two friends I didn't know. They were talking loudly and waving their hands in wide gestures. Alex was dressed in a green polo shirt and checkered cotton shorts. He was wearing thick framed, red sunglasses. Even though Alex's clothes were baggy, I could tell he was very skinny.

I know dogs don't have human faces and I know that we dog lovers, assign our dogs human features. But how else could I describe Breezy?

I looked down and saw her head close to the window, her wet nose against the glass creating two circular patches of mist. Her ears were down and as far to the back as she could possibly have them. Her tail was down, too. Breezy is a blue nose Pit-Bull, and at that moment, she looked like a steel statue of that breed, classic and immobile. It was a statue of sadness. I thought she was afraid; afraid that she might have to go back to her previous owner, Alex. Not that he ever did anything wrong to her; not at all. He saved her and loved her. But he couldn't afford decent dog food for her; any food, in fact. The ramen noodles and pizzas he shared with her certainly weren't enough.

While looking out the window and seeing Breezy's sadness I remembered the day I dropped Alex off at the hospital for the first surgery. When I came back to the Studio, I could see Breezy was almost starving. Lara and I ran to the store and bought a bag of dry dog food. We got back to the house and opened that bag. Breezy was beside herself. She didn't know what to do! On one hand, she desperately needed to eat, but on the other hand, her dog's nature was telling her to express love and gratitude. The result was funny. She was running between us and the food bag with her jaws stuffed with food and her tail swirling around like helicopter blades. She wasn't even chewing her food but only swallowing it in big chunks. That's how hungry she was. The oversized pit-bull style collar, shining with spiky metal inserts, was hurting her sensitive thin skin on her neck. She developed a painful rash there. We took the painful collar off. That day Lara also told me that Alex not only shared pizzas and ramen soups with Breezy, but his marijuana as well. Whenever he was smoking, he would blow the smoke inside her ears. I was terrified.

"How did she react? Did she mind?" I asked.

"I don't know. I don't think so. You know that Alex wants everybody to be high at all times. He says the world would be a better place if that would happen."

Now, Breezy was looking at Alex through the window. He was talking to his friends and their voices were loud. His friends were also on bikes. They gestured towards the house but Alex shook his head, '*no*'. Then they left. I was hoping he might come in and I was afraid of it at the same time. Alex squatted and tied his shoe then got up and looked around, but not towards my window. Then he hopped on the bike and followed his friends. When he disappeared around the corner, I felt Breezy's relief.

Chapter 34
Departure

The day of Alex's departure for Poland was approaching quickly. I asked him if he wanted me to take him to the airport.

"I have a ride," he said. "There are people who care about me."

As usual, I didn't know what to say. In an effort to ignore his rudeness I decided to go on a bike ride and have a little picnic. I made myself a cheese sandwich, took out my bicycle and went for a ride on the bike path. But my mind was still working on an answer I should have given him. A natural answer to this provocative statement would be '*And I don't care about you, right?*' I was pushing the pedals and imagining our conversation. I knew that answer would only satisfy Alex's hunger for spilling hatred and anger all over me. I didn't feel it was right. Sometimes, in response to a similar provocation, I would react the way it was called for and I would say:

"Yeah, and I don't care about you at all. All my life is a big proof of a total lack of care for my children, particularly you."

Alex would love that because then he could bring up the anger he had for his life and rant about it. Mostly, he would still blame me for his stays at the psychiatric hospitals. I had no answers that were good enough. They were always the same to the point of being boring. But that was all I could say.

"I didn't need your actions. I would have managed on my own." That's what he would say.

At this point of the conversation, I would usually stop talking.

I stopped my bicycle to let a large family with many children pass by. Two kids had small bikes with training wheels. The father was pushing a stroller and jogging along. I took a sip of water. I was only thinking about Alex.

I had so much to say! I just didn't know where to start. What makes things most important, therefore first in line? My hurt feelings? How else should I distinguish what I should talk about first?

I put the water bottle back in its place, and suddenly, the random parts of Alex's life started coming to my mind; the areas where I had tried to intervene and was pushed away.

Like, for example, hanging out with wrong people.

It was an ongoing problem, but I remembered one particular time when Alex must have been thirteen or so. I was going through the divorce from Matthias and Alex was still in middle school. Alex was getting good grades, worked in the skate shop and skated a lot. He was a teenager and he looked like one, with blond bangs over his forehead and acne on his face. His pants were a little too large but at least he was wearing a belt that prevented them from falling down. Alex was never in company I would approve of with the exception of his best friend, Joe. Joe changed schools though. Their relationship stayed strong, but they didn't spend as much time with each other as they previously did. Alex didn't hang out with his school friends; at least not with the ones who had good grades and were doing well.

Except for Joe, Alex was always looking for friends who

were either failing or already suspended. He always defended them. If a friend stole something, or smoked pot, or sold drugs, or ran away from home, it didn't matter. Alex always saw the reasons for the wrong actions his friend chose to perform. The list of his excuses for his unfortunate friends was long.

My bike ride was getting long and I started to be hungry. I got off the bicycle and was pushing it in front of me. I started to look for a place where I could sit down and eat my sandwich. The bike path got narrow and I saw other families coming. As I stopped to let a lady with two dogs go by, I remembered Alex's reasons.

He said his friends were poor.

Their parents used drugs or were alcoholics, or both. The mother was raising all her kids by herself because the dad was in jail. Or the other way around, with mom in jail. Somebody in the family was very sick. Et cetera…

The lady with the dogs passed and I decided to ride my bike a little further, to the end of the path, and eat my sandwich there. With new energy I hopped on my bike, but my thinking was already so invested in the past stories of Alex's middle school friends that I couldn't stop my racing mind.

I remembered one time, when I was looking for a broom I used to sweep our porch. Alex was in seventh grade. When I couldn't find the broom, I decided to ask Alex after school. Around three in the afternoon I heard his skateboard on the street. I went out and asked him if he had seen the broom.

"Yup," he said. "I lent it to my friend. His mom needed it." Alex picked up his skate board and headed for his room.

"Which friend?" I asked. "From school?" I followed him through the house.

"No. There's a house around the corner, the one with a

white fence. They live there. My friend and his family." Alex went to the bathroom but left the door open. He was only washing his hands. He was hungry and asked for something to eat.

I was thinking about it. How come he found a friend in this house? Our neighborhood wasn't one that would unify the kids and they would all play together outside. I decided I would ask Alex later. For now, I demanded the broom be brought back to the house.

The whole family from the house with the white fence showed up in the evening. They brought the broom back. In the dim light of the front door patio, I saw the small, skinny woman. That was the mother. On her side there was a boy that could pass for Alex's friend. He looked younger though, so I wasn't sure. Behind these two I could see two big teenagers. I assumed they were the older sons of the mother. All the boys had new Nike shoes. They were dressed in long, almost fluorescent, shirts. Their pants were barely hanging on their butts. The forty-watt bulb in my patio lamp was doing wonders in bringing up colors in the shiny shirts. The mother's outfit was very modest.

"Here's your broom. Thank you for lending it," she said. The tallest boy set my broom against the wall.

"You're welcome," I said and they left.

After they left, I brought the broom to the back porch and started sweeping. Alex joined me there.

"Did you see, Mom?" he said.

"See, what?" I asked.

"How poor they are. Life isn't fair, is it?"

I kept sweeping but couldn't help myself.

"They are poor, that might be true. But why and how come

251

all the boys have new Nikes? And why are their pants lowered below their butts?"

I guess I wouldn't have started commenting but Alex asked me about my thoughts to begin with, so I felt justified. Once I started it was hard for me to stop. I had to defend myself and my views.

All those thoughts were going through my head, but the hunger won. I was getting close to the end of the path. The dry river bottom was very wide in this place. The path continued the other side of it, but in order to get there, I would have to cross the sandy bottom. I decided to go down but not to cross, only sit on a big rock I'd spotted. I pushed my bicycle down to the rock and I made myself comfortable. I unwrapped my sandwich and sniffed the bread before taking a first bite. As I was chewing, the poor family story continued in my mind. Interestingly enough, I found out was happening to them not that long ago. Alex was already in college when he let me read one of his English papers. Alex's paper was already graded.

Through that paper I learned all I needed to know about the poor family from the house with the white fence.

From his paper I learned out about him printing false currency and spreading it around. The whole story was detailed in that college paper. The process was quite simple. Five-dollar bills had to be soaked in degreaser bought at Auto Zone. Then, the bills had to be washed several times in the washing machine with a strong detergent. After that, the white, half translucent bills were neatly aligned in a printer loaded with a well calibrated color container. The printer would swallow the blank bills, and after a while, spit out new hundred dollars bills.

Since the bills were fake, the two elder brothers of Alex's

friend would drive to the closest Mexican town, Nogales, to change them there. After the first transaction, the brothers, together with Alex, would quickly come back to the US. The brothers were very careful. They didn't stay in Nogales and never walked together. For a fee, they used Alex to change the false bills they previously printed. I learned all this from Alex's paper. The teacher's comment was short. It only said 'WOW!' The grade was A plus.

I remembered Alex going to Nogales once in a while. He was going together with his friend's brothers and their mother. At least this was what Alex was telling me. Since he spoke a little Spanish, he was supposedly helping the mom do her shopping. She was shopping in Nogales because it was cheaper than Tucson. That's what Alex was saying, then.

I finished my sandwich. I wiped my mouth with a napkin and crumpled it into my fist. These were things of the past. Now, Alex wasn't taking any more classes at the University. He was leaving for Poland. On my way home, I decided I needed to get his phone, somehow. Alex told me he didn't want me to take him to the airport but he hadn't returned my phone and I didn't want to lose it. I asked him if I could meet him somewhere in town, so he could give it to me.

"No way. I need it to the very end. You can come to the airport and walk with me to the security gate. There, I will give it back to you," he said.

I did as he told me. The next morning when I arrived to Tucson International, I found Alex and his newest girlfriend sitting in the main hall. They were kissing. Alex's luggage was standing a little away from the bench they were sitting on. His backpack was lying by his feet along with his skateboard. He looked like a new recruit, clean and tall. His hair was very short and his clothes looked new. He wore a blue collared shirt and long brown pants with a leather belt. The girl on his lap was skinny, with long, blond hair wrapped around Alex's neck. She had a burgundy shirt on and a short, black skirt. I waited a little, but since it didn't look like they would stop kissing any time soon, I came closer.

When it was impossible to ignore me any longer, they stopped.

"Oh, here you go," Alex said. He pulled out a phone from his pocket. "You don't need to wait. I can give it to you now."

But I wanted to wait. I didn't move. That prompted Alex to introduce me to his new girlfriend.

"This is Jane," he said. "Jane, this is my mom."

We shook hands. Then Jane started crying. She put her head on Alex's chest and sobbed.

"I know you have to go but I don't know how I will live without you. I love you." She started to kiss Alex's chest, or rather his sweatshirt. Alex caressed her head and I could tell he was as crazy and distressed as she was.

"There's Skype. And there's a phone. And you will come to Poland," Alex said.

"Yes, I will, I will." They were both crying.

I was holding his cellphone in my hand. Our business was over. I could just leave.

I don't remember if we hugged.

PART THREE

Chapter 35
In Warsaw, Poland

After arriving to Warsaw, Poland, Alex moved into his father's apartment. Matthias didn't live in Warsaw at this time. He was holding a tenured position in one of the Universities in Eastern Poland and lived there now. His Warsaw apartment was empty most of the time. It was perfect for Alex. His father would come to visit only once a month or so.

I wasn't in touch with Alex for a few weeks but it changed once he started to need various documents in order to enroll at the School of Agriculture in Warsaw. That was the school of his choice. In the back of his head, he still had a dream of a big marijuana farm somewhere in the USA. Whatever his dream was, the school was very good, well founded and accredited. It was an old school with a great reputation.

I got busy preparing his documents. I had to go to Alex's high school as well as the University of Arizona. After a while, Alex was enrolled and started his classes.

Things changed. I stopped receiving nasty emails from him. He sent nothing for my birthday, nothing for Christmas, no New Year's wishes. I sent him emails for various occasions. After a while, I stopped writing him too. Alex wasn't replying anyway. It was all okay with me as long as I knew he was doing well.

And he was.

It was amazing how his life changed. He'd really wanted to be admitted to the School of Agriculture and getting in was a major achievement. He claimed he loved his new classes.

How did I know this?

Alex didn't talk to me but he was in close touch with my elder daughter, Lara, who volunteered all this information to me.

When Alex needed something from me, like a document, he would send me an email and add a few comments about his life. These comments were meant to hurt me in a very subtle way. For example, he would praise his father and tell me what an awesome parent he was. He would say that "one couldn't ask for a better father." Alex didn't understand that this information would only make me happy and my only disturbance would be the fact he wanted to hurt me. Anyway, these were all peanuts compared to the past. Things were going well.

I was planning to visit my family in Poland in the winter and I bought a plane ticket. Lara must have informed Alex because he sent me an email asking for his yo-yos, the special ones; the ones kept in a special case. I said I would bring them, of course, and that I would be happy to see him in Warsaw.

I don't like to fly, in general, but the winter trips seem much worse than the summer ones. Maybe because I'm not used to the cold any more and I have to pack lots of clothes. I'm constantly cold, even on the plane I keep my cotton tight head covering, a beanie, on. This trip though was very exciting to me. I wanted to see, not only my sisters, but Alex too. After a long flight, I ended up in my elder sister's apartment in Warsaw. I like my sister's apartment. It's small, like all the apartments in this area of town. If we would apply American standards, we would call her kitchen tiny. But it is a very busy kitchen, even though the table is small and cooking area even smaller. I couldn't wait to sit down in the kitchen and look out the window from this third-floor apartment. I couldn't wait to hug my sister and have dinner with her, in this kitchen. It was December, right before Christmas. As we sat down, my sister told me Alex was planning to come as soon as possible.

"To get his yo-yos?" I said. I smiled. I must have been still tired from the trip, because I became sad.

"I guess," my sister said. She came over to me and hugged me. I immediately cried.

"Did he say he hates me?" I asked. "Or, did he say anything about me?"

"No, he didn't," my sister said. "Don't worry. It looks like he's doing well."

Two days after my arrival to Warsaw Alex came to my sister's apartment to meet up. It was an early evening but the window was black from what seemed a deep night outside. In the winter in Poland, it starts to get dark about three in the afternoon. I'd just came back from a short walk with the dog and was sitting in the kitchen trying to warm up. My feet were cold, especially because I was only wearing my socks. In Poland, people take off their shoes and leave them by the door before entering the apartment. I forgot my house slippers from Tucson and my sister was in the adjacent room looking for the right house shoes for me. The doorbell rang. The dog started barking but through the intercom I could clearly hear Alex's voice. I got up from the kitchen table, went to the tiny hallway and pressed the red button to release the lock downstairs. My sister lives on the third floor, and since I couldn't hear the elevator, I presumed Alex took the stairs. I waited by the door.

I was right. At first, I heard him trying to catch his breath while running upstairs. Then he showed up. He was dressed in a red winter jacket. In his right hand he held his hat. We hugged, reluctantly. Since I had only my socks on and he still had shoes, I felt very small. Alex was much taller.

"Hi," I said.

"Hi," Alex said.

I moved slightly and he came in. He quickly took his shoes off and went straight to the kitchen. My sister was already there with a pair of house shoes for me. She greeted Alex warmly and asked him to sit down. She'd just made a soup and Alex agreed to eat.

"But before we eat," he said. "Can I see my yo-yos?"

"Sure," I said. I got up and went to the room where my luggage was. I pulled out his small suitcase and brought it to the kitchen.

"Here are your yo-yos," I said.

"Awesome. Thank you," he said. He patted the case as if he wanted to open it. Then he changed his mind.

"I will enjoy opening this case at home," he said.

Both my sister and I nodded with understanding. We started to eat. The conversation was a little dry. I almost didn't talk. But when Alex got to his favorite subject, marijuana, I had not only deja vu, but also a deep understanding that some things don't change and we shouldn't expect them to do so.

I agreed that marijuana should be legal. But he insisted, and insisted. He would transform a conversation to a monologue, and after a while, it would simply become boring. Okay, okay, we would all agree, marijuana should be legalized! It still wasn't enough for Alex. In his opinion we didn't love marijuana enough. We didn't understand it was a miraculous, godsent plant. And most of all we wanted to change the subject of the conversation. This was making Alex suspicious. Why would we want to change the subject? Wasn't marijuana interesting enough? Or, maybe we just agreed with him only to please him so he would stop talking?

These were Alex's usual concerns and he expressed them all out loud, while eating the soup my sister served.

We parted, hugging. Alex thanked me for bringing the yo-yos.

#

I stayed in Poland for two weeks. This gave me a chance to meet Alex's new Polish girlfriend. Her name was Sophie.

They were in love. Shortly after meeting Alex, Sophie moved in with him and started to take care of him in a very Polish way. She cooked and cleaned. She kept him company. She was trying to make him happy. Above all, she loved him. And he loved her back. Sophie was from a small town, raised by her father and a stepmother. She didn't have a happy childhood, to say the least. Her mother committed suicide when Sophie was three years old. Sophie was never allowed even to look at the pictures of her mother. They were hidden, and when she happened to find one or two, her mother's face on that picture was scratched out. Sophie's childhood was full of abuse, physical and emotional. When her stepmother had a son, Sophie welcomed the baby with all her heart. Till today she loves her half-brother as if he were her own child. She was ten years old when he was born.

This book isn't about Sophie so I don't want to spend too much time on her story. All I want to say is she truly loved Alex and she looked up to him no matter how many problems he presented. Sophie's brother also loved Alex and Alex spent lots of time with him, being, I guess, a role model. Strangely enough, Sophie's stepmother also loved Alex and talked to him often.

I was impressed with Sophie. She was soft spoken but firm, a small, thin girl with a very white skin, almost white eyebrows and eyelashes. She had thick, long, golden hair. Her blue eyes looked like two flowers planted above her cheeks. I immediately loved Sophie with all my heart. When I left Poland after this visit, I was calmer than ever before because Sophie was in Alex's life.

I came back to Tucson, and shortly afterwards, Alex proposed. Sophie started to plan their wedding. I didn't have enough vacation time to attend, but I went again to Poland before their wedding, in the winter. Alex was in Norway, working in the tulip fields. It was a job he had arranged through his school. I met with Sophie. I gave her some money as a wedding gift and said sorry I couldn't come to the wedding. It was planned for April and I wouldn't be able to travel that month. I told her how well I wished them, of course, from the bottom of my heart. Sophie, on her part, gave me a gift Alex had prepared for me before he left for Norway. It was Italian coffee, about one pound of it. It was called 'ROSSA' and Sophie told me Alex immediately bought it, thinking of me. My maiden name, is 'Rossa' and he loved the coincidence. Alex emailed me several times from Norway, making sure I was meeting with Sophie during my stay in Warsaw. After my visit with her, I emailed him and he was happy, not only because I had visited her, but also because we connected so well. What made me happy though was that Alex and I patched things up. We talked. We communicated. We were together, again.

Chapter 36
Getting married

Sophie and Alex got married in April. They started their life as husband and wife.

They had enough money to live and study. With Matthias's financial help, they even took a biking trip abroad. They went to Amsterdam to visit Matthias's daughter from his first marriage. She lived in Holland and was more than happy to have Alex and Sophie over. Marijuana is legal in Amsterdam so Alex had a great time smoking it in the local shops. But after coming back to Warsaw, he was short on money. He didn't think they had enough to live on. Sophie's father had stopped giving her any money even though by law he was required to do so since she was in school. He wasn't giving her any money while she lived at home either but at least it had been somewhere to live He was collecting Sophie's late mother Social Security money Sophie was supposed to receive.

Sophie never demanded this money, but Alex advised her to take her father to court and demand it back. This practice isn't unusual in Poland or other European countries. The parent has to pay child support to high school or college enrolled children until the child reaches the age of twenty-six.

Sophie's father was appalled. He had to show up in court and start paying monthly child support because the judge ruled in Sophie's favor. As a result, Sophie's father stopped talking to her altogether.

Even this money wasn't enough and Sophie got a part time job. Promptly, she switched to full time while taking a leave of absence from school. Alex claimed that Sophie had problems in school, that her studying hadn't really been going well and Alex was trying to help her because school was easy for him. I don't know how much truth there was in this, considering the fact that Sophie had to pass a difficult exam to get into the program and she had done that without the support of her family. Today, I think that all Sophie's problems in school started with her never resolved abuse in childhood. They were exacerbated by Alex's lifestyle, especially pot smoking and doing drugs. All Sophie wanted to do was to please Alex.

Alex's life started to fall apart, again. His relationship with Sophie and their life together started great, along with a new school and all the excitement about the future. Alex and Sophie had plans. They wanted to have a family. They wanted to finish their degrees, come to the USA and have their own farm.

I don't know about all the events that changed Alex's trajectory but I know about several things that could have influenced it, like the friendship with his old Tucson friend, Peter.

#

Peter was a son of Matthias's work colleague. Peter's mother was my very close friend. We were both artists and both grew up in Poland. Her son, Peter, was about six years older than

Alex.

After barely making it through high school and failing at the University of Arizona, Peter ended up in Poland trying to get a degree in psychology. Peter was using drugs. He said he needed to experiment with drugs because of his university major. Eventually, he wanted to help people with addictions. Well, he was addicted to all sort of drugs himself.

I don't know how he found out about Alex's whereabouts. It might have been one of the Facebook 'blessings'. Peter had lived in Warsaw for a long time and was hooked up with all sorts of shady people, short of the mafia. He knew drug dealers, since he needed drugs for himself. I knew about Peter from Sophie. She told me that Peter's presence in their apartment, when he came to visit, was terrifying. She told me every time Peter would show up, she would pray for him to simply disappear from Alex's life. But Peter remained there.

Alex also had access to legal drugs due to his health. He was walking normally, without a cane. He was riding a bike a lot, too. But he claimed he was in pain and needed his meds back. *'In pain? Again?'* I thought. *'How come he wasn't in pain and now he's back in it?'* I was surprised and suspicious but I had other things to think about; like, for example, paying for Alex's speeding tickets and a credit card here, in the USA. It was a lot of money and I was saving every penny just to get rid of his debts. For this management of his debts, I have to say, Alex was grateful. He thanked me several times even though I didn't expect any gratitude. I hoped he would straighten his life up and come back to the USA to do what he said he loved to do, which was farming.

In Poland it's more difficult to get pain medication than it is in the US. Poland is much more conservative, and in many respects, simply 'backwards'. It has nothing to do with the doctors. It has to do with the conservative culture. It applies to pain medications, too. They are given to dying patients in the hospital or maybe a hospice, but if somebody wanted to die at home, it would be much more difficult to obtain them.

Anyway, Alex, having access to some pain meds, could sell them or exchange them, too. In a way, it put him back in the drugs market. Alex could get the prescriptions because he truly had a broken back and went through surgeries. He had all the supportive paperwork and the photos of metal screws and plates which used to be mounted to his spine.

I know that Peter introduced Alex to many other people, some of them dangerous. All of them were either dealers or had some connection with drugs. They would come to Alex's apartment, just like Peter.

Chapter 37
Love and sacrifice

A few weeks after Alex proposed to Sophie, his sister, Lara, was hit by a car while riding on her bike to her class. It happened in Phoenix, Arizona, where she was going to college now. She ended up in the ICU with a serious brain injury. I was informed of it by a phone call. Earle and I had just climbed out of the Grand Canyon that day and were on our way to Flagstaff. The phone rang when we were checking into the hotel.

Reality changed, again.

When I made it to the ICU, Lara was trying to get out of bed and crying out loudly for help. It was obvious that she didn't know where she was or what she was doing. She had a hemorrhage in her brain. She had to stay in bed. She was hooked up to an IV and wasn't supposed to move. She kept trying to stand up, though, and this led the nurses to their ultimate action of tying Lara to her bed.

As I was standing outside her ICU room, I could hear my adult daughter's cries. In her blurred speech I could distinguish words of promise, "I will be good, I won't move, I will stay in bed." The tears were flooding my face when the doctor finally came and informed me that they needed to put my daughter into a coma, for her own good. And that I should be aware of the fact that her chances of survival were fifty/fifty.

I only nodded my head and blew my nose. I was looking for another Kleenex in my purse when I saw my phone flashing. I forgot I had it on silent. I recognized Alex's number. I picked it up and told him I would call him back immediately. I was planning to do that when things in the ICU room calmed down. When Lara was finally in the coma, I walked out and called him back.

Alex was beside himself. He loved Lara with all his heart. I told him she was in a coma now, and that nobody can talk to her now. Maybe he didn't understand that it was an induced coma, because he got very upset and hung up.

He called me the next day when I was on my way to the hospital.

"You always do it, Mom!" He yelled. "I got scared for her. I thought she died! I only learned today she's alive. As soon as I learned it, I dropped to my knees and thanked God. I wouldn't want to live if she died. Why didn't you tell me that she was alive?"

I didn't understand anything. I'd told him how it was. At this point I was way too tired to be nice to Alex. I yelled back at him and told him he better listen when I'm talking next time. I was still talking to him while crossing the parking lot. I finally hung up and went straight back to the hospital room.

Eventually, Lara got well. It was what I call a miracle, aided by her incredibly strong will.

Alex was overjoyed. Now, they talked even more often. They used Skype a lot.

When my daughter got well, she told me that one time, while talking on Skype with Alex, he said that when he saw me in Warsaw, he understood I wasn't 'dangerous'. "She's just this old small lady", he said, supposedly. Even today, it makes me smile.

I would like to continue Alex's story just like I did so far. I tried this for a while but then I saw it wasn't working the way I was expecting. I was thinking about it, trying to figure out why I didn't feel I was doing this story justice.

I understood what the problem was. It was easy. I wasn't in Poland with Alex. My contact with him was sporadic and the times when he emailed me or called piled themselves up instead of spreading themselves in time. I understood, not only was I not capable of seeing these events on a time line, but in the first place, the timeline didn't matter. Even if I could arrange the events in some sequence and do a good job, it would be an artificial scheme. No matter how funny it sounds, to me, all the following events happened at once.

All I can say is that Alex was doing well in school, until…

Exactly. Until, what? Until he found friends who were doing drugs or needed drugs?

#

Nobody ever thought that a small '*yes*' would have life-long consequences for Sophie. And I'm not talking about her '*yes*' to Alex's marriage proposal.

Alex and Sophie were already married when he went to work at the tulip fields in Norway. Sophie stayed in Warsaw. One evening, when she was alone at home, she heard a strong knock on the door. After learning it was the police, Sophie opened the door. Several policemen walked in. They pushed Sophie into the kitchen and immediately started searching the apartment. One of the policemen kept Sophie in the kitchen. The apartment wasn't particularly big, so it took the police only a short while to find one plastic container with a marijuana plant in it. They placed it in front of Sophie and kept furiously searching. Whatever they were looking for, they didn't find. They took several pictures of the plant as well as the many empty plastic plant pots of various sizes. Alex and Sophie were studying Agriculture and Gardening. They were planting many seeds, herbs and flowers. They had one marijuana plant for their personal usage.

Here, I have to clarify, that having a personal plant was Alex's idea. It was his plant, too. Sophie, as a typical Polish girl who grew up in a small town close to Warsaw and would smoke pot only once in a blue moon, if at all. The milieu of people with whom she was associating herself mostly drank beer to relax. I can't say for sure that Alex was the first one who introduced Sophie to drugs but I know he had to convince her to take some 'happy pills' once in a while. He was always making sure he had enough for himself, though.

Years later, my other children who had seen Alex and Sophie in Warsaw, told me they saw them taking ecstasy or some other kind of pills and Sophie was okay with it. According to my eldest son, finishing his Medical School in Warsaw at the time, Sophie was very happy taking drugs with Alex. That was his impression.

I beg to differ. We would have to define 'happy' here. Many philosophers have tried to do it with various results but without consensus on the definition. If Sophie was taking pills with Alex, it was because of him, not her.

When the police walked in, Sophie realized that Alex would be in big trouble. She didn't want him to have more problems than he already had. She was arrested and was taken to the police station. There, under the duress of the interview where the policemen were rude, rough, abusive and intimidating, she said '*yes*' to the question about the ownership of the plant. She said the plant was hers and hers only. This statement was put in the official transcript, and eventually, changed the course of Sophie's life.

#

After the police invasion, Sophie was charged with drug production. The section of the legislation used against mass amphetamine production mafia, was used against Sophie this time. It didn't matter to the Court that Alex and Sophie had only one marijuana plant. It meant all the same to them. Alex was helpless, but Lara helped him financially. After her bicycle accident she ended up with a small settlement. The insurance paid all her immense hospital bills, and whatever little was left over, she used to help Alex. Her help was more than significant. She paid for Sophie's lawyer and all other expenses. Sophie was found guilty anyway. Lara gave Alex lots of money so he wouldn't have to worry. She was loving, generous and asked him to come back to the US. She said she would cover his ticket and expenses and that he would be able to stay in her house.

He thanked her. He appreciated the offer but didn't want to come. He said he might come some other time, but not now. I wondered about that. Why did he refuse? Was he afraid he would meet his old buddies in Arizona? Was he afraid to leave Sophie for even a short time if he chose to come on vacation? Alex told me several times he wanted to come back, and he missed the desert. So, why didn't he accept his sister's invitation?

He was calling more often now. I always felt uneasy when

seeing his name flashing on my phone. I didn't know what to expect. Most of the time my anxiety proved to be right. Alex usually called me, to tell about his problems. Often, I could tell he was high. It all made me sad. I felt powerless. How could I help him now? During one of those phone calls, he told me a story he'd been keeping to himself for many years. This was the story which clarified his sadness and depression after his trip to Poland when he was fourteen. He told me how, during his visit to the mountains where his aunt had a cabin, he was raped. He told me in detail how and what happened.

His aunt left Alex and her son in the cabin under the care of a young man whom she trusted. She didn't want the boys to be alone, which could be understood. Alex remembered the young man's name. He also told me that this person was missing one finger.

I was terrified. It was years ago. What could I do today? Catch the guy? If he didn't have a finger, it would be easy to find him in the area where the cabin was. He was a local, Alex said. Alex's cousin didn't want to say anything. He kept his mouth shut. Matthias informed the police but it didn't help. Eventually, under pressure from Matthias, the cousin said that, yes, there was such a person taking care of them at the time and yes, he was missing the tip of his finger. Alex never said if his cousin was also raped.

That was it. Nobody caught anybody. Nobody wanted to accuse anybody. Alex told me that story and he also told it to his father. It looked as if he was suddenly looking for help, which we wanted to give, but how? What could be done about something that happened so long ago which nobody else wanted to talk about? All I could do was to listen to Alex with a compassionate heart.

Chapter 38
A small cold

Alex's sister suggested Alex should try to teach English to children in Warsaw. It turned out to be a winner. Alex loved teaching and the children loved Alex. He was looking forward to the lessons and so did the children. The parents were happy, too. Alex was funny yet demanding, so the lessons were never wasted. These were private lessons in the students' homes, usually with at least one of the parents in the house. They paid well, too. Alex was grateful to his sister for the suggestion, and when he talked on Skype with her, he was describing kids and the challenges he was facing with them, sometimes. He told his sister that his favorite teaching tool was a yo-yo.

"A yo-yo?" his sister said. They were talking on Skype. Alex pulled out his yo-yo and showed it to the camera.

"Sure, this one," he said. "I will show you a trick which the kids are most impressed with."

He threw the yo-yo and showed a trick his sister already knew, but she admired him as if she didn't.

"Awesome," she said. "So, do you teach them yo-yoing, besides English?"

"Only the ones who do the homework and behave well. A yo-yo is a prize," he said.

There was one week in the spring when Alex didn't feel well, so he cancelled scheduled lessons. He had a sore throat, and although the doctor didn't prescribe him antibiotics, he still told him to stay home for three days or so.

On a Tuesday, Sophie came home from work as usual, in the evening. Alex hadn't gone to school that day but she knew he was sick so she wasn't surprised that only the small cat of theirs greeted her at the door. She assumed Alex was asleep. She took extra care in not making too much noise while preparing her tea and a small dinner. She was thinking about making a sandwich for Alex too, but decided she would ask him about it later. After a first bite, she changed her mind and went to see how Alex was doing. She peeked through the crack in the door and saw him asleep. She quietly closed the door and went back to her sandwich. After she was done with her tea, she decided to check on Alex again, thinking that by now he might wake up. She opened the door only to find that Alex's position hadn't changed at all. Sophie came closer. She called his name several times but he didn't move. Sophie started to touch him. His body was rigid. She kept talking to him, shaking and kissing him. He still didn't move. She put her ear to his chest, and as she told me later, she could swear she felt his heartbeat. Hope went through her body like an electric current. She begged Alex to wake up several times, but when he still didn't move, she had to admit that the heartbeat must have been in her imagination or it must have been her own blood pulsating under her skin. Her head was throbbing. She thought she was going insane. The reality was approaching her mercilessly. She looked around Alex's bed as if she was looking for an answer to a question she'd never asked. There was nothing and nobody there for her. In her young life, she was introduced to a completely new feeling which would stay with her forever. The feeling of extreme solitude opened its huge gates and swallowed Sophie.

She then realized that she needed to call Matthias and tell him what had happened. She acted like a robot. She picked up the phone and dialed his number. She told him. He only said he would be on his way.

Matthias, who lived far from Warsaw, called Alex's uncle who lived close to where Alex lived. I don't know who called the paramedics but they and the uncle showed up at almost the same time. Alex was pronounced dead. The paramedics covered his body and managed to carry him through the door to the hallway, then took him downstairs using the building's staircase since the apartments didn't have an elevator. The door downstairs shut with its usual noise. The uncle left. I don't know what he said to Sophie. She didn't tell me. I know he told Matthias later on that Alex already had blotches on his skin, which meant he'd died several hours prior to his being found.

Sophie stayed alone in the apartment. She looked out the window, and since their apartment was only on the first floor, she could see the paramedics loading Alex's body into the ambulance. Then the ambulance drove away. Sophie saw it disappearing around the street corner.

Chapter 39
The farewell

I didn't fly to Alex's funeral. To say that I simply couldn't would have been an understatement. I don't know what I *could* or *couldn't* do. The words didn't exist or didn't mean anything. In fact, everything lost meaning.

I was at work when I learned about Alex's death. There was an email from Matthias in my inbox. Since we rarely communicated, I opened it promptly, wondering what could be so urgent. The email was short, only two sentences informing me about Alex's death. It wasn't urgent any more since Alex was dead. Nothing was urgent. Everything stopped.

I closed the computer and went to Earle's office to tell him. No, I didn't go. It wasn't me, only my rigid body went and my wooden mouth pronounced the words to Earle. Nothing in me was me. My tongue didn't feel mine nor the lips. Somehow though, I wanted to tell him.

Andrew called me on my cellphone.

"Mom, Mom," he yelled. "Alex is dead. I got an email from Dad. He wouldn't kid me about a thing like that.

"I know," I said. I hang up.

Earle opened the door and led me out of the building. In the parking lot I felt my body enclosed in Earle's arms, his face crying to my shoulder. I don't know how and what I cried, what I did. I ended up sitting on a big rock under a tree in the park in front of our company's office. I was looking at the door to our building and thought I should go back there, inside my office, sit at my desk and delete Matthias's email from my computer. I had an almost physical urge to do that, combined with the belief that Alex's life was still here somewhere, and I needed to find it and return to him.

My eldest son was in town and so was my younger daughter Mia. They showed up promptly at our work. When they arrived, I was sitting in my car.

"I'm going home," I said.

"No, you can't drive alone," they both said.

"Earle said I can," I said.

"Ah," they both said again, and stepped away from my car. They both came on bicycles so they couldn't come with me. I drove away.

After coming home, I called my daughter Lara. She was always in touch with Alex and had supported him all through the events of the recent years. I told her the news.

"No, Mom, no, what the fuck, no," she kept repeating. I told her I would be waiting for her at home. Andrew called me again and said that he would be flying in that evening.

My heart was with Sophie. I was constantly calling her. I kept thanking her for being such a good wife to Alex. I wanted to kiss and hug her and wipe away her tears. The phone connection was terrible and she mumbled instead of talking.

With my four children we went to Costco to buy food for a special dinner we decided to have, to honor Alex's life. They were glued to me just like when they were little. We chose the best sirloin steaks and wine. We bought lots of food, way more than needed. We went back to the house and started cooking.

I invited Mr Brown, the one who had helped me to commit

Alex. Tessa had moved on with her life so I didn't even call her. I knew she was married now. I called Alex's former girlfriend, the one who went with us for the grand vacation. She came over. Alex's godmother, who is my best friend, came from Phoenix and so did Alex's best friend, Joe. Lara came from Phoenix. Her best friend, who didn't know Alex personally but had participated in the Skype conversations between Lara and Alex, came along with her. I'd met him before. He was a very good friend and a person with a big heart. He suffered with us. He brought me a blue flower vase as a gift. And one more person came, Alex's friend who one time was too high or too afraid to help me with committing Alex.

I put on my best dress and shoes. I spread the AK47 out on the floor. It was dismantled since I kept it in the box. I looked at it while drinking wine. Then I knelt by it and put it together, at least the main parts, and I threw it on my back. It felt odd to have the hard metal and wood poking into my back which was only covered with a light dress, but I wanted to feel it that way. I was carrying the gun on my back but nobody was bothered by it. I only took the gun off my back when we sat at the table to eat. We talked about Alex. We cried and laughed, but mostly cried. When my phone rang, I didn't recognize the number but I picked it up anyway. It was Matthias. I got up from the table and went outside.

We talked for about an hour. Well, he did most of the talking. He told me that the day before his death, Alex called him and was in a good mood. They were planning a meeting when Matthias would be in Warsaw the next time. He also told me about the last time he saw Alex.

I was listening, standing in the backyard, looking at the

Studio where Alex used to live and where Breezy and I lived now. Matthias continued.

He'd seen Alex on a trolley near the airport. The meeting was coincidental. Alex must have been coming back from Norway and he was on his way from the airport, Matthias thought, because Alex had his travel bag with him. Matthias told me he couldn't believe he was seeing his son. Alex wasn't only high; he couldn't even remain standing by himself. The trolley's movements were throwing him around. Matthias came up to him and got Alex's travel bag in order to help him to get home. Alex didn't want any help. On the stop close to the apartment Matthias pulled him out of the trolley and walked him home. Once in the apartment Alex fell on the couch and immediately went to sleep, still in his shoes and jacket.

After talking to Matthias, I came back to the table and had more wine. I was rejecting life, but I lived. I kept looking at my four children, constantly searching for Alex and hating myself for it. I loved all my children but I felt insane without him. I also thought how lucky I was to have restored my relationship with Alex before his death. Although, I have to say, it wasn't my first thought. I kind of took it for granted. Only after the conversation with Matthias and his complaint about seeing Alex on a trolley, *'this is how our goodbye looked'*, I started to count my lucky stars. I remembered Alex differently. I remembered him as a handsome man, smart and quirky. I remembered how I heard him laughing his honest, loud laughter, when I saw him last time in Poland. I remembered him in love with Sophie.

And, most of all, I remembered him as a child, my awesome, unique child; the one making me gifts out of old plastic bottles or colorful jar covers. I remembered the little cello he made for me when he was six. He made it out of an old shoe box and a leftover cardboard tube. He put rubber band strings on it and played me a song. I remembered when he was eight and his rat died, how he decorated her grave. On a small piece of paper, he wrote the rat's name and age. Then at the bottom he wrote a line about how loved the rat was and how much he would miss her. I remembered the very piece of paper he wrote it on getting moist from Alex's tears, the printed letters running into colorful rivers. I remembered when he was six years old and angry with me because I didn't want to give him desert before dinner. He said he would paint moustaches on all the faces on all my paintings. Alex was very determined and I was truly worried. I remembered my sweet boy crying on a trail in Grand Canyon where I took the kids for a short hike. While walking, we spotted a little bird in front of us lying on the trail. It seemed to us it was injured but then it flew away To Alex it seemed the bird fell from the trail and most certainly died. I couldn't console him. I remembered when Alex baked oatmeal cookies in middle school. It was such a success in the house that, for many months, he kept baking them for us. I remembered Alex being ten and Andrew being seven, playing in a ship built out of three chairs and a blanket. Alex made himself a simple sailor and named Andrew captain. Andrew felt so privileged he was immediately doing everything the sailor told him to do, including bringing snacks from the kitchen. I remembered Alex's voice calling "Captain, bring three more plums for your sailor, but choose the good ones, soft and sweet!"

I remembered and remembered. The images and words were dancing in my head.

In the weeks to come, I constantly thought about Sophie. I consulted lawyers about her possible immigration status. I started to spend money on various lawyers in Poland and in the USA, only to finally find out that small '*yes*' Sophie said at a time of her arrest would make it impossible for her to even visit me in the USA. I didn't know what to do with myself.

Ironically, for once things were going well at the company simply because we sold it. The amount of money we got covered a substantial portion of our debt. Earle was going to work for his new owner/employer, and financially speaking, things were looking okay. Even his cough miraculously disappeared. His overall health improved.

But nothing mattered.

I didn't have energy to lift my grief and the grief of my children. Everybody was trying to survive that blow, somehow. Grief is lonely and merciless. That's how it operates. No matter how natural it is, it seems against nature when it's happening. The passing of time is supposed to heal wounds, but what about time that freezes? What then?

END NOTE
1
Near Drowning

When I was thirteen years old, I went on vacation with my grandmother; just her and me.

I was close to my paternal grandmother. It just happened that way. When I was a child, she used to come and visit us often. She had to take a two-hour train ride since she lived in a different town. Every time she would stay a month or even longer. Also, we spent summer vacation with her and Grandpa.

Summer vacations were the best. My dad would rent a room somewhere by the sea or in the mountains, and my sisters and I would spend the whole summer there. One summer though, I went alone with Grandma. In the winter prior to that summer vacation, I was in a serious ski accident. The seriousness of it didn't result from a broken leg only but also from concussion. When the summer approached my mother decided that it would be best if I could spend time in nature, and rest. I was thirteen. My dad rented a room upstairs in an old post-German house, in the middle of the forest by a lake close to the Polish/German border.

I spent a month there with Grandma. She used to go with me to the forest. She also sat for hours on the patch of grass by the lake, watching over me while I swam and played in the water. Grandpa had already passed, so there were only the two of us.

Grandma was always agonizing over my swimming in the lake, maybe because she couldn't swim.

I was a pretty good swimmer. I'd taken swimming lessons since I was seven. In the house where we were renting a room, there were two other ladies who came for a few weeks. The young woman I kind of became friends with was twenty-five years old. She was a grown woman, and big too, especially compared with me. I was rather small. But she didn't know how to swim, and since I knew how, I had the great idea of teaching her. She agreed.

The next day we met by the lake. My Grandma was already siting on her blanket, a little further from the shore.

It all started very well. My friend followed my instructions, and pretty soon she was floating on her back. We were already in deep water. I checked the depth with my foot and I found out that I couldn't reach the bottom. I thought it was strange because we weren't that far from the shore. Gently I told my friend I would turn her around and push her, thinking we needed to get to the shallow water.

"I will just walk," my friend said.

Before I could protest, she realized she couldn't touch the bottom either. She panicked and grabbed me. She held me with an incredible force. I was trying to give her instructions, but before I knew it, I was mostly under water and my friend was simply standing on me. At first, it bothered me that I couldn't get any air. Then it stopped mattering. I had my eyes open and I could see the dark lake and plankton moving above me. I looked straight ahead of me and I saw how dark the lake under the surface was; dark and muddy. *'So, this is how it is to drown?'* I thought. I distinctly remember my thoughts being slow and calm. I wasn't nervous or panicking. I could still feel my friend's feet on my head and shoulders but it didn't bother me, except I could feel her panic. I knew I was drowning and I was marveling at the fact that it didn't hurt! I didn't feel any pain and I always imagined that drowning, or dying any way for that matter, must hurt.

Then I thought of my parents, both of them. I thought how sad they would be when they found out about my death.

It was then I felt my friend disappearing from my shoulders and I popped up to the surface. I swam to the shore where I lied down in a patch of mud, coughing uncontrollably. When I finally stopped, I rested with my cheek glued to the mud, exhausted. After a while, I sat up and saw my friend far away, wrapped in a towel. She was sitting on a small wooden pier. A young man was bending over her. I understood he must have saved her.

Grandma was far away too, still sitting on her blanket. I knew I had some explaining to do and it wasn't a pleasant thought. I waited a while to regain control over my legs and I slowly walked toward her.

"Were you playing in the water over there, or what?" Grandma asked.

I was standing by her blanket now, thinking of what I was going to say. I quickly changed my mind. Grandma obviously didn't know what had happened.

"Yes," I said, nodding. "We were playing."

"What do you have on your cheek?" Grandma said.

I squatted and she reached out. I felt her hand touching my face. The pieces of mud fell off.

"Oh," I said, wiping my face. "It's dirt."

"Looks like mud to me," Grandma said.

I forgot how long I had been trying to recuperate after this whole event ending with my face buried in black mud by the lake.

#

In the evening, we went to the room upstairs to eat dinner. Grandma ate very little as usual. She had a piece of dry bread with tea. I had a handful of fried chanterelles I'd picked in the forest on the way back from the lake. I ate them with a piece of bread.

When night came, we laid down in a big wooden bed. There was only one bed in the room and we slept in it together. It was a bed for a married couple. The framed portrait which hung right above us on the wall suggested it. The picture looked as if it had been hanging there for years, even before the war, and the couple in it, taken on their wedding day, looked as if they were married before the war, too.

"Grandma?" I said.

"Yes?"

Grandma's voice was slightly hoarse. It always sounded like that when her false teeth were out. I lifted myself onto my elbow. I could see her teeth now in a glass on the small table on her side of bed, reflecting the moonlight.

"Do you think of Grandpa often?" I asked.

"Of course I do. Every day. I even had a dream about him yesterday," she said.

"You did? You didn't tell me."

"You didn't ask."

I was thinking about Grandma dreaming about Grandpa.

"What did he say? Or do?" I asked.

"He was moving a pile of sand with a wheelbarrow," she said.

"Aha," I nodded.

"He only said that your daddy had been driving him in the car for a long time," she added.

Grandma was so consistent. She always called my dad 'addy'. 'Dad' wasn't good enough, and 'father' was unheard of. Same with 'Mom'. In my grandma's language it was always a 'mommy'.

I was thinking about Grandma's dream. That pile of sand must have been at their old house, because, where else? They use to have a garden.

"It's time to meet him soon," Grandma said. "One can't live and live and live forever. I miss him."

Far away, dogs were barking. Otherwise, it was quiet.

"So, when you will go to meet him?" I asked. "Will you at least tell me how is it there? You know…" I was careful not to say "when you die" but Grandma didn't hesitate.

"Oh, when I die, you mean?" she said. "Of course! If I will have a chance, I will do that. I promise."

"Okay, it could be a sign or something. You could move a window curtain, for example," I said. I was looking at the white window curtain now and that's what came to my mind. I saw the moon above the forest. The anti-mosquito gauze that Grandma had taped to the window dissolved the black of the sky into a deep blue-gray color. I was thinking that Grandpa, if he wanted to, could move the curtain just to show that he was with us. I was waiting.

"Time to sleep," Grandma said. "I will come, if I am able. Don't worry."

I put my head on my pillow and fell asleep.

It was two o'clock in the morning. I knew that for sure because the clock downstairs struck twice. I woke up with fear holding me by the throat. I was afraid. I felt as if I was underwater again. It didn't help that when I opened my eyes. I didn't see the room any more, only this darkness that I'd became so familiar with in the depth of the lake. My thoughts were racing and my heart pounding. *I wasn't afraid, then. What am I fearing, now?* I kept blinking, trying to erase the image of water. Then I saw Grandma's profile against the moonlight, her slightly puffy nose and flat forehead with the short hair reaching across the swollen pillow and her half-open mouth. The water was still somewhere behind her.

#

The last time I saw Grandma was one summer visit to Poland. I had four children then and Alex was still in a stroller. He was about nine months old. Grandma passed a year later. After she passed, I thought of her often, and I figured she wasn't coming because she couldn't. It was okay, although sad.

One night, though, it changed. My family life was very stressful, mainly because of Matthias. I already had all five children and was more than busy. There were periods of time when I simply struggled, not only day to day, but hour to hour. I had many bad thoughts. I didn't know how to separate from Matthias and how to protect my children from him and his abuse.

That particular night, I went to bed sad and angry. I remember myself praying for some kind of end to this stressful life, maybe Matthias changing his heart.

For this purpose, I will say that I had a dream. It wasn't a normal dream, though. I felt it and lived in it, not like other dreams. In that dream, I remember blowing my nose into a white tissue. I looked at it afterwards and I saw that all my snot was changing into quickly moving maggots. I was disgusted, but as they started to multiply and move even quicker, crawling into my hand, I violently shook them off. I could see the maggots then on our pale tiled floor, as all this was taking place in our bedroom. There was plenty of light. It was daytime. The maggots spread out quickly. Unfortunately, they were now changing into snakes. Now the full-grown dark snakes were crawling everywhere, and mostly, toward my feet. I was terrified and didn't know what to do. I remember looking for something higher to climb on but the bed was a few feet behind me, and there was no other piece of furniture close by.

This is when Grandma came in. She looked as I always remembered her; old but not too old; just like my grandma. She came into the bedroom and started to step on all the snakes. One by one, she was crushing them under her feet. After not even one snake was left moving, she looked at me and impatiently waved her hand. When she was alive it was kind of her signature gesture. I will always remember it. With this gesture she would chase me away from a half -cooked dinner I was trying to steal from a cooking pot. Or when she would see me marching outside without a hat in a freezing winter.

"You really have nothing to worry about," she said. "All is good."

And she left.

2
Familiar Feeling

The feeling of being talked to without anybody's visible presence wasn't totally unfamiliar to me. In fact, it had happened on another occasion.

At the age of twenty-one I left my home country, Poland, fulfilling my dying mother's wishes. Poland was in a bad political situation then. These were times of the Solidarity movement and the beginnings of a revolution which eventually brought down communism in the Eastern bloc of Europe. My boyfriend was very engaged in the democratic opposition so, obviously, I became very engaged in it too. We lived together in his parents' spare apartment in downtown Warsaw. In the apartment we were running a full-blown production of illegal books, screen-printing, trimming, gluing, everything. After a batch of books was done, we'd have distributors coming in and filling their backpacks with the books. They had to look as if they were going on a backpacking trip or something like that. My boyfriend also worked in distribution, with his backpack full of books and in tall hiking boots.

These were very intense times and my parents knew that I was politically involved. Sometimes I would bring them a freshly printed illegal book that they would read. They worried about me. People were going to jail for what I was doing.

Because of my parents' fear, when my mother got ill with cancer and it was already clear that she wasn't going to make it, she told me to apply for a passport. I smiled. Many people were applying for passports. It looked as if the whole of Poland wanted to leave, go somewhere else, away from the disgusting communist party and its members. I wouldn't be the only one with the filled-in passport application. The communist party wouldn't let people go. My surprise was more than enormous when I was given a passport! I couldn't believe it! Everybody was amazed at the news. The least surprised was my mother. She was in the hospital struggling with pain. That was difficult too, because of how hard the times were. There was lack of not only food, but also clothing, medications, cleaning supplies, toilet paper. The list was very long and I can't imagine an item that wouldn't be on it. There wasn't enough pain medication in the hospitals, even for the cancer patients. We had to buy morphine for Mom on the black market, or use high social or professional connections to get it for her.

My parents bought me a ticket to Spain since I had a friend in Barcelona who'd invited me there. They also gave me two hundred dollars cash, thinking that I would have to manage my own future.

I went to the hospital to say goodbye to my mom. She made sure I understood she didn't want me to come back to Poland.

"Not even for my funeral, or especially not for my funeral. Leave behind these sentiments. I want you to be safe," she said. I was sitting on the edge of her bed, looking at her hand holding a towel. I wanted to hold her hand but I didn't dare to touch her without being invited to do so. Then her face changed. I could see she was in pain and that was hard to watch.

"Okay," she said. "I guess you can go. You can hug me now."

I bent over slightly and gently hugged her while kissing her cheek.

"Go, go. That's enough," she said.

But I didn't want to go. I wanted to keep feeling her cheek against my lips. When I finally got up and started to walk towards the door, something made me turn and I ran back to her bed. I held the its metal rail, tears streaming down my face, looking at her. It was at that moment that my aunt came to visit, and seeing what was happening, started to pull me out of the room while saying, "there's no reason to cry".

It was more than difficult to leave the hospital.

I'm writing about this, because it comes back to my mind when I think about those times. But what brought me back to it in this book was the fact that I was talked to by an invisible presence one year after those events.

Barcelona

I couldn't find myself a place in the world. I left Poland for Barcelona, Spain, in August. My mother passed in October. At twenty-one years old I didn't know how to grasp my life, what to do. I was attending an art school in Barcelona. I was given a scholarship. A friend of mine let me live in his empty apartment by the famous Las Ramblas. This apartment was for sale before my arrival but my friend took the sign down and let me stay in it. The apartment was about three thousand square feet and didn't have even one piece of furniture. I had to earn everything else. I felt lonely and misunderstood. I desperately missed my sisters. All this was happening before the internet and cell phones. International phone conversations were beyond my financial reach. One time in the late evening while walking home, I saw a group of young men by a phone booth, behaving differently than just talking on the phone. After a while I realized that their intention was to rob the phone booth. While I was passing by, one of them asked me, if I would like to call anybody.

"Yes," I replied. "My sister in Poland."

"Here, use this," he said. He handed me a coin with a hole and a string attached to it.

"You only drop it down and quickly pull it out right after you will get the connection," he said.

I did as I was told and talked to my sister who was overjoyed by my phone call. While I was talking a police car showed up, and we all ran away. I never met these people again.

All this time after my mom's passing, I was very sad, and my family in Poland decided my younger sister should come and spend Christmas with me. My dad bought her a ticket for December twentieth, and I was only thinking about this day. I wasn't doing well and my sister's visit was giving me hope and real joy, under the circumstances.

On December thirteenth, martial law was imposed in Poland. My world, and the world of many other people, shattered.

From the Spanish newspapers I learned about all the democratic opposition activists being arrested and placed in jails and camps outside Warsaw. This was exactly what my mother had been afraid of for me. I was in the West, safe, but my heart was with my friends. I also had lots of guilt for being where I was instead of with them. It's a strange place in the conscience because I wouldn't go back either. Let's face it. I didn't even go to my own mother's funeral.

As confused as I was, I still didn't want to apply for political asylum and I never did.

After a few months, I decided that I needed to leave Barcelona. I got a French visa and moved to Paris. I had a close friend living there.

Paris

While living in France I became involved with the Jesuits. My high-school best friend, with whom I stayed, had converted to Catholicism, and got herself baptized. Her parents in Poland belonged to the Communist Party and never took her to church.

All this time, while living in France, I prayed a lot. Or at least I tried to learn to pray.

I lived alone in a tiny one bedroomed apartment, in the suburbs of Paris. I would take a rapid train every day to get to my child care job. My evenings were filled with cooking dinner and reading. One evening, I was doing the dishes after dinner. I wasn't particularly thinking about anything important when a voice went through me. I only call it a voice. There was no sound. I dropped the plate into the sink and tried to compose myself, but I couldn't. What happened? I asked myself, shaking. Did I hear anything? I knew I didn't hear any voice, but I also knew what I heard. I realize how crazy it sounds but this is the best description. If I push the description more toward details, I would say that all my organs moved and produced a sentence, that imprinted in me. It said: '*You will never be alone*'.

I couldn't say in which language it was said, French or

Polish, but these were the exact words.

I was beside myself. I thought I needed to do something. But what? At the same time, I didn't want to do anything but enjoy the afterglow. I tried to talk to that "voice," or tried to repeat the experience. Obviously, I wasn't able to do it. Intellectually, I understood I couldn't recreate it because it wasn't my creation in the first place. The fact that the experience was as short as the conveyed sentence didn't help. The "voice" was so powerful and reassuring that it made me long for it.

The 'voice' didn't belong to any person I knew, dead or alive. I couldn't identify it. I could only say that it wasn't a female voice. I called it God's voice then and I never changed that.

This experience has always stayed with me; an amazing feeling of a non-human intrusion. Years later, I tried to describe it to my elder sister. We were sitting in a playground outside a tall apartment building in Gottingen, Germany. This is where I met my elder sister, nine years after leaving Poland. My two small children were playing with her son and daughter when we had a conversation about my Paris experience.

"The briefness of what happened could be compared to déjà vu," I said. "But it's only for your understanding. The difference between déjà vu and this experience is that it wasn't only memory. In this brief moment, while doing the dishes, I felt an overpowering *presence*".

"And the feeling? You said something about a feeling," she said.

"First of all, a feeling of the Truth. I knew what I was told, for sure. I had no doubts. God told me that I will never be alone. I didn't even ask for his intrusion. I was doing dishes,"

I said.

United States

About a year later, I moved to the United States. I flew to Guadalajara, Mexico, first, where I got married to Matthias. We met in southern France at the math conference where I accompanied my uncle. My uncle was a professor of mathematics at the University of Warsaw. When I found out he will be going to Marseille for an international conference in Dynamical Systems, I quickly said I will join him. In Marseille I met Matthias, who also specialized in Dynamical Systems. We started dating. Now, he drove down to meet me from Berkeley, California. We decided to get married in Mexico because I'd been denied an American visa. The fluently Polish speaking consul in Paris personally told me that I would never enter the United States. I didn't have any family or assets, and he wouldn't grant me a visa. He even put a special stamp in my passport saying the visa was denied.

I flew to Mexico where my late mother's friends lived. In Guadalajara it turned out that Matthias and I didn't have the complete set of documents required for marriage. All this was covered up and bypassed by the judge who was invited to my friend's house for the ceremony. The money Matthias paid, as a bribe of course, facilitated our marriage.

As a digression, I can say that the marriage lasted twenty years, and that the divorce was almost as complicated as arranging for the marriage to happen. This is how I found myself in the United States.

3
The Voice Again

It's interesting how we misinterpret certain events in our lives, according to our expectations and wishes We choose events, but later on, we often say that the events chose us. Both of those things are true. Usually, though, we focus on only one side: our preferred side.

I was already a mother of three when I woke up in the morning in the December of 1988. My eldest son John, aged six, and his two younger sisters were still asleep. My then-husband, Matthias, was already at work. He was teaching an early morning class that semester at the University of Arizona. As I laid in my bed thinking about what I was going to do first that morning, the voice went through me.

Now, I realize of course how odd it sounds. What *voice*?

I know it's true what I'm saying, but I have a problem describing the phenomenon that happened that morning.

It wasn't a voice per se. But how else could I describe the clear message conveyed to me? I didn't say 'spoken' but 'conveyed'. For communication purposes I say that I heard a voice telling me the message, but 'talking' wasn't really taking place.

The message went through me, through all my cells. I also knew who was speaking to me. It was Mary, Mother of Jesus.

Please, allow me to explain before you think I'm insane.

I'm not insane. I don't use drugs. I don't even smoke pot; it just doesn't sit well with me. Yes, I do enjoy a glass of wine in the evening. I used to drink beer when the kids were younger. At this time, though, I didn't even drink beer. I wasn't under the influence of any kind of drugs or meds.

I need to say that.

I don't know how to describe the power of the message that went through me. It's enough to say that it threw me out of bed in one huge energy spur. I was now standing in the middle of the bedroom, my bare feet on the light gray tiled floor. I didn't dare look around. I was still overpowered by the voice which just communicated with me.

This is when things become awkward, not the very events which happened, but when I start to talk about them. The words I'm using are the only ones available to me, so of course, I'm using them, hoping for the best outcome. Unfortunately, they don't really convey the truth of the experience. They only give a rough sketch.

The voice was communicating with me in a split second. It was a female voice, specifically Mary's. The voice had no timbre and I didn't hear it with my ears. Describing the process of hearing it is the most difficult thing. The lack of words is all there is. But I still want to describe it with the tools I have, my human vocabulary. Mary's message was short but certainly it would take longer than half a second to say it. I was astounded.

At this time of my life, when raising the kids, I wasn't particularly focused on any kind of prayer. In those years of my first marriage, Matthias and I were going to church every Sunday. It wasn't for faith purposes. Matthias and I were both Polish, and while living in the USA, we belonged to the Polish parish in any city we moved to. First, it was San Francisco while we lived in Berkeley. Then it was Tucson, Arizona.

We went to church because we tried to spend Sunday in a traditional Polish way. Attending Mass was followed by socializing with other Polish families. This was the true reason for going there. It wasn't about faith.

When it comes to my own faith, though, I will just state that I know God exists. Any time when somebody asks me a question *'Do you believe in God?'* I say no, I don't believe; I know God is. Believing is cutting it short, implying doubt by the very definition of that word.

I don't want to sound arrogant. Everything I am, including my thoughts, is an expression of God's grace, and I stand by it. God can take grace away, but why would He do that? I need to clarify here that God isn't a 'he' or 'she'. I'm using the most common pronoun for communication purposes only.

I don't want to go into long philosophical discourses here. I only want to say that Mary, Mother of Jesus, woke me up that morning by clearly communicating to me that I was pregnant, and that I would give birth to a baby boy. This is the simplest and most mundane way that I can describe this event. It was her message. I cannot say how I knew it was Mary. I didn't see anybody, but there was a knowledge, with no room for any doubt, about whose presence I felt.

I ran to the kitchen to turn on the stove, carrying the message inside me. I felt as if I was physically drunk. I was experiencing a little vertigo, but my thoughts were as clear as can be. The message Mary conveyed to me played back and forth in my mind.

I will remember that whole morning till my death. I took the older kids to preschool, then my baby daughter shopping.

The next day I had a doctor's appointment scheduled. I

had a problem with my cervix and my doctor wanted to do a procedure for cervical erosion. I was told it was a simple procedure. I vividly remember the word *laser* being used in the description of the procedure. I was told it I would be able to drive myself home afterwards. I went to the doctor still feeling radiant after the previous morning's events, about which I hadn't told anybody.

In the doctor's office, the nurse prepared the room and gave me a plastic cup for a urine sample, following the rules before any procedure. Later, she took the sample from me and told me the doctor would be in soon, and I shouldn't worry about anything. After a while, the doctor came in and shook my hand. His handshake was strong. His hair was almost white but his mustache was black. He wasn't tall. His voice was deep and friendly.

"We are not going to go ahead with the procedure today," he said.

"Okay?" I said, questioning at the same time.

He told me that the urine sample showed I was pregnant. He decided that he would examine me, since I was already in the office. The nurse moved the tray with the procedure instruments away, making room for the examination. After the examination, the doctor told me that, to his surprise, my cervix problem had disappeared. No procedure would be necessary.

"It might be that the pregnancy cured you," he joked. "How many children do you have?"

"Three," I said.

"Oh," he said. "Four is a good number. That is how many I have."

I was happy not to have to go through any procedure that day. I also had a hard time believing this doctor had four children. I thought he only said that to make me feel better.

He didn't need to. I'd never thought about having four children but I was overjoyed like never before. In the midst of all this happiness my mind was constantly racing, too. *'Why another child? She said it's a boy...'* I didn't care which gender. I already had a boy and two girls. But she specifically said it would be a boy, not a 'baby', and this led to another wave of thoughts to develop. What if it wasn't a boy? Did it mean that I was simply crazy and imagining things?

I knew I didn't imagine anything. Crazy? I didn't feel crazy. But I felt it was safer not to tell anybody and I kept this experience to myself for a long time.

#

I remember the day Alex came into this world. I went into labor and Alex's father drove me to the hospital. The whole process took maybe three hours. To the last push I was only thinking about her, Mary, the mother of Jesus, and her promise.

"Here is your boy," the nurse said and she placed Alex on my chest.

I didn't only feel relief, but shame too. Such little faith and trust I had... and I was claiming I had it all! Why was I thinking about Mary's promise during labor? Why didn't I just whisper to my boy who was pushing himself into the world? Did I fear it was a girl and I would have to question my sanity?

Alex was very big ten-pound baby. I'm fairly small so everybody in the maternity unit was marveling at his size. The doctor was astonished that I came out totally unscathed; I didn't need even one stich! Alex was my fourth child, but the doctor still thought it was exceptional because of Alex's size.

Today I also think Alex's birth was exceptional. I needed plenty of stitches after I gave birth to my fifth child, Alex's younger brother, who came into the world two and half years later.

I never had any exceptional feelings or premonitions about my pregnancies. I read about women who immediately after finding out they're pregnant, know the sex of the baby, too. I had that kind of feeling once, when I got pregnant for the very first time. I was convinced it was a girl. I even gave her a name. But then I had a miscarriage. It was early in the pregnancy. After that, I gave birth to three children and I never knew what their sex was until I saw them. Being twenty-nine years old, I was too young to have an amniocentesis performed, the test that detects chromosome abnormalities. During the regular visits and ultrasound examinations, my babies were always turned in such a way that the doctor couldn't tell if it was a boy or a girl. Every time, it was a surprise. Even my fifth child's sex was unknown to me before he came to this world. I only knew about Alex's gender and it was because of an other-worldly message.

Here is something important I want to say. We often misinterpret given signs. We bend them according to our wishes and expectations. At least I did that.

Just because Mary told me that Alex was going to be born didn't mean he would get a Nobel Prize in physics. I'm talking about physics because Alex was so extremely talented. I would think the message was positive when Alex was showing his incredible talents. I avoided thinking about the message during his 'dark' periods, when he struggled with excessive anxiety, depression and obsessiveness.

When Alex's life went downhill and his psychiatric issues

took over, I started to think about Mary's message every day. I would think the message wasn't only about the wonderful things Alex would bring to my life and this world. It was also about the suffering he would cause. I think now that this is why Mary came to me in the first place. As I mentioned before, people have a tendency to read the signs according to their imagination and expectations. And they refuse to let the idea of suffering into their world.

4
The Pink Evil

We all know what dreaming is because we've all had that experience. And only because it's such common knowledge can we distinguish between a normal dream and something that isn't quite that normal. That dreamlike event would happen at the same time when a regular dream would, usually when we are in bed under the blankets, with our eyes closed and our bodies resting, in what we think is sleep.

When we wake up, we either remember our dream or we don't. Sometimes we share it with somebody and we laugh at it together, or we ponder about its craziness. Or we are still scared of it even during the day, if it was a nightmare. We can still remember the anxiety of not making it to the airport on time, or staring at the empty places in our wallet where the credit cards used to be.

What isn't a dream then? What if the event also happens at night while we are asleep or so we think? While describing the following event I will relay my experience only.

It was the summer of nineteen ninety-seven. Alex was eight years old. Our family had spent the whole past year in Poland on Matthias's sabbatical. After that summer, we were going back to the United States.

A close friend of mine, who lived in Sweden, invited me to spend a week at her summer property close to Stockholm. I was to come with all my children whom she really wanted to know better. She, herself, had one son. I was looking forward to this trip until I found out that Matthias wanted to come along. I wanted the exact opposite. In fact, I needed the opposite. It was almost mandatory that I have a break from him. He was a terrible person to be with, especially after spending a twelve-month sabbatical in the same apartment. For the whole year, he didn't have his office or schedule. He yelled and screamed on an almost daily basis, and very often, I was simply afraid of him. I was very unhappy and truly missed Tucson and our routine, where he wasn't at home during the day. He said, though, that the children and I weren't going anywhere without him. He was coming to Sweden. It was one of the places he hadn't visited yet and that was the main reason for him joining the trip.

I tried to protest, saying that my friend and I would like to have more time together, etc. But to no avail. He was coming along, period.

So, we went together, taking all the children and all our family tensions with us.

In Sweden, the situation only worsened. I don't know what happened to Matthias. I thought he was difficult at home, but on this trip, he became a total monster. I had to watch carefully, not only what I was saying but what my children were saying, too, and at all times when he was around. Money was also an issue. Matthias was controlling it all. I remember how angry he became when my then twelve-year old daughter set up a violin stand in the old town of Stockholm and played for an hour. She was a good little violinist and made lots of money. Right after she finished and put all her money into her backpack, she ran across the street to a store with summer dresses. She got one from the first rack, a beautiful green dress with black designs on it, and bought it for me. I was moved to tears. It would never occur to me to buy a dress in Stockholm.

I could write a lot about similar situations but this isn't my point. It is only the background to it. My point is to tell about one night during this trip which left me changed for life. Or, if it didn't change me, it at least gave me that chance.

I will never forget that night. Here is what happened.

The evening wasn't good, to say the least. After getting up from the dinner table, we were all to go to our small cabins. There were several of them on my friend's property. They were hidden between the tall pine trees on a hill overseeing a lake. Our family was big so we slept in three separate cabins. I was staying in my cabin with the youngest boys. Alex was nine and his younger brother was two and half years younger. When we got up from the table, the older kids decided they would stay in the kitchen to socialize. The little boys went with me and I put them to bed. They immediately fell asleep. I sat in front of my cabin and looked at the patch of open sky between the tree crowns. I was thinking about Matthias. *'Why did everything have to be so difficult? Why is he that way?'*

While I was sitting there, Matthias showed up. He came into my cabin, and no matter how hard I try to push it from my memory, I can't forget that he came to my bed and laid down beside me. I didn't want him there and I told him so. I pleaded nicely, too; there was no way. Of course, I wouldn't scream in the cabin with the two boys asleep in it. Matthias had behaved like that before, so it wasn't the first time, anyway. This sabbatical was a nightmare.

After he left for his cabin, I laid in my bed and cried myself to what I thought was sleep.

In my dream, I was terrified. I saw a big pink object floating in the air, getting close to me. It was about the size of my head. It was round, but its shape wasn't regular. It simply didn't have any sharp edges. I knew it was soft and slimy. I also knew it was evil incarnate and that I should avoid it at all costs.

But how? For some reason, I was immobilized. I couldn't run away, and that pink evil was getting close to my face. It was almost touching my cheek.

I threw myself into prayer. *'God'*, I pleaded, *'save me. Do something'*. I looked around, and to my surprise, somewhere above me I saw Jesus sitting behind a wooden desk. He had long hair and was dressed in a flannel shirt. His eyes were closed. He was sitting up straight, but he seemed asleep.

A hope poured inside me. The pink evil was dancing around my head and I still couldn't move. But now Jesus was there. He wouldn't abandon me, would he?

Out of corner of my eye, I saw another man standing to the left of the desk. I didn't pay much attention to this person since most of it went to Jesus. But when Jesus got up and went to talk to this man, I looked closer.

I recognized him. It was a Polish Catholic saint, Father Kolbe. He'd sacrificed his life for a stranger in a death cell in Auschwitz.

As a child, I'd had to learn about him during religion class in our parochial classroom. I was raised Catholic in a communist country and that meant taking religion classes after school in our parish. But the classroom wasn't the only place where I would see the saint's face. Father Kolbe was famous. His photograph was hanging in every church and he was even shown in the communist media. The most popular image was one portraying Father Kolbe in his striped shirt with the Auschwitz number sewn on his pocket. He was wearing glasses with thick frames and he was terribly thin. His head was bald.

Now he was standing and talking with Jesus. He wasn't dressed in his Auschwitz shirt any more, the only dress I remembered seeing on Father Kolbe. Instead, he had a flannel shirt just like Jesus. That wasn't the only difference from what I knew about how Father Kolbe looked in real life. Now he looked completely healthy. He radiated energy. I knew it was him. I recognized him beyond any doubt, even though he had hair now, not much, but he certainly wasn't bald.

I was amazed. Even though I was fighting my own fear of the pink evil, in the back of my mind I was marveling at Father Kolbe's looks. I had never seen or imagined him so healthy. This is the exact word that I had in mind while looking at Father Kolbe and Jesus. Both of them were looking happy and healthy. I have seen many pictures of a healthy Jesus, but I have never seen Father Kolbe in good health or even looking normal. This was a pre-internet era and there were fewer images available altogether. The ones we would see more often were "winning" our imagination. 'Winning' in the sense that they would be the ones sticking in your memory. This is exactly what was happening with Father Kolbe's picture. I only knew him with round thick glasses, skinny and sad, in the Auschwitz prisoner's uniform.

Why was he there, talking with Jesus in the first place? He wasn't my favorite saint or anybody I would think of often. In fact, I had no feelings for Father Kolbe. He made an impression on me once I learned how he died. But that was it.

Now Jesus went back to his desk, sat down and closed his

eyes again. The pink evil was almost touching my cheek.

"Jesus," I cried. "Please wake up. Please, please look at me. Please open your eyes!"

Nothing was happening and I truly thought that I was not only dying, but dying in pain and going to be embraced by the pink evil. That meant eternal suffering. I knew that whatever I was going through now would be nothing compared with what I would feel when the pink evil finally touched me.

It was then when Jesus opened his eyes and looked straight at me. He didn't even move his head.

I was so relieved! *'It will be all over, now'*, I thought, *'Jesus is seeing me. He sees my suffering. He won't leave me!'*

The pink evil was now in front of my face but a little below my eyeline, so I could still see Jesus. Now I knew I had to convince Jesus to help me.

I realized then, I simply didn't dare to do that. I was afraid to ask for the removal of the pink evil, but I knew I needed it gone at the same time. Jesus was still looking at me.

"Jesus, please give me strength to sustain my suffering," was all I could muster to say. Inside, I was screaming for removal of the pink evil and liberation, but I was ashamed to ask. I thought that if I could be stronger, I would somehow manage.

In my wildest dreams I wouldn't imagine Jesus's answer, but here is what he told me. He still didn't move his head. His words were very decisive, a matter-of-fact kind of thing:

"I won't give you any additional strength, because you already have more than enough."

I was looking at Jesus in awe. I was willing to take in anything he was saying, but I was a little bewildered by his words. I was trying not to show it, but he must have known it, anyway.

"You are strong enough. You don't need anything," he said.

Then, the pink evil was gone. My eyes were open as I was looking into the dark night, sweating.

For many years the only person who knew about this event was my elder sister. I told her about it when we came back to Warsaw.

5

A Shower Curtain and a Dream

After Alex's death, many things happened which could be called coincidences or simply events which were hard to explain. I know that they weren't coincidences. When I go to meetings of Compassionate Friends, which is an organization for bereaved parents, and listen to other mothers talk, I can see they have the same kind of so-called coincidences happening to them too. I'm always interested in the details of those mini-gigantic stories. Although to a skeptic they might seem coincidences, they are not. We are so much more than a mere bunch of atoms randomly moving through the Universe.

I will add three events to my story. Sometimes, it's hard to judge what is interesting to whom, and I certainly wouldn't want to bore anybody with details mostly interesting only to me.

A few days after Alex's death, I woke up at night. I was quietly lying on my mattress in the bathroom. I kept my mattress there because of the smell my oil paints filled the studio with. Staring at the dark ceiling above me, I heard a noise. It seemed as if it was raining. I knew it wasn't raining. I listened with interest. Then I saw my shower curtain move. It started to shake from top to bottom. I understood the noise was made by the shaking plastic curtain. It was dark so I couldn't see the top of the curtain, but I could clearly see the middle going down to the bottom. I don't know how long it lasted. It seemed like quite a while. I observed the silver light gliding across the shaking curtain. I waited. I don't know if I fell asleep before the curtain stopped shaking.

In the morning, I looked at the curtain and I carefully touched it with my fingers. It's hard to describe the respect I felt.

A few days later, I was in a mobile phone store, waiting in line. I needed to fix my phone which was giving me trouble. There were several people ahead of me so, after securing my spot, I stepped out. I walked around the plaza without any special goal but when I saw a Bed Bath & Beyond store, I walked in. I always liked that store and walking around without buying anything seemed like a good idea. I went to the clearance rack because that's what I always do. There it was! An extra-long shower curtain. It was clear, just like the one I had, and it cost only five dollars! I'd paid almost eighty dollars for my shower curtain. The reason for that price is that my shower is extremely high up. The rack is mounted above eight feet from the ground. I was shopping for a curtain fitting these dimensions for a long time before I'd found the right one. So of course, seeing a shower curtain that would fit my shower for so little money got my attention. I bought the curtain and I returned to the phone store.

Later in the evening, I took the new curtain out of the bag just to measure it up. I stood on a chair inside my shower and rolled down the curtain. I looked at the hooks on a metal rod attached to the wall and I understood what Alex was doing to this curtain while shaking it at night. The best thing to do by way of explanation, would be insert the picture I took of it, so here it is.

The hooks of the curtain after shaking

I looked in disbelief. I called Earle. He also looked at the photo I'd taken.

"I know you well. I know you would never hang a shower curtain like that," he said.

Not only I would never do it, nobody would do it. I remember how carefully I was in choosing my old curtain, and when it finally arrived in the mail, how careful I was while hanging it.

I didn't touch this curtain for years and I certainly didn't look up at the hooks. Only going to the store and buying a new curtain made me look up and see what really was happening with the hooks while the curtain was shaking.

It was clear that the placement of the hooks had changed. It was amazing to think that, when I was actually witnessing this event the night before, it didn't occur to me to look up and check. But then, why would I? I only saw the curtain shaking. While it was shaking though, in the dark place close to the ceiling a true unearthly miracle was taking place and I was in the same room! *'How would this have looked if I had actually looked at that moment at that dark corner with my very own eyes? Would I have seen the hooks moving?'* I wondered. I'm convinced that Alex directed me to Bed Bath & Beyond. I very rarely go to that store. And he made sure there was a very specific shower curtain on a sale rack, so I could buy it and finally *see* what he came for that night.

I left the hooks in their strange places. I look at them daily, always marveling. The misplaced hooks look to me like a pure expression of Alex's creative personality, his way of communicating with whatever tools he had. I thought I could feel that he'd wanted to present himself with a small project, similar to the ones he was making as a child using old cardboard boxes, masking tape and some paints. Only now all he could use was the shower curtain… and from the different dimension I presumed he was in.

The second event was a text message.

I had a good friend, Anna, who all my children knew very well. She was Polish and so was her husband. Both our families lived in Tucson, and we visited each other often when the kids were young. We were "aunties" to each other's kids. Due to unrelated life circumstances, we stopped seeing each other and both settled for life without being close friends. Our children grew up and left town. A few days after Alex's death, Anna called me. She'd found out about his death through friends of friends. Anna proposed a meeting and the next day we had coffee after five years of not seeing each other.

After our meeting, I came back home around five. My phone rang. It was my daughter, Lara, the one who lived in town.

"I had a very strange dream," she said. "It's actually strange I fell asleep in the afternoon in the first place. It never happens to me."

"Wow. I'm glad you slept," I said. "You must have needed it."

"I don't know, Mom," she said. "It was all so strange. I suddenly couldn't help myself. I had to lie down and close my eyes." She sounded puzzled.

"Okay?" I said. I could sense she couldn't wait to tell me the reason for her phone call.

"So, I had a dream that I received a text message. Out of

313

all people, Mom, I received a text message from Auntie Anna."

I felt chills running down my spine. Anna was only a memory in the adult lives of my children. She wasn't present even in our conversations. I froze in the middle of the room. I could tell how surprised my daughter was receiving a text message from Anna, even in her dream.

"So, in this text message," my daughter said. "Auntie said that Alex had talked to her. He said some non-sensical things. Like, he was apologizing that some scarf went up to his head. He said this in Polish, '*przepraszam ze mi chustka poszla do glowy*, I'm sorry that the scurf went to my head. He also said that, in the beginning things will be rough, but then everything will be all right."

To this day I think about Alex's message and 'the scarf that went up to his head'. I couldn't imagine what he might have wanted to say. Scarf? To his head? I had many theories but all of them were a little stretched. I put all my questions and doubts aside and accepted what was given to me. Alex was a very creative person. All his life, he communicated things quickly and in a rather straightforward way. I assumed he must have had a trust in me and his sister to bypass words that weren't needed to understand his overall message. And the message was that things will be all right. Even if it didn't totally make sense that day, the message came.

6
Third Event

About three weeks after Alex's death, around eleven at night, I started to prepare to go to bed in the Studio. I usually slept there. On the main easel I had a painting which smelled of fresh paint, so I put my mattress in the bathroom on the floor. That way I could close the bathroom door and not inhale the odor. The Studio bathroom is very spacious, with a big window. It's more like a room. There was enough space in it to fit a mattress in the corner against the wall and the closet had sliding, mirror doors. When I was lying down, my head was by the mirrors and my legs were about a foot away from the shower.

That evening I brushed my teeth, changed into my pajamas and lay down on the mattress. I was very sad and started to cry. At first, I tried to tame my sadness but quickly found myself crying even more. I wiped my face with the sleeve of my shirt, while searching for a roll of a toilet paper I thought was somewhere close to my mattress. Then, the sadness tripled and came over me like a tsunami. I totally gave myself over to it.

"Oles!" I cried, calling Alex in Polish. "Oles, Oles, my little Oles!" I kept repeating his name. I can't say that I was particularly calling him to come. I was just calling his name.

I'm having great difficulty in describing what happened

next because it seems so surreal. It was all very real to me. I must say I wasn't drunk. It's funny how I need to make sure everybody knows that. I guess I'm afraid somebody might immediately try to explain what happened and therefore jump to the wrong conclusion.

As I was lying on my mattress, I heard a strange kind of grunting sound coming from outside the window. The window was right above me. It was closed. I opened my eyes and thought I saw a human neck, moving slowly ahead in kind of jerky motions. I knew that there would be a head attached to this neck, nevertheless only the neck was truly visible to me. All this time, the grunting sounds were audible. Since I was lying down almost on floor level, I kind of saw this neck from below. The grunting sounds were expressing an extreme effort. The neck scared me and the sounds, too. In my mind I knew that the neck was approaching my Studio French doors. I knew they were locked. For some reason though, I was expecting the doors to open up. I was waiting for the loud metallic sound of the first security gate opening up, and then, the squeak of the French doors.

The neck disappeared from the window. I didn't hear any sound. Instead, I felt a presence in the Studio and got even more scared. The door of my bathroom was closed. Lying down on the mattress, which was placed directly on the floor, I could see the narrow gap under the door filled with a dim light. The light was always there at night. It was coming from my neighbor's security night lamp. It was turning on and off as the cats were strolling under it and the wind blew.

I stared at the gap under the door already knowing that someone was in the Studio. Then I saw two shapes crossing the dim light. '*Feet?*' I thought. The presence could be felt right behind my bathroom door. Suddenly, I knew. I jumped out of bed and threw a robe on. I opened the door and there was Alex.

I can't write about it without crying. We clung to each other. Alex was pretty tall. I stretched my hands up and wrapped them around his neck, and felt his skin and hair. He looked so happy. He was radiating health! There was really nothing I could say, like, he should have been skinnier or have a little more fat, or anything! He was simply perfect. His whole face was smiling. He was wearing his red winter jacket, the one I saw him wearing in Poland when I went there the last time. Altogether, he looked as I 'd seen him last over at my sister's house when I gave him his case of special yo-yos. Only now, he was radiating health and beaming with joy.

"Finally!" he exclaimed out loud and we hugged again and again. It was a long hug and I felt his strong hands wrapped around my back. I felt his neck and head. Our cheeks touched. We were both, ecstatic.

"Let's sit somewhere so we can chat," he said. He took my hand and we went inside the Studio and sat on the floor. While we were sitting, I asked Alex if I could touch him again.

"I'm only asking, because, you know," I said, but I didn't finish. I didn't want to say '*because you are dead. Your body was cremated half the world away from Tucson and your ashes are in a grave in a Polish cemetery*'.

"I know, I know," he said to my unfinished comments. I understood that he knew what I was thinking. "Of course, you can touch me. Here, touch my knee."

We were already sitting on the floor. I reached out and touched his knee. It was there, as solid as mine.

"Tell me, how was it," I said. I wanted to find out how

was his experience of dying, how he felt while going through it and all.

Then Alex said something that didn't make any sense. Almost every day I ponder what he could have meant. He said it in Polish. In fact, the whole conversation was in Polish but translating the words didn't clarify the mystery.

"Czulem chlopstwo," he said. The direct translation would be like, '*I felt 'peasantry*'. It didn't make any sense to me. Was he feeling like a peasant? Why a peasant? I had questions but I didn't want to interrupt. I was thirsty for every word of his, even if it didn't make sense. I was listening intensely, still in disbelief, I kept touching his knee.

"And then?" I asked.

Alex shifted slightly.

"Then, I went to the forest," he said. His voice now was quiet and the excitement gone. I felt he was telling me a story. I was waiting.

"I was in this forest for a long time," Alex said.

He lifted his head and looked at me. It was dark, of course, with only a little light from the neighbor's outdoor lamp and some other light sources like my microwave, phone station, a switch, etc. All the objects were visible in the Studio and so was Alex.

I don't know what happened next. I don't remember anything. It was the morning and birds were chirping and I was standing by the bathroom sink. I dropped to my knees. I didn't want to get up. My mouth was open and the tears were pouring on my tongue. My loud cries echoed in the Studio while I was trying to accustom myself to the fact that there was a day outside, around seven in the morning, and that I needed to go to work.

I remember myself driving on a sunny street that morning choking on my tears and making sure I stayed in the lane. I called my daughter, Lara, from the car and told her what had happened. I told her that I felt as if I were drunk or high.

"I must be high in some sense. I know that it's different from anything I've known so far in my whole life," I said.

Whenever I recall that night, I feel the same way. Sometimes I cry, sometimes I don't. I sleep in the same Studio, only now in a real bed which isn't in the bathroom. I look into the darkness at night. I know that Alex won't come now unless something unusually important occurs. I don't think it will be any time soon.

7

Falling Down

There are certain events in life which stand out. Some of them become milestones. Before that milestone event though, we often don't even know about the possibility of an intersection. We think the road is straight.

It was several months after Alex's death. I was cleaning the very top of the kitchen cabinets in the Studio. With my bare feet, I was walking on the edge of the granite countertop, touching the spider webs in the ceiling's corner. I decided I needed to wet the rag one more time and therefore needed to come down to the sink. I knew where the ladder was standing since I'd just climbed it. I reached out with my foot, trying to find it, and then I don't know if I missed it or it moved. It didn't make a difference any more since I was already flying in the air. I missed the open baby grand piano by maybe an inch and my body smashed against the bare tile floor.

I screamed with pain that went through me, left me, and then came back with double the force. It felt as if a screw had been driven into my hip and arm. Wanting to defy the possibility of a disaster like broken bones, I jumped up, and while still screaming, started to walk around. Earle heard my screams and rushed to the Studio. When he walked in, he only saw me walking around, crying in pain.

"What happened?" he said.

I told him. What I didn't tell him was that I was convinced a miracle helped me, not only to survive the fall but also to be able to get up and walk around. I didn't break any bones.

Next day I went to see a doctor. After examining my bruises, he said he was amazed I didn't break any bones. I definitely was injured and ended up with steroid shots in my hip. I was limping and couldn't go for a walk for a year, but no bones were broken.

I felt as if Alex had caught me while I was falling from the countertop. I know; it's only my feeling. Anybody who saw the countertop, the piano, the tiles and imagined me falling, couldn't believe nothing major happened to me.

8

The Sinusoide or a Wave

About one year after Alex's death, I went to bed in the Studio. It was about ten in the evening. For a whole year I had been intensely praying for Alex and for his well-being, no matter how inadequate it might sound. I was praying for all the other people who had already passed, whether they were my family, friends, or not. For the animals, for creatures, for life, for everything and everybody who was afraid and suffered. I was praying for wisdom and patience, for guidance, for never turning away from God.

The light by my bedside was still on when I saw my feet moving up. Obviously, it was hard to believe, but my feet were up in the air, and it seemed as if I had nothing to do with it, meaning I hadn't lifted them. Before I could think of it any longer, the energy wave that I would later call Sinusoid went through me.

Please be patient. I used to read books from authors who would describe strange events and swear they were true. It was hard to believe them at the time. Today, I believe them all because I had difficulty in believing myself. I don't need to believe myself. I know what I went through.

The Sinusoid was essentially a wave. It could be described as an energy wave or as something more familiar to a human being; for example, a wind. As it was going through me, starting by lifting my feet, my body became that very wave or rather was just *waving* itself. I felt the Sinusoid's perfection. I knew in my mind that the low apex of the Sinusoid was exactly opposite the high apex. On the coordinate system the x and y would have the same value, only the y would be negative. The graph illustrating these numbers would show my Sinusoid.

After the Sinusoid made its way to my head, half my body was lifted upwards and then violently my whole body folded like a Swiss army knife.

I cried and asked for mercy. I called out to Mary, Jesus's Mother, and Jesus. I called Alex. I called God himself. I thought that I was very loud but I have no proof of what sounds I was making. I was folded together like a pocket knife but it wasn't the end. An unknown force kept pushing down my back. I feared I had no power to sustain that force. The pressure against my back felt as if I were carrying the whole Earth with all the life on it, with simply everything, good and evil, but mostly evil. The force kept pushing and I was out of breath. It wasn't only the Earth on my back any more, it was the whole Universe. Even that wouldn't be enough to describe the weight of it. The Sinusoid pushed so hard, that eventually I wasn't able to utter a sound. I was now sitting on my bed, face between my knees and unable to breathe. I lacked air and was terrified.

When I lost hope, the force let go. I sat up and drew a breath, terrified. I got off my bed and walked around the Studio, crying. I didn't want to lie down. My fear of the Sinusoid surpassed my need for rest and sleep. And it wasn't only for this one night.

The next day, I started my research. What was that? I knew what I went through but I didn't know where to look for answers. The first place of course, was an internet search. But even there I was cautious. My fear prevented me from doing an open search. All the time I thought that the Sinusoid would come back with double the rage. I allowed myself to do what my instinct told me and stopped praying, or at least meditating. This decision didn't come easy. I was still talking to Mary and Alex, but I didn't sit up to deliberately open my mind like I used to. I was determined to follow my instinct. I had a funny feeling that I'd let something in and this something was around me and could enter me any time. I was seeing waves everywhere. Everything was a wave. In fact, I understood that I was a wave myself, only materialized. It was a scary feeling. I was convinced I am the same as everyone else but that for some reason the wave chose to show itself in my body

At the end of the week, after not sleeping and barely functioning, I went to see my doctor. '*At least he knows me*', I thought; '*he knows I'm not making things up*'. It was true. I'd had the same doctor for years. His wife is my best friend and our families see each other on some social occasions.

He listened as I was telling my story. He was concerned about a possibility of a seizure, but he excluded it. He proposed antidepressants but I didn't want to take them. He ended up prescribing sleeping pills. I took his prescription. I desperately needed to rest.

9
The Crash

About one year after the Sinusoid event, I went to visit my eldest son, who now lived in Chicago. He was a resident medical doctor in the hospital there. We decided to go on a one-day bicycle trip.

We went for a long ride along the Fox river in the Chicago suburbs. I was using my daughter-in-law's bicycle since she was out of town. With the helmet well secured on my head, we started our thirty-something miles trip.

It was a beautiful autumn day right before Halloween. The warm sun was shining through colorful tree leaves. We stopped for lunch, and after that, we had about ten miles left. The path was mostly flat, running along the river. But even this "flat" path had its ups and downs. One of those downs was a little deeper than other places, and there wasn't any warning suggesting slowing down. I was going down very fast thinking I would naturally slow down while riding up after the deep dip. At the bottom though the surface changed. Some special material that maybe would prevent water from freezing, or at least disrupt that process, had been placed there. When I hit it, I lost control of the bicycle. I was braking like crazy, but I couldn't stop. I was approaching a tree at what I thought was the speed of light. Finally, I could the tree's bark so close it looked to me like its quantum structure. There was no escape.

This was it.

My thoughts were very fast. I never imagined I would be able to think so fast. But then I detached from my thoughts. I only started to observe them. I was surprised to discover two separate roads on which my thoughts were going and I was on both of them, simultaneously. Both of those thought-roads were very vivid.

On the first one, I was reliving Alex's snowboarding accident. I felt I was him and was going to hit a tree, just like him when he broke his back on the mountain. I felt the unstoppable speed of his snowboard and his effort to control it. I felt his fear as well.

The other road was as vivid and final, too. I thought it was as straight as the first road, but it turned out to be a circle, since it brought me back to my life. After traveling this road, I was still me, but completely changed. As I was speeding towards the tree, my values were changing. Suddenly I saw a meaning in everything I had to go through. Even Alex's death felt like a gift given to me, so I could become who I am today, a person who cares about time spent with loved ones. A person who cares only about love.

It seemed to me I was going to die while speeding towards the tree. I struck it. The helmet saved me. If not my life, then certainly my health. If not for the helmet, I could have been paralyzed or even dead. I think about it sometimes, especially when I happen to look at the picture of my damaged helmet. My son, who stopped another cyclist from calling for help, took that picture for me. He told me later that he never stopped having faith in me. As a doctor, he was professional at assessing the situation. He was afraid. The crash looked bad. Riding behind me, he saw it all. But as a son, he simply refused to conceive an idea of his mother being permanently hurt. Obviously, since I wrote this book, I didn't die.

This accident, though, was essential in my grief. It helped me understand love. The moment I crashed I heard a message. I didn't hear it with my ears. It was coming from my very guts, and brain and soul. *'Is this it? This is how it ends? How strange. How simple. But… I didn't tell people, family, everybody, anybody and everything I know, how much I love them.'*

Epilogue

I never found out what was the cause of Alex's death. It was assumed that he overdosed on the opiates. The toxicology report was never done. Alex died in April and I finally went to Poland in the summer. I went to talk to the coroner's office, only to be informed that the toxicology hadn't been performed. I asked why, but it seemed that no one wanted to talk to me. The responsible district attorney was on vacation. He only picked up the phone a few days after my visit to his office. I told him I would come back and talk to him, but he didn't want to see me. He apologized that the report hadn't been made, but that the police hadn't seen any foul play, and therefore there wasn't a real need to perform toxicology testing. The autopsy didn't show anything extraordinary. All the organs were in place. I was too devastated to argue. Alex's body had been cremated for several months before I arrived.

I never finished my teaching degree. I stayed full time with our plastics manufacturing company. I developed my skills as a Computer Aid Designer in our flat work and three-dimensional models. My back ground graphic design had to be substantially upgraded for CAD work. I continued working as an artist, though. I always painted, and I still do it today.

CPSIA information can be obtained
at www.ICGtesting.com
Printed in the USA
BVHW072051070223
658049BV00001B/95